KULEANA

KULEANA

A Story of Family, Land,
and Legacy in Old Hawai'i

Sara Kehaulani Goo

FLATIRON
BOOKS
NEW YORK

www.flatironbooks.com

Wai'ānapanapa State Park black-sand beach photograph © thetahoeguy / Shutterstock

Designed by Jen Edwards

Library of Congress Cataloging-in-Publication Data

Names: Goo, Sara Kehaulani, author.
Title: Kuleana : a story of family, land, and legacy in old Hawai'i / Sara Kehaulani Goo.
Other titles: Story of family, land, and legacy in old Hawai'i
Description: First edition. | New York : Flatiron Books, [2025] | Includes bibliographical references.
Identifiers: LCCN 2024061209 | ISBN 9781250333445 (hardcover) | ISBN 9781250333438 (ebook)
Subjects: LCSH: Hawaiians—Land tenure. | Hawaiians—Kinship. | Maui (Hawaii)—History, Local. | Goo, Sara Kehaulani. | Hawaiians—Ethnic identity. | Hawaiians—Biography. | Multiracial women—United States—Biography. | Reporters and reporting—United States—Biography.
Classification: LCC DU624.65 .G66 2025 | DDC 996.90092[B]—dc23/eng/20250228
LC record available at https://lccn.loc.gov/2024061209

Our books may be purchased in bulk for promotional, educational, or business use. Please contact your local bookseller or the Macmillan Corporate and Premium Sales Department at 1-800-221-7945, extension 5442, or by email at MacmillanSpecialMarkets@macmillan.com.

First Edition: 2025

10 9 8 7 6 5 4 3 2 1

This book is dedicated to my kūpuna, for their wisdom and guidance, my entire 'ohana who live today, and for the Kahanu generations to come. My story is also dedicated to the lāhui of Hawai'i, whether they live on the islands or around the world, who respond to its calling. May all who understand and embrace aloha 'āina fight to keep our culture alive.

CONTENTS

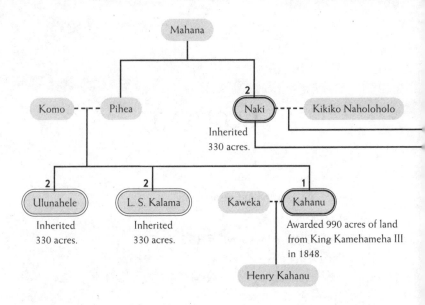

Mahana

Komo - - - Pihea   **2** Naki - - - Kikiko Naholoholo
Inherited
330 acres.

2 Ulunahele   **2** L. S. Kalama   Kaweka   **1** Kahanu
Inherited   Inherited   Awarded 990 acres of land
330 acres.   330 acres.   from King Kamehameha III
                                                in 1848.

Henry Kahanu

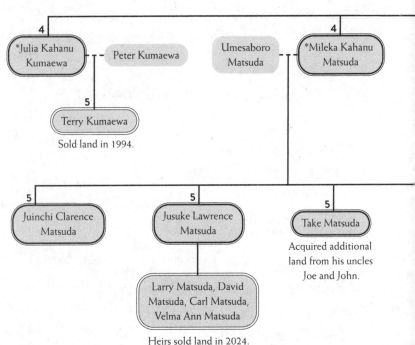

4 *Julia Kahanu Kumaewa - - - Peter Kumaewa   Umesaboro Matsuda   **4** *Mileka Kahanu Matsuda

5 Terry Kumaewa
Sold land in 1994.

5 Juinchi Clarence Matsuda   **5** Jusuke Lawrence Matsuda   **5** Take Matsuda
                                                                    Acquired additional
                                                                    land from his uncles
                                                                    Joe and John.

Larry Matsuda, David
Matsuda, Carl Matsuda,
Velma Ann Matsuda

Heirs sold land in 2024.

HISTORY OF THE KAHANU FAMILY LAND

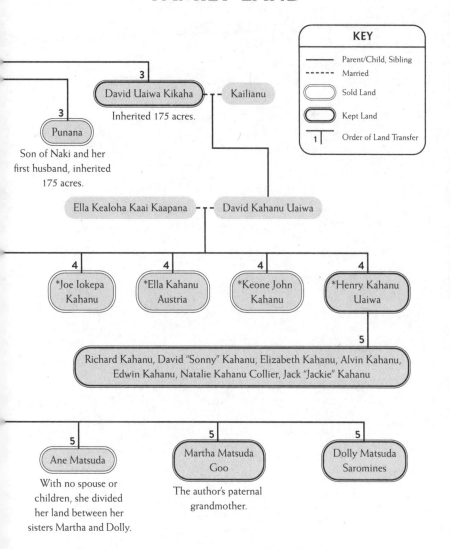

KEY

———	Parent/Child, Sibling
- - - - -	Married
(oval)	Sold Land
(oval)	Kept Land
1	Order of Land Transfer

3 David Uaiwa Kikaha - - Kailianu
Inherited 175 acres.

3 Punana
Son of Naki and her first husband, inherited 175 acres.

Ella Kealoha Kaai Kaapana - - David Kahanu Uaiwa

4 *Joe Iokepa Kahanu

4 *Ella Kahanu Austria

4 *Keone John Kahanu

4 *Henry Kahanu Uaiwa

5 Richard Kahanu, David "Sonny" Kahanu, Elizabeth Kahanu, Alvin Kahanu, Edwin Kahanu, Natalie Kahanu Collier, Jack "Jackie" Kahanu

5 Ane Matsuda
With no spouse or children, she divided her land between her sisters Martha and Dolly.

5 Martha Matsuda Goo
The author's paternal grandmother.

5 Dolly Matsuda Saromines

*All of Ella and David Kahanu Uaiwa's children inherited an undivided 130 acres. In 1972, the family, along with the Hana Ranch, donated 61 acres, including the Pi'ilanihale heiau, to the National Tropical Botanical Garden.

KULEANA

Introduction

ʻĀINA

Along the rugged shores of Mauiʻs east coast, bright blue waves crash into the black rock coastline that, from above, frames the rainforest like a postcard of paradise. A light breeze smells like the wild guava trees that grow abundantly on the island mixed with salty air whipped up from the ocean: a perfume found only here, in the middle of the Pacific. And around every bend in the winding road that weaves through here, a breathtaking waterfall spills from the cliffs above—sometimes into a natural swimming hole that tempts you to stop to take a cool dip.

This is one of the last remaining places of the *real* Hawaiʻi untouched by international hotels or tacky bus tours.

These are my familyʻs ancestral Hawaiian lands.

For centuries, these lands were the crown jewels of Native Hawaiian royalty who relished the lush green landscape ideal for growing crops and the shoreline known for its plentiful fish, sharks, octopus, and shellfish. This land is also full of stories—or passed-down mo'olelo (moh-oh-leh-loh)—that tell legends of bloody battles waged between island chiefs who fought for control over this rich bounty. Other mo'olelo explain the formation of dozens of beautiful pools with waterfalls that cascade, one pool to the next, down the mountain; or the cave whose water mysteriously turns pink once a year. Perched along the coastline sits an enormous Native Hawaiian temple called a *heiau* (hey-ouw). Made of rocks meticulously stacked nearly four stories high, the heiau is a remnant of the ancient Hawaiian religion and culture that thrived here centuries ago.

More than ninety acres of this land, from the road to the sea, now worth many millions of dollars, are still owned by my family—the Kahanu family. This is just a fraction of the original, much larger landholding given to my ancestor by King Kamehameha III in 1848.

And for the most part, this land has remained exactly as it was some 175 years ago. Raw, undeveloped, wild. It is overgrown with thick hala trees, whose broomstick-like roots stand high above the ground and whose thin, sharp leaves serve as nature's barbed wire fence, keeping out curious hikers. Spindly papaya trees peep up in the distance, serving up their yellow fruit for the birds that chirp loudly but can't be seen. A single dirt road, which floods several times a year after sudden bursts of thunderstorms, divides the land parcels belonging to my grandma—our family, her descendants—and my aunties and uncles and cousins.

Our ancestors are buried, in marked graves, a few hundred yards from the base of the ancient temple—permanent evidence of our connection to a mysterious, centuries-old structure that was once central to the people of this island. On the land adjacent to it, a few landmarks and memories are all that help delineate where one cousin's property starts and another's ends. All we know is that our family—the Kahanu family—promised to take care of this land, and the heiau, for generations. No matter that no one has money to build a house on their parcel of land or pay the water company to build a line to it. No matter, because having this land allows us to hold on to a small piece of the past. That past was a time before the United States of America existed and when Hawai'i was not a vacation spot but an island nation with its own system of chiefs, gods, and kings, thriving and isolated by vast oceans on every side.

This land is not merely land, at least in the way Western eyes see it. The land is heritage. The land is evidence of our survival. The land—the 'āina (aye-nah)—is our kuleana (koo-lee-ah-nah)— our responsibility.

Kuleana is a word you don't hear much as a visitor to Hawai'i, but you do if you're a local. It comes from Native Hawaiians' strong identity and relationship with the land that was both their responsibility and privilege to take care of. In the ancestral tradition, families each had responsibility for some part of the place they lived, the food supply or cultural practice. For example, certain people had kuleana for growing taro or crops in a certain part of the island, or for taking care of a fishpond or teaching hula. In ancient Hawaiian society, each person had an assigned role that they learned, practiced, and perfected with pride. In turn, society depended upon them to fulfill their role so that the larger society could function and become dependent upon one another for survival.

Kuleana was this principle, and this way of life was essential for living on an island surrounded by a vast ocean as far as the eye could see with little contact to the outside world. Native Hawaiians had to develop a way to survive and thrive by making the most of what nature could provide on land and sea. Before Western contact, that meant developing a system by which each island was divided into a dozen or more pie-shaped pieces, with each slice containing a section of waterfront and a section to the top of the mountain.

In Hawaiian, the word 'āina means "land," but it also means more than land. It also refers to food that comes from the land. Take care of the land, and it is implied that the land will take care of you. Mālama i ka 'āina (mah-lah-ma ee-kah aye-na).

Within each piece of pie, certain people were responsible for fishing, for building canoes, for cultivating the crops, for making adzes or stone tools, and building hale (hah-lay), or house structures, and household items. There were also kāhuna (kah-hoo-nah), or priests, who were healers or overseers of the heiau. In American popular culture, you may have heard a reference to "the big kahuna," or priest. But the kāhuna were specialists in spiritual wisdom and practice who spent years training and also descended from elite families.[1] The 'āina was overseen by konohiki (koh-no-hee-kee), or chiefs, whose job was to ensure that each section of the island was producing enough food for others to eat; the hale were built with care; the canoes were fashioned with skill for fishing or travel; the fishponds were built with precision. Today, as people talk about climate change, we imagine a utopian world of sustainability. But Hawaiians perfected and lived this concept because they needed to survive while living in the middle of the ocean, two thousand miles away from any other continent. They mastered sustainability because they needed to in order to survive. It's what enabled them to thrive for hundreds of years.

Today in Hawai'i, you often hear kuleana in a more casual, modern way to mean "responsibility," as in signs that read, "It's your kuleana to pick up your own trash." Responsibility, in the Western sense, often comes with a sigh, an obligation—a burden, even. But kuleana means a much deeper, prideful responsibility—a privilege, even. Kuleana, in the family sense, is passed down from one generation to another in a continuous line. It's not something one randomly decides to pick up; it's often connected through history that came before you and will be assigned to those who will come after. At least, that's the way I understand it.

In our family, my grandma and other elders always talked about our kuleana for this special land on Maui that King Kamehameha III had granted to us to take care of. But why us? Nearly two centuries after the royal land grant, several forces have made our family's ability to hold on to this land much harder. First, the land was transformed by foreigners who upended centuries of native farming, aquaculture, and self-sufficiency to develop sugar plantations, and later, pineapple. After the illegal overthrow of the Hawaiian government by the United States, foreigners who understood real estate laws, probate, and taxes figured out how to buy land that belonged to Hawaiians who hadn't paid taxes on their property because they didn't know they needed to. And today, owning Hawai'i land is one of the most prized assets by the world's wealthiest, who are gobbling up acreage in a race against one another, driving up land values and property taxes for those who actually live here. Every decade, my kūpuna (koo-poo-nah)—my ancestors—lost hundreds of acres of that original land grant. Some would say it's a miracle that any portion of it survived in our hands through today. Given the history of colonialism and pressures of capitalism, some would say it's just a matter of time before we are forced to give up the last remaining acres of it.

And in 2019, we were confronted with that moment.

It started with an email from my father on a Monday night, after I put the kids to bed.

Sara,

The Hāna property taxes went up 500%. If we can't find a way to pay, then the trust funds will be depleted in 7 years and we may be forced to sell it. This is how Hawaiians are losing their birthright lands.

Dad

I was sitting at the kitchen table in my brick colonial home on a cool autumn night in Washington, DC, a city I had lived in for nearly twenty years.

"What?!" I said aloud in my dark, quiet kitchen. Goose bumps rose up on my arms. Inside, I felt sick, uncertain. *This can't be true,* I thought. *Surely, we can do something about this. This can't be happening. Why now? Why so suddenly, so randomly now?*

I was so far away. The ground beneath me had shifted, as if time itself was grabbing me by the shoulders, shaking me to do something. I felt a screaming sense of urgency ring in my ears. Yet also in my gut, useless and clueless about where to start.

I felt—how else to describe it?—like a fish out of water, caught very far from where I belonged or was needed.

I was separated by an ocean from our family's land. I was separated by a continent from our family's land. I heard my grandmother calling me back home, yet I wasn't sure how to get back.

Two decades ago, I moved to Washington to pursue my dream and become a reporter for *The Washington Post*. In my early twenties, I'd been chasing that dream, hopping from one city to another working a string of newspaper internships. I'd been making my way across the United States, from west to east, throwing myself into one unfamiliar city after another, from Saint Paul, Minnesota, to Detroit to Boston and, later, on to Washington, DC.

Having grown up in the suburbs of Southern California, I relished living in a new city and approached each one like I was an anthropologist studying a new world. I spent my time figuring out their rhythms, reading books about their histories and major industries, and studying the characters who ran them. For American reporters, it was a rite of passage to move from town to town, from smaller to larger metro daily newspapers, until someday, hopefully landing at a big paper like *The New York Times* or *The Wall Street Journal*. My mentors and college professors each could name all the papers they'd worked for like they were tattoos on their bodies, markers they had earned on their way to "making it." So when I, at age twenty-four, was offered a full-time job at *The Washington Post*, I felt like I had skip-leveled my career by some miraculous fluke. It didn't matter that the job was to cover a suburban county in Maryland that I couldn't find on a map. It was a coveted job as a reporter at a newspaper where most reporters aspired to work. I was going to write stories that were delivered to hundreds of thousands of homes with my name on it: Sara Kehaulani Goo, reporter, *The Washington Post!* And I was determined to make the most of it.

I'll never forget the day I drove into the city. I was behind the wheel of my tiny, silver Toyota coupe, filled to the brim with plastic bins of clothes, boxes of bedding, and lamps. The sun was setting, and I turned around the corner of New York Avenue and glimpsed a sight of the US Capitol dome. The sky was pink and orange, and the dome was shining like a picture in a movie where you hear "God Bless America" in the background. "Holy shit!" I screamed to no one but me, shocked to see it up close. I thought of all the promise of democracy represented in that dome, and of the people who built it and the history made within it. The last time I'd visited Washington, it was as a tourist with my parents and cousins when I was in middle school. I remembered touring the Capitol and the Smithsonian, awestruck by the enormity of it all. Now I'd be part of the history, too, or at least witness it up close as a reporter. Reporters love to say that our job is to write "the first draft of history." I felt the duty and honor of everything in that one moment. Pinch me.

Today, I know people have strong feelings about the news. They have come to distrust it, disdain it, and think of journalists as biased pundits whose agenda is to take political sides or sell sensationalism. But that's not the journalism world I entered, nor was it what I set out to do. By today's standards, my reasons for pursuing journalism were simpler, inspired by legendary reporters like Bob Woodward and Carl Bernstein. I'd grown up so far away from the powerful that I yearned to understand for myself how the government works, how companies work, and how to hold them all accountable. I wanted to tell stories—true stories—based on research and interviews to get to the bottom of it. While other friends wanted to go to college and pursue careers to make money, I wanted to make a difference. I saw journalism as a civic duty and essential to democracy—that people deserved information so that they could make decisions and make up their own minds. I didn't even necessarily want to cover politics. I just wanted to get close to the action, and I loved the thrill of doing it for a living.

It was electrifying to be living in the nation's capital and, more importantly, the country's nerve center for news. And once I got started at the *Post*, I lived off the daily adrenaline of chasing down members of Congress, asking tough questions, and rushing back to the newsroom with just minutes left to write my stories in time for the 6:00 p.m. deadline. I came to work inspired and awed by the incredible reporters I met and worked with, some of whom won Pulitzer Prizes each year. My twenties were spent chasing story after story of the first decade of the new century—covering the terrorist attacks of 2001, the airline bankruptcies, the rise of companies like Google, Facebook, and YouTube, and the financial crisis that began in 2007.

Soon after I moved to DC, I met Michael, and I was excited to find someone who didn't live in the news world that I spent so much time in. For as stressed and adrenaline-filled as I was at work, I also needed someone who could provide me some balance. He dazzled me with how smart he was, having traveled the world, trekking across Nepal and living in Europe. He loved playing guitar and cooking nice meals for me. We got married, bought a home together, started a family, and suddenly—the years passing by like minutes—I realized I was becoming an East Coast person. Moreover, my parents had followed me to the DC area several years later to be closer to us and our kids—their first grandkids. It was like one day I woke up and realized that my family center had shifted east.

I found myself at times wondering how twenty years flew by so fast. Even though I loved it, I hadn't intended to be in Washington forever. It never really felt like "home" the way Southern California did, or the way Hawai'i did. It never felt like a permanent place for me. In my mind, I was still the young person charmed by the city, here on a stop that had somehow turned into a cul-de-sac. Washington—especially for professionals who work in politics and media—is full of people who have moved there from somewhere else to chase their career dreams. Now, I've lived more of my life on the East Coast than the West Coast. In more ways than one, I was far from the Pacific.

As the years ticked by, I'd had moments of gut pangs. Moments of feeling out of place and a yearning—a calling coming from the west to go back "home." This ramped up after we had kids. I began to worry whether my young children had any connection to the Hawaiian side of their family and their roots. When they were born, it was important to me to carry on the family tradition by giving our children Hawaiian middle names. But now I feared that our family visits every few years to Hawai'i might not be enough for them to feel connected to the place, when our daily lives were consumed with the busy schedule of work, school, after-school sports, piano lessons, work-related travel, and home improvement that was grinding up every hour of every day into a scheduled spreadsheet matrix that controlled our lives. I'd started to feel in between two worlds. Day-to-day, I was living a successful, fulfilling city lifestyle far from Hawai'i—putting on a collared shirt, a winter coat, hustling to get the next news story, the next rung up the career ladder, shuttling my kids around to sports practice. I was happy, I told myself. But inside, I felt something unmoored.

Living in Washington enabled me to achieve all my professional dreams and the stereotypical American dream. My husband and I were able to buy a single-family home on the edge of the city. I could buy groceries and things we needed without worrying too much about money. We saved for family vacations every summer. Life had been good, and I had much to be thankful for. On paper, we looked like every other successful family. But when it came to what mattered, I felt a sense that I was failing as a parent. Would our children ever feel Hawaiian—or Hawaiian enough?

If I'm honest with myself, I was struggling to work through my own identity. Genetically, I'm the definition of East meets West. My mother is Caucasian, whose ancestors likely came over on the *Mayflower*, and later generations became Midwestern farmers. My father's side is the story of Hawai'i and the East, with one side immigrating to Hawai'i from Okinawa, looking for work in the booming sugarcane plantations; the other side settling in Hawai'i from China to start a small laundry and tailoring business, hustling their way to a better life.

Even though I carry on the Chinese name Goo, culturally, my father and grandparents did not pass down much in the way of traditions from China or Okinawa, where my great-grandfather was from. That's because their roots were from the melting pot of Hawai'i, which drew immigrants from across Asia in search of work and opportunity for more than a century. In the mainland United States, if you look Asian, people expect that you speak an Asian language and assume that you or your parents are immigrants. But neither of those things is true for me. I joke with my white friends that truthfully, I'm about as Asian as they are Irish. Meaning that my Chinese and Okinawan side moved to the territory of Hawai'i in the late 1800s and early 1900s, respectively. In Hawai'i, my family's long history on the islands is a much more common story of mixing different countries of origin over the course of many generations.

Aside from all the tangled East-West heritage inside me, there was one small side, the Native Hawaiian side, that I wrestled with most. It spoke loudest of all inside of me because it left behind not just a story and a culture that went back hundreds of years but a physical, actual place.

As I sat with that email open in front of me, that voice I heard all those years calling me to Hawai'i was now screaming like a five-alarm fire. If we lost the land, I'd lose not only my connection to Hawai'i, but I'd never be able to share that with my children and their children. I saw not just the danger in losing connection to a place but more so the end of a family legacy—forever.

My Hawaiian grandma and her siblings each inherited about ten acres of Maui land from their mother, who inherited the land from her grandfather, who inherited it from his father, then aunt, and then from the original ancestor—whose name we only know as Kahanu—who received the land from the king. Grandma was always clear that this land should remain in the family. She had dreamed of building a small home on her land so that she could spend some of the last years of her life where it had started. And she wanted us—her children and grandchildren—to feel as connected to the special place as she did. She came close to achieving that dream, but it never happened. Today, the land sits as it has for more than 175 years—a beautiful, wild rainforest with a rocky coast—just as it did when Native Hawaiians lived here undisturbed by a Western world that would change their way of life forever.

But now I began to wonder what kuleana meant to me—and whether it was even possible to fulfill—when I had built a life so far away and so far removed from it. Of course, genetically, I'm part Native Hawaiian because my great-grandmother was full Native Hawaiian and her native language was Hawaiian. And even though I grew up in Southern California, I was raised in many of the cultural traditions: eating Hawaiian food, watching my aunties dance hula, and listening to Hawaiian music. We had many aunties and uncles and cousins we'd visit in Hawai'i, and over the years, our family ties grew closer to family there. In their retirement years, my grandparents moved back to Hawai'i, settling into a local community of largely other Native Hawaiians in O'ahu. And when I'm in Hawai'i, I feel welcomed into one big 'ohana (oh-hah-nah).

Even so, to people in Hawai'i, there's a clear divide between locals and mainlanders, or visitors from the continental United States. And there's another pecking order based on race, with ultimate street cred in how Native Hawaiian you are and, at the bottom, how haole (how-lee), or white—or technically, "foreigner"—you are. In Hawai'i, I'm hapa (hah-pah), or part, a mix of those two. I'm a mainlander who lives a very different cultural and social reality from locals who live on the islands. Even if I look Hawaiian, in Hawai'i, my mainland accent gives me away. I'm not a "local" who can talk pidgin beyond my "Eyy, howzit?!" But I also know enough and understand enough that they know I'm not a haole. I've always felt like a member of the Native Hawaiian tribe on the outside looking in, trying to fit in and learn, mouthing the words to the song but not confident enough to sing it loudly. Still, Hawai'i and its cultural practices—the music, the hula, the food, even the language—stir something deep inside me that is hard to describe except to say that it feels part of me even as I'm still learning it. I feel connected to it, called to it deep in my soul. It feels like I belong, and I want more of it. But my ability to be present in it is never long enough, never quite fully immersed.

The possibility of losing Grandma's land suddenly pushed all these nagging questions to the front and center of my life. It forced me to confront an uncomfortable question about my place in this culture and lineage. Was I kanaka maoli (kah-nah-kah mah-oh-lee)—Native Hawaiian—or malihini (mah-lee-hee-nee)—visitor? I felt lost somewhere in between.

———

The Kahanu lands are one of the rare properties still in the hands of Native Hawaiian families on Maui since the US government illegally overthrew the kingdom of Hawai'i over a century ago. Like countless others, our family had already lost hundreds of acres in the first land grab—from the sugarcane plantations where sons of American missionary families and European entrepreneurs pushed out Native Hawaiians and other residents from their homes to cultivate and export sugar. These families—the Cookes, the Castles, and the Baldwins—became the wealthiest in the islands, some of whom still own some of the largest properties.[2] Alongside the sugarcane plantation owners are the big ranchers—the Robinsons, the Parkers—who befriended Hawaiian royal family members and made deals with them, and today are also among the largest property owners. In our family's case, our land first became owned by a sugarcane plantation (Kaʻeleku Plantation), which was later bought by the Hāna Ranch.

The second land grab came swiftly from the US government, which eyed Hawaiʻi's strategic location in the Pacific as an ideal military base—and later used one Hawaiian island, Kahoʻolawe, exclusively for bombing target practice. Pearl Harbor was infamously attacked by Japanese bombers, which brought the United States into the Second World War. But well before that, the beautiful harbor was known as *wai momi*, or pearl water, for its plentiful pearls tucked away in oyster beds that were plucked by Native Hawaiian divers. Its immense coral bed was dredged, gutted, and now used as a naval base. The largest landowner was once the royal family of Hawaiʻi—the crown lands—which became US state and federal lands with the overthrow of the Hawaiian government.

Today's land grab is from yet another powerful set that roughly tracks the world's wealthiest on the Forbes list: Zuckerberg, Bezos, Ellison, just to name a few. In 2012, tech billionaire Larry Ellison bought out the first land grab owners by purchasing nearly the entire island of Lānaʻi from the former owner of Dole Food (yes, the pineapple company). Over the past three decades, the world's wealthy out-of-state landowners have driven up the price of land. About one-quarter of home sales in Hawai'i and one-third of property taxes are paid by nonresidents.[3] For any local person, this land grab means less property available and higher prices. To put it simply, Hawai'i property is at a premium and locals are competing against the wealthiest buyers in the world.

So, at first glance, our family tax problem could be viewed as a version of any problem that locals who live in a tourist destination experience to some degree: rich investors gobble up real estate that they don't occupy most of the time. Meanwhile, all the locals who work every day mowing the rich people's lawns or cleaning their homes get handed higher and higher taxes for their own property. And with each passing year, rising property prices make it harder for those on a working wage to afford anything. Each year, it becomes more difficult for local people to afford to rent, let alone buy a home of their own.

The real story, though, is more than just about real estate. The real problem is that Hawai'i is still a modern-day colonial state that has, generation after generation, displaced the Native Hawaiian people from the land, their natural resources, way of life, and culture. It has removed them from their 'āina. It has been a slow, quiet crisis that no one is paying attention to because Hawai'i is so far away—out of view, out of mind. It is also a burning, urgent crisis because now Native Hawaiians are struggling to remain in Hawai'i and keep their culture alive.

As of 2020, there are more people of Native Hawaiian ancestry living outside Hawai'i than those who live on the islands.[4] As a global tourist destination and real estate investment for the world's wealthiest, Hawai'i has become an untenable place to live for local people. It has the most expensive housing costs in the nation. Less than a third of local residents can afford to buy a condo, much less a single-family house, as prices have risen 2.5 to 8 times their value since 2000.[5] At the same time, the number of people living without shelter in Hawai'i has grown—in part because people literally can't afford a place to live.[6] Countless others are forced to live with multiple family members in cramped conditions just to make ends meet. When the median home sells for over $1 million but the median salary is $50,000, the math is simple.[7] Hawai'i has New York City real estate prices but Arkansas salaries. For a state that was once an independent nation, the Hawaiian people have seen, decade by decade, an unending downward slope in their ability to remain living in their own homeland. They can't afford it anymore. So they move to Las Vegas, which locals affectionately and smirkingly call Hawai'i's "ninth island." Everyone in Hawai'i has family in Vegas.

It begs the question: What is Hawai'i without the Hawaiian people?

Drive a half mile from any beach resort, out of view of the tourists, and you will see tent encampments filled not just with people unhoused but families—including some working people who sleep in a tent and shower at the beach and then get on a bus every day to work at those hotel resorts. Four in ten people who are homeless in the state today are Native Hawaiians or Pacific Islanders.[8]

We learn in American history books about the displacement, violence, and broken promises to Native American tribes as if that sad story is in our past. But each day, each year, native people continue to be displaced from their land and their livelihood in Hawai'i, whose only American narrative is as a paradise tourist destination. What's overlooked, out of view, and too uncomfortable to see is the separation of Native Hawaiian land from Native Hawaiian people. My family's story is one small sliver of that story and the odds stacked against native families to hold on to their land, their ability to live and practice their culture and let it live on for the next generation.

There are small glimmers of hope in this larger struggle. With the COVID pandemic in 2020, Hawai'i temporarily shut its borders, and its tourism business and it immediately felt the impact of what happens when millions of tourists stop coming. The people saw that their beaches were cleaner. The fish and coral returned. In a place where 85–90 percent of the food is imported by boat or plane every day, Hawaiians began growing more crops to feed themselves.[9] They started important discussions about how the island economy needed to serve the local people, not just the tourists and investors. This has fueled what had already been a broader resurgence of reclaiming what has been lost—rights to land, to water, to protecting natural resources, and reviving the culture, language, and traditions. It's no wonder more Native Hawaiians have been running for—and winning—local public offices and leading effective advocacy groups in recent years.[10] There's been an awakening.

The wildfires that swept through the town of Lahaina, Maui, in August 2023 traumatized all of Hawai'i. The fires not only killed more people—more than one hundred—than any US fire in recent memory within a matter of hours, they exacerbated a housing crisis in which there was nowhere to put the thousands of people who survived. The problem was not that there wasn't enough housing for survivors; it was that the available houses, condos, and townhomes go for $500 a night and are for tourists, not locals. Since the fires, everyone who has survived has had to move multiple times from hotels to temporary housing. More than 1,500 families who lost their homes in the fires have had to leave Maui altogether, creating much larger questions for the island of how it can serve both local people and tourists and how to find a new balance.[11]

Against that larger backdrop, our family had a tax problem and a deadline. The last thing I wanted—or that anyone in my family wanted—was to be the end of the line, the generation that lost the land forever. Without any explanation, the tax bill on our ancestral lands had arrived in an amount due that was multiples above the year before. Now, it was our turn to hold on to our land in that broader macroeconomic story.

Later that night, after tucking the kids into their beds and putting away the dishes, I lay in my own bed with a million thoughts in my head. I was five thousand miles away. What could we do? It's not like we could walk to the county tax office in Maui to solve the problem or even hire a local lawyer to help advise us. *Should I book a flight to Hawai'i and figure this out?* The stress of not having any clear path to help my dad and the reality of knowing that I—with a busy full-time job in the news industry and three kids and a dog to manage—likely couldn't get away even if I wanted to began to sink in. At that moment, Hawai'i felt as it has over the course of my life—like it was calling me and yet just out of my grasp.

I didn't know it at the time, but this email would spur our family into action for the next several years, in agony over what to do with our property. Could we buy ourselves some time—and tax relief—by changing the zoning on the property? Should we buy an Airstream or glamping yurts and rent out overnight stays through Airbnb to help pay for the taxes? Or should we confront the inevitable decision to consider leasing or selling it? The rising taxes forced us to face uncomfortable truths—it was unlikely that anyone in our immediate family would likely live in this remote part of

Hawai'i, and no one wanted to put up the money or invest the time to do anything with it.

Compounding the tax problem were all the people who would immediately need to be involved. My grandma's land was held in a family trust set up by my late grandparents, who had eight children, four of whom had multiple adult children of their own—and I'm just one of twelve of those children. Who would have a say, and how would we set up a structure that would not disturb the family peace? It was like sorting out a family will with the person not yet deceased—among eight stakeholders across four time zones, each with varying financial means, personalities, and levels of interest in Hawai'i—including some who hadn't visited the islands in many years. In other words, a total headache.

This journey would lead to difficult choices, frustration among family members, and anger at the shape-shifting legal and governmental forces trying to take away our land or control how we use it. I considered whether to stand back and let my dad and his brothers and sisters sort it out. But the land—and my sense of duty to fulfill my Hawaiian grandmother's wishes to hang on to it—called me to act. It also forced me to wrestle with something we don't often talk about: What do we owe those who came before us and those who will come after?

In his email to me that night, my father didn't need to explain. I understood the panic behind his words. The clock was starting. The good news was that we likely had a few years to come up with a plan. The bad news was that it was not going to be easy.

Saving the land was far from guaranteed.

PART ONE

THE ʻĀINA AND THE SECRET

1

THE HEIAU

I was eight years old when I was first exposed to the family secret, on my first trip to Hawai'i.

It was a cold, dark morning when Dad nudged my sister and me out of our bunk beds to get in the car for the drive to Los Angeles International Airport. "Ready to go to Hawai'i?" he whispered, patting my arm.

I grinned before opening my eyes and then became instantly alert with excitement. Once we got to the airport and boarded our plane, Mom snapped photos of the three of us kids—me, my younger sister, Haley, and my little brother, Benjamin, wearing pajamas—crammed into a row in the coach section, with our faces full of anticipation. I can still recall the blood racing through my forearms as I gripped my mother's hand on one side and Haley's in the other, bracing for takeoff as the plane rumbled down the runway with increasing speed. "This is the best part!" Mom said, as joyful as we kids were. We felt the momentum of no return as the plane lifted our lumbering load off the ground and the cabin creaked in a thousand small places. Overhead, luggage thunked around. It was not only our first Hawai'i trip but also my first time in an airplane, ever.

I was really looking forward to playing on the sandy beaches of Hawai'i, swimming in any pool we might come across, and maybe even attending a luau with real hula dancing. But as it turned out, our trip would not quite end up like that.

That night, after our six-hour flight to Honolulu, Dad drove us to a single-family house in Pearl City, not far from the airport. We could hear a loud party going on inside, with laughter and the island sound of a Hawaiian guitar strumming. An enormous pile of worn rubber flip-flops, belonging to feet of all sizes, fanned out near the front door. "Okay, no shoes allowed," Dad said, explaining the Hawaiian tradition of removing your shoes before entering a home, which was new to us. He pointed at my feet and that of my sister and brother.

In our socks and bare feet, we walked into a living room full of tanned, smiling relatives who looked a lot like us. Dad led the way, greeting everyone with a loud "Aloha!" and a hug and a kiss for each and every person in the crowded living room. "This is your auntie," Dad said, beginning to introduce everyone in the room. "This is your cousin. Your uncle." Over and over, wow, there was a line of aunties and uncles! On a back patio, a group of older men were playing 'ukulele, guitar, and one man held a small guitar on his lap and slid his finger, which was inside a metal tube, across the strings. A small Christmas tree decorated with tinsel sat in the corner, and about a dozen cousins and aunties resumed a loud game in which they opened and then stole Christmas gifts from one another as the laughter echoed around the room, competing with the music.

One of the aunties beckoned us to a small table in the kitchen, where the familiar sweet tang of teriyaki beef caught my nose. Mom nudged me to sit next to my sister and brother, and we filled our stomachs with piles of rice, macaroni salad, and the sweetened soy sauce–flavored beef. Bursts of laughter erupted from our cousins as we ate and watched from the kitchen table. I couldn't remember everyone's name, but I already felt at home because the food tasted exactly like my grandma's. It was, in fact, nearly identical to the meals she cooked for us when all my aunties and uncles got together at Grandma's house on the mainland. Only now, we were with family members who lived an ocean away. My stomach and eyes connected the dots. This was our big Hawaiian family.

Our first couple of days of the trip included more introductions to relatives and house visits. But it wasn't until we took a short flight to Maui that I learned more about our family's deep roots to the land— and a special place. For the drive to visit Grandma's hometown of Hāna, my parents assembled my younger sister and my baby brother and me into the back seat of a white rented Buick. "It's a very windy road," Mom warned us, knowing my tendency for car sickness. "But just look at the horizon, look at the road ahead, and we'll go slow."

Tourists today know this road as the Hāna Highway. It's written up in visitors' guides as the most adventurous and scenic road in the world—a narrow strip that hugs the sharp cliffs of Maui's eastern coast across more than fifty-nine bridges, many of which are a single lane and pass along natural streaming waterfalls. *Fodor's* says it's "raw and lush and beautiful, and at every turn there are waterfalls, black sand beaches, iconic surf spots, and locals selling all sorts of fruit breads. It feels like *real* Hawaii, with its blissful lack of big resorts and its low key, barefoot vibe."[1] It sounds romantic, maybe even fun. But for me, at least at age eight, it was a form of torture.

Although we were driving along the coast, it was hard to see where the road was headed. The road began gently enough, with long curves, and I could see the popular windsurfing spot to my left, where surfers took air and leaped high off the waves. But soon enough, that vista disappeared and became a series of nonstop switchbacks—620 from beginning to end—with increasingly harrowing turns. My head begged for relief and throbbed, and my stomach felt as though it were perched on the edge of my throat.

I looked at the steering wheel in Dad's strong hands and noticed that they never stopped moving: he spun the wheel almost all the way around clockwise, then spun counterclockwise, then repeated and repeated. Large trucks heading in our direction brushed so close to us on the narrow path that I could've high-fived the occupants as they sped by. Impatient local drivers filled with teenagers sitting in the backs of pickup trucks flashed their lights for us to pull over to the side. Just as soon as we let them pass, we'd join the road again to find ourselves behind a shiny rental car like ours flashing its red taillights. All the while, through the windshield, I could not detect what I desperately wished to see around every curve—the holy grail—straight pavement.

"Look at the road, the horizon straight ahead," Dad said again, trying to help. But there was no horizon. The road ahead kept disappearing behind a sharp bend, and the spinning, spinning, spinning felt like we were moving curlicue by curlicue up a Dr. Seuss mountain. Cigarette smell from the Buick's beige cloth seats added even more nausea to my misery. Around each bend, my stomach threatened to lurch out my lunch. I took deep breaths, hoping for a sign that it would end soon.

"We're almost there," Dad said.

"Can we pull over?!" I begged. But in many places along the barely two-lane road, there was no place to pause. The pavement hung on to the vertical mountain cliffs on one side; on the other, a deviation of the tire by mere inches would mean diving straight down hundreds of feet to the ocean below. For much of the drive, the road narrows to a single lane as it crosses over bridges, so drivers must wait their turn to cross.

"Ooh, look!" Mom called from the front seat as we drove over a bridge and caught a quick glimpse of water trickling from a tall rock. But just as I found what she was pointing at, the car yanked us around another sharp curve. I dug my fingernails into the seat in front of me and hung my head, cursing the road, this trip, my parents, and the fact that I had not yet had the chance to swim at the beach or see a luau. "See the waterfall, kids?"

This is paradise?

Hawai'i, I decided, *is like hell.*

After three of the most excruciating hours of my life, that road spat us out to a lush open landscape and the relief of a horizon. The road's sharp curves eventually widened. The bridges became fewer and farther between, and the road finally opened up as the landscape shifted from cliffside edges to flatter, greener, and more rural terrain on either side. Small homes and signs of civilization, like a roadside coffee shack, appeared to our left. Much of the green landscape was filled with overgrown grass and scattered trees, as though a series of small farms had been let go to grow wild. Dad pulled the Buick off to a side road that headed down toward the ocean. Then the road turned to a dirt path lined with slim wire fences along either side. A few horses and cows grazed in the distance.

I was proud of myself for making it the entire journey without hurling out the window. But I was still green when Dad suggested we get out and walk a bit to get some fresh air. Once I put my feet on the ground, I said a prayer of thanks to God and took a few deep breaths, bent over, my hands on my knees. I smelled the recent rain on the pavement. Dad motioned for Haley and me to follow him as he began to stroll away from the car along the side of the empty dirt path.

Soon, I noticed the bushes and nearby trees bore fruit that I had only seen in the "exotic fruit" aisle at Albertsons in California. Papayas as big as my head. Guavas that could be picked ripe from the tree. Bananas the size of fingers that tasted tangy sweet, like an apple. Dad plucked some guavas growing wild next to the road. He pulled one apart to expose its light pink, fleshy seeded insides. When I bit into it, immediately, the torture of the drive began to fade. The fresh, earthy, sweet juice made me want to apologize for all the cursing I had done a few miles back. My stomach started to find its footing.

We picked more guavas along the road. My head stopped throbbing, and it felt good to reconnect my feet to the ground. Haley and I, along with Mom holding Benjamin, followed Dad along the road a short distance until we came to a metal gate. Out of nowhere, a small white truck pulled up next to us and parked. The driver's-side door creaked open, and a small, tan man with thick, brown square-framed glasses looked out and smiled at us.

"Heyyyy!" he shouted.

"Sara, this is your uncle Take [Tah-kay]," Dad said, walking toward the man and meeting him with a warm hug and a kiss on the cheek.

"Alo-ha," he said, reaching out for a hug. "I am Uncle, you grandma's bruddah."

For the rest of the day, and week, Uncle Take served as our guide to the place where he and Grandma, along with their four other siblings, grew up. Today, he wanted to meet us at this spot to show us something important, Dad said. Uncle and Dad immediately began to laugh and talk about "the land" and Grandma. I found myself edging closer to Uncle Take, trying to eavesdrop on the conversation and enthralled with his manner of speaking and his strong, authoritative voice. It was nothing like how Grandma talked, or anyone else I knew.

"You folks want to go down hey-ow?" Uncle Take asked, now looking more serious and raising his eyebrows behind his thick-framed glasses that he kept pushing back up his nose. Haley, Benjamin, and I all nodded up to him, not sure what he was talking about. He was speaking in pidgin English, a creole language created through Hawai'i's history of immigrant groups who needed a truncated version of the English language to communicate. To my eight-year-old ears, though, I didn't quite understand why Dad said everyone spoke like a "pigeon." I found Uncle's words hard to follow. I was always a few beats behind.

"First ting," he said, there were some rules about this thing, the heiau. He bent over to us kids and raised his pointer finger at my younger sister and me. "Remember, it's ka-*pu* to take stones. No take da stones. Bad luck!"

What stones? I didn't know what he was talking about, but I promised to obey with a nod. Dad hadn't really prepared me for this part. I instantly trusted Uncle Take—even if I couldn't understand him completely, I felt his warmth and knew that he would not take us into harm's way. Yet I had no idea where we were going. It sounded like an adventure of some kind to a place that must be important, because it had rules.

Beyond the metal gate, we walked down a narrow path behind Uncle Take's slightly hunchbacked gait over thick roots and alongside trees I had never seen before—their trunks looked like giant broomsticks, with thick bristles that rose from the soil high into the air, taller than I was, and grew into one tall trunk. The air smelled fresh and green, like the rugged, wild overgrowth of trees surrounding us. We walked for several minutes in the quiet. With each step, I began to feel as though we were pushing farther into the jungle and away from where civilization could hear us or know where we were. I listened carefully to the tone of my father's voice for any sign that he might be worried. But his voice never left the casual, reunion tone as he bantered with Uncle Take. The path we followed was created by Uncle Take's white scuffed sneakers as he walked slowly with his bowlegged gait, followed by Dad, four-year-old Haley, and me. Mom, carrying my two-year-old brother, caboosed farther back. We smacked the mosquitoes on our legs as we walked in silence, totally unprepared for what we were about to see. "Huh-huh," Uncle Take said in his deep, staccato baritone. "Mos-kee-do. Dey know you not from here. Me, dey no bother." He pulled out a rusted aerosol can of Cutter and hissed it around our calves with the smell of chemical funk.

Then we stopped and looked up. First, it appeared like an enormous tidal wave of black, emerging above a thick curtain of green jungle several stories tall. Only when we got closer, this temple—or *heiau* (hey-ow), the Hawaiians call it—revealed itself like a mysterious man-made mountain high above our heads. Thousands of thick, porous lava rocks—way too many for me to count—ranging from the size of a watermelon to the trunk of an enormous tree had been neatly lined up and stacked to create this giant wall. Someone—or many, many someones—had taken the time to fit them all together like a jigsaw puzzle. Standing at the base, the rocks formed a structure that was taller than the trees above my head, taller than our

California house, for sure, and maybe even two of our houses. I stood quietly as my mind swirled with questions. It was hard to imagine how these stones got there—who put them there, and why?

Whoever made this mountain of stacked rocks must have spent months or even years doing so, because I couldn't even quite see where it began and where it ended or how far back it went. The moss growing on some of the rocks had turned white with age, a hint that whoever did this must have lived a very long time ago. In some corners, the rocks had tumbled out of place or had become loose, but that only revealed more piles of other rows of rocks that stood behind to keep the structure intact. And what puzzled me most: What was this mysterious structure made of rocks? Why was it hidden in the jungle? How old was it, and why did the Hawaiians build it? Was there something inside, or could we climb to the top somehow to find some more clues?

The rocks extended as far as I could see to my right and left before they disappeared behind the jungle, which hung around the structure as if it were about to eat it up. Above our heads, the stones formed steep steps—I counted one, two, three, four, and, yes, it appeared there were five or more of them—like a staircase made for a giant with legs as tall as Dad to scale the thing. Each step was almost as tall as I was.

The heiau intimidated me, and I realized we had come upon something few people had probably ever seen before. I certainly never had. Should we be here? Should we tell someone? Should we *never* tell someone? I waited for an adult to tell me what it was, but everyone was silent.

Standing at its base, I felt the quiet presence of something— I'm not quite sure what, but something not quite spooky—no— something sacred. Peaceful. It felt like a hush; I wanted to be quiet next to it, like I was in church. This place had stories, but it was not telling.

"Dad, what *is* this? What was it used for?" I asked, and Dad paused—unusual for him. He looked at Uncle Take for a response.

"You know," Uncle said with his baritone voice. "Dis place is called da *heiau*. Pi'ilani [Pee-ee-lah-nee] heiau. Pi'ilani was da chief. In Hawaiian, *heiau* means 'temple.' Very old heiau. And dey really don't know what dey use it for. Some people say dey did these tings there like human sacri-fice and dat stuff, but we don't know. Me, person-ally, I don't tink they do dat, but we don't know for sure.

"Let's go," Uncle Take said, motioning for us to follow. There was more.

He led us to a small path that cut through more thick branches of tall trees with giant sharp leaves that looked like machetes. I waded my small feet around the trees' broomstick legs, while the relentless bloodsuckers ignored the Cutter and pinched the backs of my calves with each step and buzzed in my ears, teasing me that I couldn't stop them. I was torn between wanting to linger, to take in this black monster and ask more questions. I wanted to touch the stones, to break the very rule Uncle Take had told us not to break, if only for a second, and perhaps glean a clue. Yet the nasty mosquitoes were eating me alive, one annoying bite after another. To get away from them, I wanted to run straight for the car. Yet I couldn't go back now. We were going up.

The path turned up a steep hill onto small black lava stones that led to the top of the heiau. I could barely contain myself; I was eager to see what was on top and how big it was up there, hoping for a clue to explain or identify the use of this giant structure. As we climbed up a side path, I wobbled over each rock, wondering if I could keep my balance and also worried whether the entire mountain of rocks would roll out from under me. Bit by bit, I noticed the face of the terrace was created with multiple terraces, each one sharply defined. Even though each terrace was made with irregularly shaped rocks, they fit together to form perfect edges, displaying the skill of their mysterious creators from ages ago.

"Uncle Take?" I nudged myself closer to him. "Why are there big steps up the front?"

But he just shook his head and shrugged and seemed almost a little embarrassed that he didn't know. I looked over at Mom and Dad, whose eyes were as big as mine as they walked around in wonder, even though I sensed this place was familiar to them. My sister whined about mosquito bites.

"You've just got sweet blood, honey," Mom told her.

Even Benjamin was quiet at the heiau.

The higher we hiked, the trickier it became to balance on the odd-shaped rocks. I wobbled, trying to navigate on top of the stones, some of them sharp and shifty while others were the size of softballs. It was almost as if the walkway was built to throw you off-balance on your way up this mysterious site. We stopped, and I took another deep breath. My eyes struggled to make sense of the view. Much like the heiau was structured at the bottom, at the top there was another enormous and equally puzzling vista of black rocks that expanded flat into the distance. It was clear that the enormous height of the heiau was equal to its expanse at the top, about the size of a football field. And as we explored more closely and carefully, there appeared the remains of a village or ghost town of . . . something. Near the middle of the landscape, a two-foot-high wall built of lava stones had been formed into a perfect yet incomplete square, like the outline of a house with a missing space where a large front door should be. But there were no walls, no roof, no signs of anything inside—just stubs forming the outline of a large dwelling—as if everything had been swept away a very long time ago. Two other areas appeared to have similar short wall structures—smaller in size and located a stone's throw from the larger one.

The structures stood on top of the black lava without any further clues. What were these spaces used for? Were they homes or the remains of some buildings, like the house of a king? Were they markers for a religious event? Or were they as Uncle Take suggested—*gulp*—some place where humans came to be sacrificed to the ancient gods? The whole vision was foreign, but it was clear that this place was some version of the Wild West ghost towns I had visited with my family on vacation in Nevada—only much, much older. I tried to picture Hawaiian people standing where I stood now, maybe hundreds of years ago. How did they use this place? What did they look like? How long ago did they build this structure and why? Were these people, whoever they were, somehow connected to *me*?

Uncle Take pointed across the way at our family's gravestones where "tūtū [too-too] man," his great-grandfather, and many other people with long Hawaiian first names and the last name Kahanu were buried. Uncle explained that our family once lived not far from the heiau, but as kids, they were forbidden to go near it or tell anyone about it. It was *kuli kuli*, or hush-hush. "We not talk about it—my mother say—kuli kuli!" The heiau was like a sleeping giant, hidden by a blanket of green trees and bushes for centuries—I'd later learn—but kept quiet by the locals. And it still felt like our special secret on this visit. We were the only people there, surrounded by the sounds of birds rustling in the trees and the distant crashing of the ocean below.

Uncle Take said this heiau was part of our Kahanu family land "from the mountain to the sea" from our ancestor. The heiau is named for Pi'ilani, a Maui king from long ago, he explained. And the breathtaking view of the ocean from the top of the heiau certainly looked like it was fit for a king. The aqua blue waves crashed into the rocky coast just a short distance away, and Maui's jungle lay below like a bright green blanket. In the distance, on a clear day like today, you could see the outlines of the Big Island of Hawai'i.

Something about standing on top of the heiau made it feel wrong to walk on it or even explore it much, and I didn't want to linger. It felt like perhaps we shouldn't be walking on the site. What if it was some kind of burial ground or I knocked a stone over with my foot? Would someone yell if they saw us up there? The lava stones were uneven, sharp, and difficult for my feet to find a comfortable stance on. I felt exposed standing among the mass of black rock, as if the sun's intense heat might suddenly zap me like an ant under a magnifying glass. The ancient rocks, combined with the ocean salt, smelled ashy and volcanic. I tried to listen. The heiau felt sacred, quiet, and full of secrets.

"You can feel the mana of dis place," Uncle Take said.

At that moment, and for years afterward, I would receive only half-satisfying answers to my many questions about this ancient hidden temple in the Hawaiian rainforest, located a stone's throw from my family's land. But I knew that someday I would return to find out.

———

"Goo?!" Laughter. "Gooey Goo!" Laughter. "Goo-goo. Ga-ga. Are you a Gooey girl?" More laughter. Kids, and adults, loved to make fun of my last name. "Are you Chinese?" When you grow up with a last name like Goo, you learn pretty quickly about the downsides of being Chinese in America.

I'm Native Hawaiian and Okinawan from my paternal grandma's side and Chinese from my paternal grandpa's side. Mom's side is Western European—English-Scottish, Irish, and German. In other words, I'm a mutt where East meets West. But I learned from an early age that none of that matters when your name is Goo. Kids would pull their eyes back to make them slanted and tease me about this name that, to Americans, refers to unidentifiable sludge. The constant teasing made me dislike and even resent my own last name. It got so bad that one day I came home from school after another day of teasing and announced to my parents that we, as a family, should change our last name.

"Okay, well, what do you think we should change it to, then?" my mom asked.

"Anything," I said. "Anything else."

I decided we should vote on it, and I took an empty tissue box and converted it to a ballot box where everyone could submit Goo alternatives. I filled it with strips of paper that suggested names like Smith and Jones and my mother's maiden name, Champlin. Something whiter, less remarkable. Something that didn't make the kids laugh at school. "More normal" as defined by the suburban California playground.

Part of what was so unfair about being teased for the name Goo as a kid was that I didn't really feel that I could "own" being Chinese in the way that other Chinese American kids I knew could. Grandpa's side of the family is Chinese, and he grew up in a Honolulu neighborhood where lots of Chinese families lived. But Grandpa was not from China. Neither was his father. He was the grandson of Chinese immigrants and knew only enough words to order in a

Chinese restaurant. They say that it takes three generations to lose a language, and what I didn't realize at the time was that our family didn't fit the more typical Chinese American profile, which was having parents who immigrated to the US from China or Taiwan, and then raised their Chinese American kids in the US. I am fourth-generation Chinese—which I'd learn from other Americans meant that they expected someone with the name Goo to speak Chinese. When it came to Chinese culture, I knew very little. I remember my aunties talking about how I was born in the year of the dragon, and I loved looking up each animal's characteristics for Lunar New Year. I learned to eat with chopsticks at a young age, and Grandpa made the best fried rice for breakfast and lo mein noodles for dinner when he visited. I remember a few trips to eat dim sum in Chinatown with relatives. Sometimes, we'd go to buy sweet pork buns that Grandma called by their Hawaiian name—manapua (mah-nah-poo-ah)—but also known in Chinese as *char siu bao* (char shzoo bou), soft-baked white buns with sweet barbecue char siu meat inside. "It's like a Chinese hamburger!" Grandma would say. And perhaps unlike other American families, we ate white rice with dinner most nights.

I wasn't ashamed to be Chinese American so much as I felt a bit like an impostor. Other Chinese American kids I knew could speak a few Chinese words, at least, or their parents did. They even got money tucked into red envelopes during Lunar New Year. Our family didn't do that. Instead, what I got was all the teasing that came with having a "weird" Chinese last name and few of the benefits (Grandpa's tasty homemade lo mein was one of them). In high school, I got to know other Asian American kids who looked like I did, but in Southern California, they all had a mix of backgrounds that were so different from mine—their parents or grandparents came to California from Japan, Korea, Taiwan, and Vietnam.

Later on in life, I'd learn more details about my great-great-great-grandfather Goo Lip's story of how he emigrated from China and opened a prominent tailor shop along the main street of Lahaina, Maui. I look Asian American, and I have a Chinese name, but in the white American world as well as the Chinese American world, I didn't feel *enough* of either to feel that I fully identified. Among Asian Americans, people who look Asian but who are out of touch with Asian culture are called a "banana"—yellow on the outside, white on the inside. When I first heard this derogatory term, I felt a sting. *Gulp*. Is that what I am—a banana?

The Okinawan side—which my dad and aunties and uncles referred to as the "Japanese side"—was even more distant than the Chinese side. In fact, only later in life while doing more family research did I realize that my great-grandfather Umesaboro didn't immigrate to Hawai'i from Japan but from Okinawa. Of him, four generations removed, I knew practically nothing and practiced nothing from our culture. It was as foreign to me as any other country. I don't think I even knew where Okinawa was on a map, never mind its fraught history of how, like Hawai'i, it had been taken over by another nation. Later, I learned that Great-Grandpa Umesaboro's Okinawan family had disowned him for marrying a Native Hawaiian woman—my great-grandmother Mileka (Mee-leh-kah)—and disapproved of the interracial marriage. He never returned to Okinawa and never took his family, including my grandma, to meet them. When Grandma retired, she and her sisters, as well as Uncle Take, took their first trip to Okinawa and met relatives there for the first time. That one and only visit to her father's homeland was special to her and emotional. But the rejection of my great-grandfather's interracial marriage cut us from any cultural traditions and ties, too. On my first trip to Asia as an adult, I passed through the Tokyo airport, and the man at customs spoke to me in Japanese. I could pass. But it felt like I'd been smoked out. I wasn't really Japanese, nor could I even pretend. I just looked the part. As someone who is mixed race, I learned very early on that to others, I could pass as a lot of things if I kept my mouth shut.

As a kid, I also quickly learned from other kids that being Japanese or Chinese was not as "cool" as being Hawaiian—at least in Southern California. My darker skin and last name indicated that I was more than just Chinese American. "Ooh, you're Hawaiian?" is something I've heard all my life. It's usually followed by, "Cool!" Especially growing up in a small beach town where surfing—not football—was the sport to which lots of kids gravitated, having a bloodline related to where surfing was invented came with a certain status that seemed to cancel out my less familiar Asian background. Among white kids, I figured out pretty quickly that there was a pecking order to one's racial background. And since I'd been to Hawai'i and seen the heiau and family land and visited all my family there, I grew up feeling more Hawaiian than Chinese or Okinawan. The Native Hawaiian part spoke up the loudest inside me not just because it was the side that my parents and grandparents had made sure that I had a connection to, but because it was also reinforced by my peers as the unique part about me. And so I found myself, even in elementary school, constantly correcting the narrative that people had about me and my race. I turned "Goo-goo!" taunting into "Actually, I'm Hawaiian and Chinese American." Friends would come to my defense: "Yeah, shut up. She's Hawaiian." That ended it. This was my coping mechanism, my survival tactic as a child and teenager.

Grandma and Grandpa Goo had made sure that their children and grandchildren knew about Hawaiian culture. After all, they had left Hawai'i to raise a family in California, and they missed many things about it—the food, the music, the beauty of its flowers and landscape. They did manage to find a way to move back to Hawai'i, on O'ahu, after they retired. Growing up, we never had a typical American-style turkey for Thanksgiving. Instead, every family gathering was a mini luau, with a version of shredded, salty smoked kalua turkey for Thanksgiving. Grandpa would marinate the teriyaki steak, which he'd cook on the grill, and spareribs, which he'd slow cook in the oven. The house smelled like tangy-sweet ginger-and-garlic teriyaki. Grandma would indulge us by making or buying a half dozen desserts that reminded her of home—coconut cream pie, custard pie, haupia (how-pee-yah)—a coconut gelatin-like dessert—and fresh vanilla cakes with lilikoi, or passion fruit, icing. Our family gatherings were always fun, weekend-long hangouts filled with jokes, laughter, and lots of food from the islands.

Sometimes on these special occasions, I got to see my three aunties—Maureen, Doreen, and Kathy—dance hula. As teenagers, they studied hula and performed up and down the California coast in these incredible hula costumes that Grandma had kept stored in the attic. They danced in grass skirts with bikini tops and also long, brightly colored aloha-print dresses. They danced slow numbers wearing giant flowers in their hair as well as faster ones, where they held and tapped gourds in their hands to the beat of the song or swung poi balls from their hands. They even knew how to dance Tahitian-style—the fast, hip-shaking rumble. I would sit absolutely mesmerized by their hula, the most beautiful and captivating kind of dancing I'd ever seen. Watching them made me yearn to dance hula myself, and the little that they'd teach me—say, after we'd eaten our Thanksgiving dinner—intuitively felt like it was a part of me.

"Roll your fingers, leading with your middle finger." Auntie Maureen would demonstrate by moving her hand like the shape of a wave. I'd spend hours practicing how to do it just right.

"Don't sway your hips," Auntie Doreen (Auntie Maureen's twin sister) would tell me. "You're really just bending your knees down really low, and it makes your hips sway from side to side."

The family gatherings, with Hawaiian food and hula, gave me a taste of Hawaiian culture before I got a chance to visit for the first time. And when we returned from our trip to Hawai'i, I felt like my identity as Native Hawaiian and connection to the culture further deepened. With that impressionable visit to the heiau, I'd been let in on a secret as Uncle Take took me to an ancient place with a mysterious history that our family had kept quiet for a long time. Not only that—I felt I'd experienced a very different kind of Hawai'i from the one I'd heard about in books and movies. Just a few years earlier, the movie *Indiana Jones and the Temple of Doom* had come out. Visiting this mysterious, enormous, and ancient place with Uncle Take felt like I'd gone on an adventure like Harrison Ford had (except without any bad guys chasing us), traipsing through the jungle to unlock ancient artifacts. In my suburban town in Southern California, lots of kids like me got a chance to visit Hawai'i on summer vacations. But even compared to them, I knew that my trip was very different. Uncle Take had shown me the *real* Hawai'i, not the fake Hawai'i that the mainland tourists see. This was where my 'ohana, our family, was from. I felt accepted and trusted to know about this special family place.

When we returned home to Southern California after that trip, I was eager to learn more about the heiau or any Native Hawaiian history. I remember visiting our local library and searching through the card catalog to find information about heiau—"A hey-what?" the librarian asked. I yearned for books or magazines that would give me more information about the ancient structure I'd just seen, or the history of Native Hawaiian people I craved to understand. As a kid who loved reading and using my library card, I was disappointed to find that there was nothing. Shelves contained books about World War II, the bombing of Pearl Harbor, and tourism. The tourist books had very small sections about the history of Hawaiʻi. In elementary school, we learned all about the history of California, the missionaries and the native tribes, the California independence movement, and the gold rush during the entire fourth grade. But it was confusing as a kid to find that books simply didn't exist about the place and the people of Hawaiʻi. It's possible that I just couldn't find the books or that they didn't have them at our local library. Back then, we didn't have the internet or Amazon to find answers with a quick online search. Years later, when Google and Wikipedia first came into existence, I *still* couldn't find anything about Hawaiian heiau. Even when I was a kid, this blank space felt wrong.

If Native Hawaiian history didn't exist in a book, did that mean that there simply wasn't anything known about Native Hawaiian people and their history? Did it mean that they didn't leave enough of a mark on the world or that their stories didn't count—weren't important enough? Did it mean that no one cared? I was too young at the time to ask these bigger questions that I'd ask later on in life, when I managed to find some books about heiau published in the academic press. I just knew that, early on, this somehow meant that the world didn't know their story because I couldn't find their story. Even Uncle Take didn't know their story. He had said something about "human sacrifices"—which sounded scary and barbaric. But he also didn't know if it was true. Maybe kids in Hawai'i grew up learning about heiau and the Native Hawaiian people in school like I'd learned about California in school. And if that was the case, I wished I had one of their textbooks. I yearned to find a book that would tell me the history of my family's people.

All I learned about Hawai'i in grade school was that it became our fiftieth state, and there were photos in my school textbook of people in Hawai'i looking happy about the "statehood" news. One photo showed a group of people holding a sign saying FIFTY—IT'S NIFTY. The book said nothing about the United States government illegally overthrowing the independent nation of Hawai'i and imprisoning its queen—something I learned about in the news in high school, when President Bill Clinton apologized for it. It said nothing about Native Hawaiians and how, centuries ago, they might have spent months and years building these enormous heiau, rock by rock, down a human chain from the mountain to the sea, as a sign of their chief's power and utilizing it as part of their religious rituals. It said nothing about their way of life and how a group of people voyaged by canoe and settled on the Hawaiian Islands centuries before. It said nothing about how they survived and thrived, in isolation in the middle of the ocean building the ahupua'a (ah-hoo-poo-ah-ah) system. That first trip to the heiau sparked so many broader questions that I'd think and wonder about—I knew there must be answers somewhere, but I couldn't find them. For years after that first trip to the heiau, all my questions remained in a capsule without answers.

Looking back now, this experience—and the unanswered questions—planted the seed for me to become a journalist. That burning itch to find answers would lead me to return again and again to my family's roots in Hawai'i. I simply wasn't satisfied with not knowing the answers. Moreover, I knew that there was something *wrong* with not having answers, like some kind of injustice to having a question mark about a people's history that was also part of my family's history. There was something wrong with not having any books on the shelf about a place and a people. It felt wrong that the books, movies, and stories about Hawai'i focused only on two familiar facts: that Hawai'i is an expensive, bucket-list beautiful place to visit, and Pearl Harbor was bombed by the Japanese, which led our country into World War II.

Yet I had been to an ancient heiau and understood there was a lot more to this place and its people that could not be seen in either of these two narratives. This is where my curiosity was born that would keep me interested to get to the bottom of this story and many other stories. This curiosity would lead me into the news business, where I realized that I could ask questions and find answers for a living. It would take me across the country to later become a newspaper reporter—leaving my hometown along the beaches of Southern California to the freezing Midwest to the centers of power on the East Coast, building a career around the opportunity to dig for answers and writing them into news story after news story. For many years, this insatiable curiosity would take me further along into a journalism career that would move me farther away from Hawai'i. But my time capsule questions about Hawai'i from that first trip made such an impression. The land would pull me back now and then throughout my life, scratching that itch and calling me back.

2

MAUKA TO MAKAI

"Mountain to the Sea"

In his email to my siblings and me, Dad wrote that the taxes on the Hāna land had gone up by multiples in just one year. Now it was time for us to act.

At first, Dad thought it was some kind of mistake: In the "Amount Due" section, the single-page bill said $2,000 instead of the usual $300. It was not preceded by a letter giving us warning. There were no words to explain the change in the amount. It was just a bill that came in the mail, with an extra zero in it this year. Dad just opened his bills and was like, *Wait, what? Is that a typo? Is it for real?*

Among the eight children in his family, Dad and Auntie Maureen oversaw Grandma and Grandpa's affairs after they died. The first thing we needed to figure out was why the taxes had suddenly gone up and what to do about it. The why, it turned out, was pretty straightforward. With a few emails and phone calls to

Maui County, Dad learned that the county tax office had recently started using satellite imagery for taxable properties, and when they took aerial photos of Grandma's land along the east coast, they determined that our family property, which had been zoned for agricultural use, didn't seem to actually be used for that purpose anymore. The photos, which were included in a file online, indeed show the entire area as a dense carpet of wild, green, tropical forest. Fair enough.

The good news was that my grandparents had set up a trust and set aside funds—about $20,000—to take care of taxes, maintenance, and any other expenses that might come up related to Grandma's land in Hāna after they died. Their goals were crystal clear to their eight children, as Grandma repeated over and over again on family occasions whenever it came up: the land should remain in the family as long as we could afford to do so. And by that, Grandma was repeating a family pact that was passed on to her from her own mother and all the Kahanu descendants who still had parcels of that original land grant.

Grandpa and Grandma lived off Grandpa's pension and were very frugal their entire lives, so setting aside $20,000, I imagine now, was not easy for them and must have taken years to squirrel away, bit by bit, to ensure the land's future would be in good hands with the next generation.

Dad said he and Auntie Maureen would start with a legal tactic to fight the big tax bill. A few days after he sent my siblings and me that email—the one that was both matter-of-fact about taxes going up and certain about the need for action—I wanted to know how I could help.

With a little research, I learned there was some good news: there was already a law on the books in the state of Hawai'i designed to help Native Hawaiians hold on to ancestral lands from the Mahele (Mah-hell-ay). All we had to do was qualify for what's called a *kuleana land tax exemption*, and we'd automatically get our taxes lowered. It wasn't lost on me that the name of this tax relief—*kuleana*—was what we were trying to preserve.

Dad reached out to the Native Hawaiian Legal Corporation, a Honolulu-based nonprofit organization whose mission is to advocate for Native Hawaiian rights to land and resources. A generation before, Grandma and her siblings had worked with the legal group when they pushed for the restoration of the ancient heiau and to protect our family's ancestral burial grounds near it. So, Dad figured, he'd appeal to them for assistance.

"I hope [you] would work with me to provide a way to help native Hawaiians avoid being forced to sell their native lands because of property tax codes that ignore the unique origins of our island heritage," Dad wrote to the legal group in a 2020 letter.

"I don't mind paying my fair taxes. Lord knows I pay a lot of taxes. My main objective is to find a way to protect Native Hawaiians' ability to keep their heritage lands and pass them on to future generations. I don't think history will be well served if Native Hawaiians are forced to sell their land to the highest bidder, who often builds a home, drives up the area appraisals which raises taxes on more native heritage lands even further."

A month later, we got the legal group's brutal opinion. "Conclusion: Ineligible."

"The subject parcel is not a 'kuleana' as defined under the Kuleana Act of 1850. As a Mahele Award between KING KAMEHAMEHA III and KAHANU under the Mahele of 1848, it is not a kuleana as defined by law. Only lands defined as 'kuleana' are eligible to request a tax exemption."

The legal group had a lot of sympathy, but their reading of the law was that basically our ancestor was a chief who received land from the king. The kuleana land protections were for maka'āinana (mah-kah-aye-nah-nah), or commoners, who were "native tenants." Never mind that both konohiki and maka'ainana are Native Hawaiian.

To me, the practical application of this law was a ridiculous way to split hairs. In other words, the spirit of the law was behind us, to keep native lands for native people. But legally speaking, in the interpretation of this law written in 1850, our ancestor Kahanu had too much status. So we didn't qualify.

Strike one. It was time to go back to the drawing board and see what else we could do.

In their letter to my father, the Native Hawaiian Legal Corporation had one suggestion for a path forward that was more practical than legal: "Although your property does not qualify for the kuleana property tax exemption, you may be able to lower your real property tax bill in the future by making agricultural use of your property and applying with the county to be assessed at an agricultural rate."

Dad knew that would be our next plan, but it wouldn't be easy, either. To get our Hāna property zoned for agricultural use, we'd have to start some kind of farming operation on it.

"Maybe we can borrow some cows and just take some pictures," Dad joked, "then I'll send it to the county."

I laughed, trying to picture my dad, who had spent his entire career working in a white-collar job for tech companies and who had never met a cow in his life, trying to find one, wrangle it, and move it to our Hāna property. More daunting was the prospect of farming my grandma's plot of land in the rainforest from five thousand miles away. How the hell would we do that?

Dad started cooking up plan B.

———

On the west side of O'ahu, a group of tourists wobble on their stand-up paddleboards as they paddle out on the flat water of the lagoon. In the morning sun, they try to balance on their knees on top of the boards. A yoga instructor, on her own paddleboard facing them, demonstrates how to carefully balance a yoga pose without falling into the water. Meanwhile, a group of retired locals takes a stroll down a mile-long walking path behind the yogis, coffee mugs in hand. A gardener behind them, with a golf cart, monitors the grass, cut at perfect golf-course height, and tends to the bright pink bougainvillea that line the walking path. This is the daily morning routine at the postcardlike beaches of Ko Olina.

Ko Olina is where the American tourism industry has crafted the most perfect resort that tourists want to experience when they think of Hawai'i. But nothing here is authentic. The massive six-hundred-acre site was started by a Japanese developer in the 1990s but abandoned a decade later after an economic downturn. Later, other developers turned what was a local part of the island—far from the crowded beaches of Waikiki—into a quieter, safer resort enclave by building a series of beach "lagoons." The beautiful soft sand is free of rocks or shells because the sand was sifted from those imperfections and then shipped in from a nearby island. The series of four "lagoons," each fronted by a hotel resort or time-share condo building, were dug out and constructed into perfect crescents built so that no waves could enter. Instead, a man-made jetty creates a buffer from the ocean. Inside that barrier, developers created several flat, swimming pool–like bays filled with ocean water. One lagoon sits next to a wedding chapel and venue for destination weddings. Another features a busy luau venue to watch Polynesian dancing. The movie *Blue Crush* was filmed here. These sites are picture-perfect.

At Lagoon 1, Disney opened a resort called Aulani, with rooms starting at $500 a night, and built a floating river and pool alongside its lagoon. The Marriott at Lagoon 3 offers rooms at $600 a night and above. Every morning, tour vans pull up at the hotel lobbies, ready to whisk visitors away for day trips around the island. And in the afternoon, more vans arrive from the Honolulu airport, unloading new visitors straight off their planes, many of them ready to experience Hawai'i for the first time. For many guests, Ko Olina offers a quieter experience than the busy miles of shopping, hotels, and packed beaches at Waikiki. When I'm on O'ahu, I actually enjoy swimming in the lagoons and jogging the walking paths at Ko Olina, like lots of locals do, but it also has the feeling of being on a cruise ship—you're experiencing Hawai'i in its most polished, orchestrated setting.

If you drive just a few miles past the beautifully manicured exit to Ko Olina off the highway and keep going west, you'll find a very different Hawai'i where the tour buses never go. In fact, it's hard to get a taxi from the airport to take me here. It's the local side of O'ahu. It's home to large swaths of Hawaiian homesteads—crown lands that were set aside for the purpose of allotting some land for Native Hawaiians after Americans overthrew the government. It's home to the local people, including many who work at Ko Olina, or who drive the tour buses, or who work at the airport. For the most part, the locals are working in jobs that support the tourism industry, many living with kids and parents and grandparents under the same roof, trying to make ends meet paycheck to paycheck.

O'ahu's west side is also where you will find many local people who don't have roofs over their heads at all. Instead, they have tents or metal awnings curved into Quonset huts. Just a few miles down the road past the resorts, there are equally breathtaking beaches with gorgeous views of the sunset and the warm, glistening ocean set against the backdrop of the island's dramatic mountain cliffs. Only on this beach, there are no $600 rooms. No "perfect" sand that has been shipped in. Instead, green and yellow and red tents dot the beaches for miles upon miles where people are barely hanging on. The main road follows the beaches, and each beach has a bus stop, where a man wearing his "aloha shirt" hotel uniform with his name tag waits to board the bus with a barefoot man wearing dirty shorts and no shirt struggling to stand up. These communities are home to some of the largest concentrations of Native Hawaiians in Hawai'i. This is the poorest part of O'ahu, where society is hurting: the highest area for homelessness, drug addiction, poverty. This is the Hawai'i that my grandparents returned to after raising their kids in California. It simply wasn't the same. And it's getting worse every year.

Native Hawaiians are at or near the bottom rung of society in their homeland, but they were just the first to be squeezed out. Today, most local people—both working-class and college educated—who live in Hawai'i are feeling it is near impossible to make a decent living, afford housing, and save money to get ahead. It's where the American dream is broken—not just a struggle to achieve but totally out of reach. It's an economy where a gallon of milk costs nine dollars but the minimum wage was only recently raised to fourteen dollars an hour.[1] No wonder there's an acute shortage of teachers, medical professionals, and other essential workers—they simply can't make it work. No wonder that there are now more people of Native Hawaiian descent—53 percent of the 680,000—living outside Hawai'i than in Hawai'i.[2] They see that the only way to get ahead is to leave.

"It's a constant conversation we have and so many of our friends have," says my friend and fellow journalist Ke'opulaulani Reelitz, who was born and raised in O'ahu, with her husband, Jason Ubay. "Do we stay or do we go? We want to raise our family here; we have all our family here. But we know we could earn more and have more on the mainland."

"Like most of us in Hawai'i, we're all living paycheck to paycheck," says Samantha DeCorte, who won a state senate seat in 2024 to represent west side communities of O'ahu. She ran, in part, because she sees a crisis in housing, especially for Native Hawaiians. "I'm living paycheck to paycheck. And we're probably all one paycheck away from being homeless."

How did it get this way? It happened like a slow boil, generation after generation.

———

The earliest inhabitants of the Hawaiian Islands—an archipelago located nearly two thousand miles away from the nearest continent—were also some of the world's most impressive pioneers. They crossed the vast Pacific, likely from the Marquesas Islands, in double-hulled canoes, using careful, memorized maps of the stars and ocean currents as their guide, around 1000 to 1100 AD. Although their motives for voyaging so far out to sea are unclear, it is clear they were confident they would find a new home. They filled their canoe with the essentials of building a new, sustainable life—plants, food, animals, tools—and created a successful settlement that thrived for hundreds of years. The ocean provided a bounty of fish, octopus, and shellfish, like the opihi (oh-pee-hee), a limpet that clings to the rocks on the shore. Whales passed by every winter on their annual migration. The fertile soil made it easy to grow sweet tropical fruits like guavas and coconuts. They cultivated patches of taro and sweet potato and grew breadfruit trees from saplings that they had brought with them. Hawai'i's steep mountain peaks, formed by volcanoes, were rife with freshwater streams, rivers, and waterfalls to quench their thirst. Hawai'i's unique, isolated environment provided its new inhabitants with everything they needed. It was, in the ancient stories, a land of plenty.

What brought them to Hawai'i, no one knows. But they stayed and managed to not only survive but to grow and become a population estimated to be as many as seven hundred thousand[3] strong by the time the first Westerners "discovered" them. In 1778, a couple years after the rebellious Americans had declared their independence from Britain, two British ships, the *Discovery* and the *Resolution*, sailed to the Hawaiian Islands. Aboard was an explorer, Captain James Cook, who arrived while on a mission to try to find a mythical northwest passage between Europe and Asia that the explorers hoped would expedite commerce. The Hawaiians, who had never seen a Western ship before, mistakenly thought the white sails of Cook's ships were signs of the arrival of their god Lono, and they showered Cook with food, hospitality, and a feathered cape reserved for the most honored chiefs. The men became fascinated with Cook's weapons, and the women swam to his boats, offering themselves to Cook's men in exchange for intriguing Western tools and objects of curiosity. Cook, who landed in Hawai'i after exploring Oceania from New Zealand across the Pacific, wrote, "I have no where in this Sea seen such a number of people assembled at one place."[4] No wonder Cook and his men stayed months to enjoy the paradise and his high place as a demigod. Until, that is, the Hawaiians realized he was not a god and killed him.

Although Cook never returned to England, his men did, and they documented extensively what they saw and learned in drawings and notes. They spread word to the rest of the Western world about what they found in Hawai'i. Indeed, Cook's visit forever changed the islands: her ecosystem, her way of life, and especially her native people. The *Discovery* and the *Resolution* were only the first of many, many ships that soon followed, not only from England but France, the Netherlands, and America.

And the Hawaiian people—their culture, their society, their population—would be devastated. First, the diseases would come. Cook's own records from his first trip indicate he knew some men aboard his ships had venereal diseases, and he worried that their arrival infected the Hawaiians. They did. And there was more to come: smallpox, syphilis, tuberculosis, leprosy, and all the others, just as they had ravaged the Hawaiians' native cousins in America a century before. By one estimate, twenty-two years after Cook's visit, and as more foreign ships arrived to "discover" the bounty of the islands, nearly half the Native Hawaiian population died from foreign diseases to which they had no immunity.

At the time of Cook's fateful visit, and for centuries before, the Hawaiians lived simple lives of fishing and farming, with a very stratified social culture and strict religious beliefs that were intertwined. Although many people today know the Hawaiian Islands once belonged to a kingdom under monarchy rule, the early Hawaiians before the 1800s were ruled by chiefs, each of whom oversaw a large section of land. In Maui, for example, the east and west parts of the island were at constant war with each other.

The Hawaiians were smart about how to thrive on a set of isolated islands. Each fall, during the makahiki (mah-kah-hee-kee) season of harvest, the chiefs would circle the island, visiting each ahupua'a to receive food and goods from the subdivision as a form of tax. Some scholars have compared the Native Hawaiians' system to Europe's early feudal system, where there is one landowner and laborers are assigned areas to maintain and pay taxes. While this analogy is somewhat true, the chiefs overseeing the lands were also accountable to the people in their section of land to ensure they shared their food and resources and that the area thrived and continued to grow under the chief's rule. Within each ahupua'a, the chief appointed other, lower chiefs to oversee critical responsibilities, such as land irrigation, the construction of fishponds, and the harvest of certain crops. Each system was impressively sophisticated for ancient, remote people, Hawaiian scholars say. The Hawaiians did not have metal, but they used the sharp edges of rocks, shells, shark teeth, and wood to create basic tools that helped them become expert fishermen, farmers, and warriors.

The ahupua'a system enabled the Hawaiians to thrive in a system where there was no concept of landownership—or ownership of anything, for that matter. But there was a system of stewardship. Each person understood their kuleana for taking care of their part that would serve the broader whole society. If the farmer walked away from his crops, he would have nothing to feed himself and nothing to exchange with others. If the fisherman failed to bring in his catch or failed to maintain his fishpond, he also would fail himself and the people of his ahupua'a. For centuries, this system enabled a group of voyagers who settled the islands with just a few tools, plants, and animals in their canoe to become a strong nation of people who had little need for the outside world because they perfected a way to depend on themselves. Today, we hear a trendy term for this concept. Whenever I hear the word *sustainability*, I think of the Native Hawaiians and their ahupua'a system. It would be upended within just a few years of Captain Cook's arrival. His men returned to Europe and spread the word about the beauty and bounty that is Hawai'i.

Then, in 1848, King Kamehameha III's Great Mahele Act—or land division—put forward a system that for the first time allowed land to be owned, sold, and traded. Native Hawaiians—including our family—received some land, but that was the exception more than the rule. Quickly, foreign white farmers and businessmen who lived in Hawai'i saw an opportunity to acquire land to grow cash crops. To Native Hawaiians, the concept of landownership was foreign, and they quickly lost out on opportunities to understand and afford a system that now required them to register for a title on their land, pay a surveyor and, later, taxes. A couple of decades later, as the United States was engaged in a civil war, sugarcane plantations rapidly expanded across the landscape of Hawai'i, owned by what became known as the Big Five—Castle & Cooke; Alexander & Baldwin; C. Brewer & Co.; H. Hackfield & Co.; and Theo H. Davies & Co.—for the five largest sugar companies, many owned by the sons of Christian missionaries who were among the first to settle in Hawai'i. Seizing an opportunity of the US's Northern states' inability to access sugar from the South during the Civil War, the Big Five profited from favorable export agreements to the US mainland via the West Coast—and gobbled up hundreds of acres of land on the islands to cultivate sugar.

Within a couple of decades of the Mahele in 1848, many Hawaiians found themselves without access to the 'āina.

Sugar plantations not only changed the Hawaiians' way of life and locked out most from access to land—they had other downstream effects. The Big Five realized that they not only needed land for their crops, they needed access to water rights to cultivate them.

They claimed freshwater resources, literally acquiring mountain land and moving freshwater streams, building ditches and tunnels and diverting their paths downstream to irrigate their fields. This forever changed the ecosystems in parts of Hawai'i that were once lush with their own water resources for traditional taro patches and other parts of their ahupua'a system. Where land was once lush, it is now dry. Where Native Hawaiians could farm to feed themselves, the water was now used for cash crops to ship somewhere else and make a profit for the haole plantation owners. Vibrant ahupua'a in communities across all the islands, including Lahaina on Maui, which was devastated by wildfires in 2023, were now as dry as deserts.

The Hawaiian people were without land, and then they were without fresh water.

After the sugar, came the overthrow. In 1893, a group of American businessmen conspired to overthrow Hawai'i's government and imprison its leader, Queen Lili'uokalani. They were imperialists who viewed Hawai'i as a strategic location for trade, and they wanted to protect their investments in the lands, in agriculture, and in merchant shipping by moving Hawai'i under the flag of the United States. In preceding years, various attempts to attack and overthrow the kingdom had been made by the French and the British, who used ships to try to take over the Honolulu harbor. The Americans took their shot because they saw Hawai'i as a strategic island nation that could expand their empire and their business interests. They also saw it up for grabs and wanted to wrest control, lest it fall under the control of a European power. "The Hawaiian pear is now fully ripe, and this is the golden hour for the United States to pluck it," wrote American minister to Hawai'i John L. Stevens.[5]

Once the group of Americans put Hawai'i's queen under house arrest in her own palace, they took down Hawai'i's flag flying out front and raised an American one. Initially, the US president at the time, Grover Cleveland, declined to recognize the overthrow. (Less than two decades earlier, the president of the United States had held the first US state dinner by hosting the president of Hawai'i, King Kalākaua.) The people of Hawai'i gathered tens of thousands of signatures in the Kū'ē Petitions, protesting the overthrow, and a group of local men staged a rebellion effort, but it was no use. They could not take on the might of the US military. It was a bloodless coup. In 1898, a new US president, William McKinley, made it official that Hawai'i would become a territory of the United States.

No land, no water. No independence.

Fully in command of the 4 million acres of the Hawaiian Islands, the US government now examined how it would use it. It left private ownership in place and took over most of the kingdom's crown lands—about 1.5 million acres that had been owned and controlled by the royal house—and transferred them to US, and later state, government use. The US had relied on its exclusive use of Pearl Harbor through an 1887 treaty with Hawai'i for trade, especially sugar, during the Civil War. After the kingdom's overthrow, the US decided that it needed a military foothold in the Pacific Ocean and turned to one of the most prized assets, Pearl Harbor—home to a beautiful estuary with naturally deep waters—and dredged it to become its naval base.[6] It also took a small island off the coast of Maui, Kaho'olawe, and used it for the sole purpose of bombing practice for US military planes. Schofield Barracks and Hickam Air Force Base were built up for military use. The US military quickly became a major source of investment in Hawai'i and employment. But it also has a record of ignoring Native Hawaiians' sacred places and, in many locals' view, lacking respect for the land and culture.

In 2021, the US Navy's fuel storage tanks leaked into the ground-water of Oʻahu, making the tap water smell like gasoline and unsafe to drink or bathe in. After public protests and investigations, the military branch finally agreed to clean it up and take responsibility for the harm it has caused. For many, this was just another modern-day example of the US military taking what it wants from Hawaiʻi, without respect for local people and local land.

At the urging of one of Hawaiʻi's last royal family members, Prince Jonah Kuhio, who also served as Hawaiʻi's first representa-tive to the United States Congress after annexation, the US hon-ored some of the crown lands to be set aside for Native Hawaiians in the form of a homestead program. Prince Kuhio's vision was that these lands would enable people with at least 50 percent Native Hawaiian blood to use the land to live on or farm on, in the form of ninety-nine-year leases. Today, this system is still in place, with more than thirty-six thousand families living on land managed by the Department of Hawaiian Home Lands. (Prince Kuhio was married to a woman named Princess Elizabeth Kahanu.) Follow-ing Prince Kuhio's death, the homelands agency suffered from de-cades of mismanagement, and these lands now have a waiting list of thirty thousand Native Hawaiians with little chance of getting access.

Against the odds, in 1996, Grandma's name came up in the lot-tery of the homelands agency, and they notified her that she could have access to a property in a new section of homelands on the local side of Oʻahu. As it turned out, the neighborhood division was called Princess Kahanu Estates. Dad helped her qualify for a mort-gage and pay some of the cost to build a home there, which enabled my grandparents to return to Hawaiʻi when they retired. But again, our family was the exception to the rule. In 2022, the Hawaiʻi legislature authorized more funds to acquire more land for the first time in decades, in part to address the state's homelessness and housing affordability program. The state acknowledges that most Native Hawaiians on the list die while waiting.

America's wealthiest people are increasingly becoming among Hawai'i's largest private landowners, gobbling up land at astronomical prices and exacerbating Hawai'i's economic displacement. Media mogul Oprah Winfrey snapped up about 1,000 acres on Maui. On the island of Kauai, AOL cofounder Steve Case bought 38,000 acres of what is known as Grove Farm, a former sugar plantation, which is now a mixed-use development of agriculture, housing, and industrial use. Also on Kauai, Mark Zuckerberg, who cofounded Meta, formerly known as Facebook, has spent over $150 million to acquire upward of 1,600 acres for ranching and conservation.[7] As part of acquiring some land in 2017, he sued several Native Hawaiians who had claims to some of these lands, but later backed off after complaints from the local community and news coverage.

But perhaps none have outdone billionaire Larry Ellison, who cofounded the tech firm Oracle. He bought nearly the entire 90,000-acre island of Lāna'i from an investment firm—essentially the same land that was originally owned by James Dole, who turned the island into an enormous pineapple farm in the 1920s. Today, Ellison has made the island into a high-end resort destination, where he serves as employer and landlord to nearly everyone who lives there.[8] Some billionaires have chosen to make Hawai'i their home—at least some part of the year—and to use their land for "good" purposes, such as encouraging farming or conservation. But many do not.

The net effect of the world's richest people gobbling up Hawaiian lands is clear: there's less land available, and it's less affordable for everyone else. And in recent years, prices have escalated so high that they have impacted land values and property taxes for locals. This includes Amazon founder Jeff Bezos's $78 million purchase of a home and property and small bay on Maui, a $45 million estate purchased by a hedge fund manager on Maui, and another $36 million private estate sale on Maui. Like other places, real estate prices have their boom and bust seasons in Hawaiʻi, except they drive up higher here than anywhere else. All told, these purchases mean that billionaires who don't live in Hawaiʻi own more and more of the land that is now unavailable for locals who can't afford to buy, can't afford to build their own equity. For those who do own a home, it drives up their property taxes. That is how America's real estate system works, but for people who live on islands with finite land and places to live, it explains why local people have nowhere to go but live on the beach, or move away from Hawaiʻi. They are literally priced out. Homeless in their homeland.

Land. Water. Homes. The Hawaiians lost and lost and lost. Today, they are still losing.

So it was within this context that Dad, and his brothers and sisters, set out to find a way to hold on to our land in Hāna. Sharply rising property values had driven up property taxes. We only had a few years before we'd deplete the money our grandparents set aside to pay for taxes. And we knew that we'd have to somehow navigate a bureaucracy in Hawaiʻi that was byzantine, unfamiliar, and slow. In other words—given the history and today's real estate market—the odds were against us.

3

DREAMS UNFULFILLED

The sun burst through the glass-shuttered window of my grand-parents' spare bedroom in Nānākuli, a small town where locals live on the west side of O'ahu. I had put a pillow over my head hours earlier to block the sound of the public transit bus engines wait-ing for schoolkids. Fast slaps of their flip-flops—or slippas—hit the pavement as they ran to the impatient bus at dawn.

"Coo-coo-COO, coo-coo-COO" is the wake-up anthem of Ha-wai'i's brown doves, who announce a new day. The temperature had begun to rise inside the small bedroom where I slept, even with the light breeze that came through the windows. Last night's long flight from Washington, DC, felt like a fog.

I stretched and then walked down the sun-faded carpet stairs and passed by Grandma and Grandpa's bedroom with their perfectly made bed, admiring a glimpse of Grandma's hand-sewn blue-and-white Hawaiian quilt bedspread carefully tucked in at the pillows.

"There you are!" Grandma greeted me with her trademark giggle, which sounded both nervous and sweet. She stood in the kitchen in the way I remember her most vividly now, a dish towel draped over her right shoulder, her eyeglasses hanging around her neck on a cord.

Despite the eighty-degree heat, she wore polyester slacks with pantyhose underneath, no shoes, on the linoleum floor. She placed her hand on her petite hip. "Sa-ra," she called. "Come eat."

On the kitchen table, she had sliced a fresh pineapple onto a paper plate reinforced by one of those plastic trays made specifically to support the heavy contents. I have only seen these at family gatherings in Hawai'i. She added a sliver of papaya and a sliver of mango, whose juices overflowed down the skin of the fruit. Both were plucked from the trees she had planted in the backyard. "Don't eat too much pineapple. Your tongue will go numb," she warned. The juices slid down my chin as I bit into the fruit.

I always eat too much pineapple. It just tastes sweeter and better here than anywhere else.

A fresh plumeria flower that Grandma plucked from the tree in her front yard waited on the table in a shallow dish of water. Its sweet, candy-like perfume made me want to pick it up and bury my nose in it, inhaling its soft white petals with the yellow center. In fact, I couldn't resist and did just that, catching droplets of water on my nose. It had the smell of a juicy melon.

Ahhh, Hawai'i.

Suddenly, I was transformed from a twenty-four-year-old woman just starting out my independent life in the big East Coast city into a little girl being pampered in my grandparents' house. Back in Washington, DC, I had just moved into my first one-bedroom apartment, which I rented all by myself. Even though it was a basement row house that cost almost half of my salary, I was finally feeling like an adult who didn't have to live with roommates or share a kitchen. But none of that mattered at this moment. I enjoyed being fussed over like this. In front of me, Grandma slid me another plate—a thick slice of soft, sweet Hawaiian bread, which she had warmed in the toaster oven and then slathered with butter.

She never skimped on the good stuff: Grandma Goo was one of those people who believed that butter needed to be seen to be tasted. And she loved her sweets. She pulled up a chair to the kitchen table and poured herself a black coffee and milk. I widened my eyes as she tipped forward the sugar container—yellow Tupperware with an open flap—and sugar streamed into her mug like a waterfall. "One, two, three!" she counted and then tipped it back. She smiled at me and giggled her trademark giggle that now I miss so much. Our deep, dark, almond-shaped eyes were almost exactly the same.

It was our shared love of sweets, especially when I was a kid, that began a special bond between us—a grandmother and firstborn grandchild. But it was also much, much more.

On this visit, I had decided, on a whim, to fly to Hawai'i and visit my grandparents because I wanted them to show me the islands they knew so well, but having grown up in Southern California, I knew only as a regular visitor. I also desperately needed a break from the fast-paced news of DC. I hadn't had a vacation in nine months. Hawai'i seemed like the perfect escape.

It may not seem like an ideal vacation for a young twentysomething to spend her precious paid-time-off days to be with Grandma and Grandpa alone for ten days, but something about Hawai'i had been tapping me on the shoulder. It was time to come back. I was really loving my new life in Washington, DC; I felt like I was an independent adult who had achieved the first sense of success in a big job at *The Washington Post*. My days were spent reporting for the newspaper—interviewing people every day, researching and asking questions to get to the bottom of the story, and writing it up for the next day's edition. And yet I realized I had so many unanswered questions about my own story—especially in Hawai'i. Getting there now would take an eleven-hour flight and cost me around $900—the kind of money that takes time to save and plan ahead. And I sensed that time was short even though my grandparents were still active and in good health. In the years I spent chasing professional dreams on the East Coast, they wanted to know when I was coming back.

It occurred to me that I could put my everyday reporting skills to work in a new way. I could interview them, get to know *their* story, to know the Hawai'i that they grew up in and had returned to. So I packed a narrow reporter's notebook and my tape recorder into my suitcase as if I were going on any other reporting assignment and made my way here. I left for Hawai'i on September 1, fresh off the top of the month, eager for a change of scenery and pace. I'd return on the eleventh, a Tuesday, when I happened to find a less expensive flight home.

My grandparents were thrilled about my arrival and had taken great time and care to map out all the places they loved across three islands in Hawai'i. In O'ahu, they took me to Chinatown to eat dumplings and to visit the jeweler where Grandma liked to buy jade bracelets. On Maui, we visited Uncle Take, Grandma's brother, and the heiau. And on the island of Kauai, they took me to see a botanical garden with preserved native Hawaiian terraces and crops.

They relished showing me all the things they loved about

Hawai'i, playing tour guides but also narrating their own stories about each place. And so, this trip was a little different from any other vacation I'd ever take. I felt spoiled as the only granddaughter on this special trip—in our large family where I had seven aunts and uncles and numerous cousins, it was rare to have my grandparents' sole attention. I'd spend many hours in the back seat of their old Ford Taurus wagon, leaning forward with my cassette recorder perched between the front and back seats while they talked. I scribbled notes and tried to not get carsick while Grandpa took the wheel and they took turns talking story with me. Grandma and Grandpa would bicker and interrupt each other constantly—"No, Father, that's not what happened, not what I remember," Grandma would say. "Let me finish, Mart," Grandpa would say, using his nickname for my grandma Martha. Despite all that, I got, as reporters say, great material.

One day, we drove about forty-five minutes from their home in Nānākuli to the North Shore, known for the big waves that draw surfers from all over the world. Pipeline is famous for the dangerous, enormous surf that arrives here every winter. But my grandparents wanted to show me something else.

In the little town of Hale'iwa, a small white arch bridge leads to a protected beach bay. Grandpa turned into the parking lot. "This," he said, "this is where I met your grandma."

"Aww," I said. "Tell me the story again." We got out of the car and walked along a pathway at the beach. It was morning, so there were few people there except some locals. A man was getting his canoe out of his truck, readying for a morning workout. A woman was sitting on a towel on the beach with her toddler.

"I didn't know it, but I learned that there was a train that you could take to the beach, here on the north side," Grandma said. "So

I went, I was excited to go, with my sisters. I wanted to take the train ride."

"And I was in the army. My buddies and I, we had the day off. So we went and took the jeep to go check out the beach."

"And I'm sitting there, enjoying myself on the beach, you know, right around here." She pointed to the soft sand under the shade of a tree. "And there's these boys come up, you know, this one with a camera," Grandma says, pointing to Grandpa.

"I wanted to take a picture of her."

"And I didn't like that," she said. "I don't like having my picture taken. Well, anyway, these boys, they wanted the girls to go with them, you know, in the truck that they had, on a ride around the beach. I didn't want to. But some of the girls I went with, they did."

"Oh yeah. I forgot about that."

"So I took the train back home," she says, giggling at the memory.

"Your grandma, she was kind of, you know, hard to get."

That would have been the end of the story. But months later, they saw each other at a sock hop at the armory building in Honolulu. "You know, my sisters and I would go dancing two or three times a week. That whole jitterbug craze," Grandma said.

"I was at the dance with a girl, but once I saw Mart, I went up to her to see if she remembered me," Grandpa said.

"Oh yeah, how could I forget? The man with the camera." Grandma laughed.

"My girlfriend, she was so mad. I was paying all this attention to Mart."

"And he showed me. He had *that picture*."

"I still have that picture of your grandma in my wallet. So I took her home," Grandpa said of the other girl.

Grandpa met up with his friends after the dance at the Kau Kau

Corner, a drive-in restaurant popular with twentysomethings at the time that stayed open late and served food on a tray hanging off the car door. Grandma and her friends were there, too.

The rest is history. They would go on to get married and then raise eight children in San Bernardino, California. Now retired, they had sold their house in California and managed to return to O'ahu. Looking at them, interrupting and completing each other's sentences, I got a sense that this visit wasn't just for me. It was a chance for them to go back to where they started. I could see it in their faces.

There was more that they wanted me to see—or really, taste—on this trip. Grandma, with her sweet tooth, made sure to tour me around to all the bakeries she loved.

"Today, I thought we'd go get some malasadas," she said with a big smile, referring to Hawai'i's special kind of fresh doughnuts.

But no ordinary corner bakery would do. We got into the Taurus wagon and drove into Honolulu, to Leonard's, the special Portuguese bakery Grandma loved that offered hot round doughnuts filled with haupia (coconut cream), chocolate, or custard.

"Oh my god, Grandma, I don't even know which to choose," I said once we got into the storefront packed with people peering into the trays of doughnuts behind the glass. I could smell the sweet sugar and feel the heat from the hot oil in the back.

"No, no. We'll get a sample," she giggled. "Then you don't have to choose."

We didn't even make it out of the parking lot before digging into the pink box of goodies. Each malasada was puffy and shaped like an oval—a doughnut but without the hole—about the size of the palm of my hand.

Grandma went for the custard. And Grandpa took a plain one

that was dusted in cinnamon and sugar. I picked out a malasada filled with haupia—which is the name of a Hawaiian coconut dessert that has a texture between pudding and coconut cream pie filling—mostly because I was intrigued how that would work in a doughnut. I took a bite of the soft, warm doughnut lightly sprinkled with sugar on top. The doughnut was light but not sweet, and the sugar dusting offered a slight crunch. Then suddenly, warm coconut cream oozed into my mouth.

"Wow," is all I could say, with my mouth full. Now the haupia cream was spilling out of the rest of the doughnut in my hand, urging me to eat the rest quickly. The tiny napkin was useless as I ended up licking the haupia and sugar from my fingers, happily mopping up my delicious mess. In the front seat, Grandma and Grandpa were doing the same.

"'Ono [oh-no], no?" Grandma said, using the Hawaiian word for *delicious*. Yes. The malasada tasted like Hawai'i—a burst of the warmest, sweetest, happiest thing I'd ever eaten.

No wonder I felt like the most spoiled granddaughter, twenty-four years old and all grown up but wanting to remain the kid in the back seat whose grandparents give her all the sweets. Good thing we still had several more days together.

"Where are we going next, Grandma?"

The best part, and the part of the trip I looked forward to the most, of course, was to see Grandma's land in Hāna.

———

Grandma's land is in the ahupua'a called Honomā'ele (ho-no-mah-el-leh), on the east side of Maui. Grandma's mother, Mileka, who was full-blooded Hawaiian, had grown up in this remote part of Hawai'i where our ancestors have been for generations. From Hāna, we drove down the small road off the Hāna Highway and past the entrance to the heiau. I wanted to see that, too, but today was about "the land." Asphalt turned to a dirt road, pockmarked with deep ruts and jutting rocks that Grandpa had to swerve around to avoid getting a flat in our rental car. On either side of the road, tall green trees and bushes were held back by thin wire fences. Very quickly, we entered a part of Hawai'i that was very much off the tourist path.

"Slow down, Father," she told Grandpa. She always called him Father, even years after raising their eight children together and with none of them currently in their presence. She rolled down the passenger-seat window and peered out, looking for her land. "That one's Take's, there," she said, pointing to the left. "And Bobbie's one, I think that's it." She pointed to the right. I nodded, but there was nothing to indicate where one property began and another ended, because it was exactly the same landscape—wild green brush held back by the fence.

Suddenly, on the right, we could see a small clearing in the dense forest.

"There, Father. Stop," she instructed. We got out of our shiny, clean rental and found ourselves surrounded by a quiet tropical forest on a dirt road, with no one around.

A small red tag was tied to the wire fence. Grandma moved a wooden post so we could walk through. It kind of felt like we were trespassing, not supposed to go into the forest. But Grandma knew the way. She had covered her petite body with long pants to fend off the mosquitoes, and a white bucket hat over her thick, shoulder-length black hair. Her rectangular eyeglasses dangled from a cord around her neck, as always.

"Sara, come," she said. Mosquitoes buzzed around my ears. I cursed them and swatted them away.

We passed through the gate to find a freshly cleared gravel road, about the width of a truck, that gave us a pass through the jungle tunnel. The bright, hot sun disappeared as we walked into the cool shade of the path, which amplified the sound of the mosquito den we seemed to have entered. I was a walking piece of red meat ready for their bloodthirsty attack.

Quickly, it was as if we'd entered another world. Birds chirped from above, but I could not see them. The air smelled fresh and green, like the brief rain shower that blesses this part of Maui nearly every morning for about fifteen minutes. The narrow walkway was unsteady underfoot as we stepped carefully on wobbly, broken chunks of lava rock. Soon, the canopy opened up to the bright blue sky again, and we were greeted with a gorgeous view of the roaring ocean in the distance.

I followed Grandma downhill on a narrow footpath toward the shore, careful not to lose my footing. Grandpa followed behind me, with a camera around his neck, pausing to look for a good shot. I yearned to see the shoreline, as I remembered being here as a child many years earlier. Grandma was taking me to her favorite part of the land—a place she called "the arch," a natural formation of black lava that extends into the ocean like a bridge. You can walk on top of it, as my cousins do, and cast a line or throw net for some good fishing. Standing on top of the arch puts you a good twenty feet above the shore break, where bright white wave foam crashes through the hole below.

We held hands as we stepped up to the top of the arch, laughing as the spray occasionally broadsided us. Oh, how I'd missed the smell of the salty ocean. And I had forgotten about how wild and relentless the waves were here. I slipped my arm around Grandma, slightly shorter than me, feeling the softness of her arm's golden skin. Her wrists were adorned with gold and jade bracelets I noticed many older Hawaiian women wore. She lifted her arm and pointed to the land we had just walked across. Only now, we turned around, our backs to the ocean. From where we stood, we had an impressive view above the massive Haleakala volcano, whose top was hidden by the clouds in the distance and whose steep slope appeared to wear a carpet of bamboo forest. It's a rare view where the wild, lush tropical jungle meets the rugged, rocky shoreline. The green forest seemed to glow almost fluorescent in the hot sun. "This land was once all Kahanu land, from the mountain to the sea," she said. Mauka to makai (mow-kah to mah-kai), in Hawaiian.

I took in the view and tried to imagine our ancestors living here, their simple lives of fishing from the shore and growing taro on the land. I looked to my left, down the shoreline, where the relentless aqua waves pummeled the black rock coastline. Not a house in sight. Not a hotel in sight. Not a person. Just the land, the trees that grow here, and the animals that live as they have, alone, undisturbed for centuries.

So this is what Hawai'i used to look like. So this is what Captain Cook saw. So this is what my family has known and cared for all these years. I longed to know more about their way of life and our connection to it.

"From the mountain to the sea" was such a broad description. I wanted Grandma to show me a map to more precisely define it in my mind, with surveyors' markers and boundaries. She said the land was a gift from one of Hawai'i's last kings. Our ancestor Kahanu, a man whose name has been woven through our family tree for generations; Grandma said he was a chief for the king.

"How did we get it? And how far was it, exactly?" I asked her. She explained that her mother—also named Martha, or Mileka in Hawaiian—had given her and her siblings the land that she received from her own tūtū, or grandfather. But beyond that, she didn't have clear answers.

One thing she was clear about: this remote corner of the world was the place of her birth, her mother's birth, her grandparents' birth, and so on, and so on. This land was from her mother, a woman whose first language was Hawaiian, who told her and her siblings to take care of it and keep it in family hands. It was also our family's kuleana to take care of the heiau, the ancient temple that was part of the family's land.

When I was a teenager, I remember Grandma holding court at family gatherings, talking about her dreams to build a house on this plot of land someday. She played the lottery every week to try to win enough to pay for the construction, and she socked away meager savings from her social security check, too.

Standing on a rocky path, she pointed to a flat area, up the hill—that's where she wanted to build a house. It would be set back enough from the shore, a nice flat spot to build a family home. Maybe even a small bed-and-breakfast. She could serve guests fresh papaya from the land. And that's where the garden would be, behind the house site, a place for all the Hawaiian flowers and plants she loved. In Hāna, with its daily rain, she remembered as a child throwing seeds on the ground and tiny plants popping up just a week later. The soil here could grow anything, and fast. Here, she could plant all her favorite local fruits: mangoes, apple bananas, mountain apples, guavas, and all her favorite plants: red ginger, ti leaves, gardenias, orchids, heliconias, and plumerias. Maybe she could even have a small fruit stand along the side of the road. She was ready to return to her birthplace in Hāna. She was ready to finally realize her dream after a lifetime of saving for it.

"I want a place for you folks to come, for all my children and grandchildren, and someday, you'll have children, too." I smiled and looked at her. Having kids of my own seemed a long way away, since I didn't have a boyfriend and I had more things I wanted to do in DC first.

As with me, Grandma's life had taken her farther away from her home.

Grandma had left Hāna as a teenager after two major events that would forever shape her life. First, when she was a young teenager, her mother left Hāna for Honolulu, divorcing her father for reasons never fully explained. Mileka took all the youngest children with her, including Grandma, on a boat to Oʻahu, to live with relatives. They traded the remote, simple life of Hāna for a new urban world, busy with cars, people, and traffic. Only my uncle Take, Grandma's brother, stayed behind with their father in Hāna to help run the store and restaurant that they owned.

Second, Grandma contracted tuberculosis, which had broken out in Hawaiʻi at that time, and the only medical care provided was at Leahi Sanitarium, where she was sent to live and be treated for nearly two years. Instead of attending the big city high school, she was tutored in the sanatorium and spent her days bored, with little to do. When I asked Grandma what life was like in Hawaiʻi during World War II, she had little to share because she said she felt disconnected from it, her days bounded by the walls of the hospital.

After high school, though, Grandma made a full recovery. And when the war was over, she met Grandpa on the beach and at the sock hop. They married, and moved to California when he got a job at Norton Air Force Base. Over the years, they maintained ties to Hawaiʻi and sent their kids to Hawaiʻi during the summer, where they'd gather with all their Hawaiian cousins. Her dream was to build a small house here that would finally bring her home. It would be an anchor for generations to come to know this place as she did. This was more than a dream for herself, I learned later. It was an extension of her mother's and grandmother's, who fought to keep the land over the generations but never had enough money to build something on it. It was an anchor to keep us connected to it, as she saw her uncles or aunties sell or lose theirs.

It was a dream for us.

We turned to find Grandpa some distance away, pointing a camera at us. "Smile!" he said. I took a deep breath to soak in the moment. I wrapped my arm tighter around Grandma and wondered if her dream would come true.

———

When it was time to go back to DC, I got this feeling that I always do when I'm about to leave Hawaiʻi—like I was not ready, and I did not want to leave this moment, this world, and this reality, because I knew being transported back to the East Coast would be like being sucked through a reality tube where I'd have to become a different version of myself, plopped into an entirely different world. It wasn't just about moving on from the warm sun, the beautiful beaches, and the vacation. It was the soul of Hawaiʻi that I felt connected to, that felt exactly right, that filled me up. I wanted to cling to it just a little longer. I wasn't ready to be jolted back into my one-bedroom apartment in the gritty city that, just ten days earlier, I was so proud to have come from.

On my last night with them, I went to bed in my grandparents' guest bedroom, thinking of all the things we did together, and wondered what I'd do with all the information that I'd written down, all the stories they'd told me. I had learned so much from them. And yet, I still had so many questions. Why didn't my grandma know more details about where our land came from? Who was this ancestor Kahanu, and why did the king give him the land in the first place? What was the significance of this heiau? Over the last several days, I filled my notebook and then had to find scraps of paper to jot down all the things that spilled over. But I felt like I was about to leave with an equal number of new questions that I hadn't gotten to the bottom of yet. I began to think about the next year ahead and when, realistically, I would be able to afford to come back. It was expensive for me to make a trip like this, but equally challenging was just finding the time. I only had two weeks of vacation every year, and getting here and back ate up two of those days.

My American Airlines flight was scheduled to depart Honolulu on September 11, 2001, at 9:00 a.m. Five days later, I'd turn twenty-five. But of course, I did not go back to DC that day. Instead, Grandma knocked on my bedroom door with an urgency that startled and confused me. "Sara, your mother's on the phone," she said, carrying a cordless phone in her hand.

I rubbed my eyes. "Okay." I grabbed the phone.

"Sara, you *cannot* get on a plane today. There's been a terrorist attack. Or something. Planes have crashed into the World Trade

Center. It's not safe." My mother's voice was urgent, afraid. I had no idea what she was talking about.

Hawai'i time is six hours behind the East Coast, so by the time the islands woke up, the news of the terrorist attacks of 9/11 did not unfold with the minute-by-minute confusion of terror as one building, then another, then another were hit by commercial airplanes. They had all burned by then, and America understood we had just been attacked. Attacked, like Pearl Harbor. I went downstairs to watch the television, and it was like watching reruns of a horror movie. I could not get my head around the idea that terrorists had hijacked planes that flew into downtown New York City and the Pentagon on suicide missions and that the World Trade Center buildings were just . . . gone. Scenes of people running for their lives, covered in ash and smoke, seemed unreal. It was too much to take in at once and understand what was going on.

Immediately, I could feel my heart rate go up, and the journalism instincts began to build adrenaline in my body. I needed to help with this story, any way I could. I wanted to wake the whole island up with news of the terrorist attacks. I called my boss in Washington, and asked if there was anything I could do. She told me to go to the airport and see what was going on, as the Federal Aviation Administration had called for a first-of-its-kind ground stop, ordering all planes in the air to land immediately. I wouldn't be flying today. For the first time in history, as far as I was concerned, no one else in America was flying, either.

The events of 9/11 sucked me in for the next few days. I ditched my role as Hawaiian granddaughter and flipped the switch to become a *Washington Post* reporter. I borrowed my grandparents' car and spent days reporting from the Honolulu airport, interviewing tourists stuck there. I also reported from the bizarrely deserted beaches of Waikiki, called up the Pacific command, and sent short files to the paper—I have no idea if they ever made it into stories. I even called up *The Honolulu Advertiser* to see if they'd let me work from their office, as newspapers often helped one another out. It turned out that one of my college journalism professors had since become the editor of the newspaper, and he welcomed me in; he cleared off a desk and let me use their phones to make some additional calls and file my short reports, or "takes," as we called them at the *Post*.

The terrorist attacks of 9/11 yanked me back to a new reality and a new focus not just for that news moment but for the following three years. When I returned to DC, my editors assigned me to write about the impact on the airline industry and the government's efforts to secure our country now facing a new kind of terrorism threat it had never experienced before at home. I would go on to cover the new Transportation Security Administration. I'd fly on planes with undercover air marshals. I'd write about new companies trying to sell their bomb-detection equipment to airports. I'd write about a new workforce of tens of thousands of airport security officers. And pilots who trained to fly with guns in the cockpit. It was an awesome assignment that gave me a sense of duty, and I was good at it. My work, along with my colleagues', was later nominated by the *Post* as one of their submissions for a Pulitzer Prize, and my articles were used in the book later published by the 9/11 Commission. I was so proud to be assigned to cover this important historic story for the *Post*.

And yet I knew it was pulling me away from learning more about the place I loved and the family's story that I so wanted to fully understand. The Hawai'i story faded to the rearview mirror. I'd get back to it someday, I told myself. That story could wait a little longer. It would have to.

———

On a late January night in 2005, the phone rang in my Washington, DC, condo.

"Hello?" I whispered into the phone. Who could be calling so late? The clock said 11:00 p.m. Maybe Dad, who was in California at the time, forgot about the time difference again.

"Sara, hey, it's Dad." I never heard my father's normally bold voice so weak and quiet. I felt a tightening in my gut about what he was going to say. "I wanted to let you know Grandma passed away, just a few hours ago."

A week before, Grandma had suffered a stroke and was in the hospital. She suddenly had trouble speaking after leaving a movie with Grandpa. We knew the prognosis was not good.

Still, hearing the news of her death stunned me. Dad described her last moments. Each of my aunties and uncles—eight grown children in all—had flown in from across the country and gathered at her hospital bedside. They all filed into her tiny hospital room, all eight of them and Grandpa, and held hands around her bed and sang her favorite Hawaiian song as she left this world.

> *Aloha 'oc, aloha 'oe (Farewell to thee, Farewell to thee),*
> *One fond embrace, 'Ere I depart, Until we meet again.*

Tears streamed down my cheeks as I thought about my aunties and uncles singing Hawai'i's most famous song, one written by the last queen, Lili'uokalani, as Grandma took her last breath. I hung up the phone and looked out my window at the city street below.

Sirens blared from blocks away, reminding me of my city life that was so far away from Hawai'i, from the place Grandma wanted me to know. Pictures of our times together flickered through my mind like a movie reel.

I wished we'd had more time. Just a few years before, we were traveling the islands together, visiting all her favorite botanical gardens in Hawai'i along the shore. I wore a white linen dress and ran into the ocean, starved from living so far away. I laughed like a little child jumping over the soft, warm water and the white foam I could hear fizzing quietly at my feet. My dress got soaked at the bottom, but I couldn't care less. I looked back at Grandma from the shore; she and Grandpa were laughing at me, feeling the joy in my joy, as if they were remembering a time they did the same. I can still see her broad smile and hear her infectious laugh. I can still smell the sweet plumeria flowers she would pick from her yard every morning, that she had waiting for me on the table so I could tuck it behind my ear like a local girl when I visited. I still hear her repeating the names of every Hawaiian flower we'd come across— the ti leaves, the red and yellow ginger, the sweet tuberose, and her favorites, the orchids—purple and white with yellow spots inside. She delighted in teaching me about the flowers that made Hawai'i so special and beautiful—most of them not found anywhere else on the planet.

I thought about that visit to Maui, to her land and to the heiau, that we had made together. Her dreams for her own land rang in my ears. And then the terrorist attack—the news that urgently ripped me back to my city life.

Now, I tried to let it sink in. There would not be any more granddaughter trips back like the one we had had. Now there was a void, not only to feel the warm, cocoa butter smell of my grandmother's arms embracing me—and not only her love and affection, and the matriarch of our family, but my kumu (koo-moo), my teacher in all things Hawaiian, was gone.

Now what?

Grandma's death shook our family. In a way, we would never be the same, as if the center of us was cut from the middle and we'd have to still go on and figure out how to exist by piecing it back together. Gone was her infectious laugh, her delicious custard pies, her secret recipe for Chinese chicken salad, and her clarity about building a home in Hāna on her kupuna's land. Gone was my guide to all the beautiful endemic flowers and plants of Hawai'i. Gone was her knowledge of the best jade shop in Honolulu's Chinatown, the best places for malasadas and saimin on the west side. Gone was her sweet singing voice in the pews of the Catholic church in Nānākuli, where she took me every time I visited. Gone was the living, breathing link to my heritage and our kuleana lands. It felt like a hole had been ripped in my heart, the key to our special place and what made our family special—my beloved grandma was gone.

"One of the last things she told me before she passed away was: Never forget where you came from. Don't forget the land," my youngest sister, Emily, recalled to me. "She was talking to me and said, 'I don't have much time left. I want to make sure you realize where you came from.' I didn't see her alive after that."

———

Sitting in my condo, I hung up the phone and watched the raindrops slide down my windows in the darkness, a fitting scene for the grief and distance I felt. I was lucky to have had twenty-eight years with her on this planet, to have taken notes and recorded all the things she shared and memories of all the places we visited. Our special visit now felt so precious—a gift that I'd treasure for the rest of my life. But losing her also left me adrift, uncertain and unclear about what this meant for my own relationship to Hawai'i now that I lived so far away. It felt like something was slipping out of my grasp. She had been my guide to what it meant to be Native Hawaiian just as I was searching to understand my identity as a young adult woman. We had just gotten started. Now where would I go? Out of commitment to her, aloha for her, and the deep connection I felt to Hawai'i, I wanted so badly to hold on. I was not sure if that was even possible without her here to guide me.

A few months after Grandma died in 2005, Michael and I got married in Maui. He had proposed to me under the cherry blossoms along the Potomac River in Washington, DC, that spring. We were so in love that we didn't want to wait to get married. We figured, why not pick a date six months away and just do it in the most beautiful, meaningful place we could find? That spot was on a hill overlooking the Pacific ocean in Wailea, where about sixty of our friends and family sat in white chairs looking out at the incredible view. We were blessed that so many people we loved traveled thousands of miles to be there and that we also had a couple of dozen family members on Maui who joined the festivities. During the short wedding ceremony, we presented our kūpuna with fresh flower lei—one for Michael's father and mother, one each for my parents and Grandpa. We also honored Uncle Take and Auntie Lei, who came from the other side of the island, by draping a lei around their shoulders. One by one, they each came forward as the 'ukulele strummed, and Michael and I took turns draping the delicate flower lei over their heads in a moment to honor our elders.

It's funny the way life can bring you moments of intense grief and joy all at once. In that instant, I never felt so much happiness, looking deeply into my new husband's eyes and thinking about the promise to be by his side for the rest of my life. I also had never felt such a simultaneous sense of loss. When Grandpa walked to the front, I draped the lei over his shoulders and hugged him. His once-strong body now felt as though he might collapse.

He whispered in my ear. "Your grandma, she . . ." he started to say, and tears filled his eyes and his voice caught. He didn't need to finish his sentence.

"I know," I whispered. "Love you," is all I could get out.

He walked slowly back to his seat, shoulders slumped, and sat down next to Grandma's empty chair now draped with a beautiful flower lei. I looked at the wedding crowd and saw in their faces that everyone in attendance felt the pang of Grandma's absence and the pain of Grandpa's loss, my loss, and the unfinished grieving of our entire family. I had imagined Grandma would have been sitting in that front row next to him, so proud to bear witness to me, her firstborn granddaughter, a mainland girl coming back to Maui for her wedding day.

The empty chair now said it all.

I somehow managed to hold it all in and tried to bring my emotions back to my new husband standing in front of me. Our wedding day was a time to celebrate both our families and all those who loved us and supported our new life together. And even if Grandma wasn't there, I took comfort in feeling the presence of her blessing. My heart felt a deep squeeze inside—the combination of intense sadness and joy—and it felt appropriate and maybe even necessary for this time stamp in our lives where we'd both move forward and honor where we came from. I looked out at Grandpa, Uncle Take, and Auntie Lei, smiling through tears at me as if to represent her, and the nod of approval of their joy on behalf of their generation.

Through them, I felt her. Maybe they could help me find a way to pick up where Grandma and I left off. I swallowed the lump in my throat and told myself that I'd come back to that later.

I turned my gaze toward my husband and felt so sure that my life was full of more blessings than I could have ever wanted.

———

A few years after my visit with my grandparents in 2001, and with the help of relatives, Grandma was able to finally pay for a bulldozer to come and clear enough of her land to make way for a narrow dirt road and a flat area that could serve as the perfect spot for a small home where she and Grandpa could live, at least part of the time. Over time, she said, we could add onto it and ensure that "you folks," as she'd say, could visit and know Hāna like she did. It was finally happening. Years of praying and saving and planning. She never did win the lottery. But she was on the cusp of fulfilling her dream to find her way back to Hāna.

The Hāna home was never built. Soon after the land was cleared, Grandma and Grandpa learned that a nearby property owner had complained to the county that she had bulldozed a small section of her land without proper permitting. After the work of clearing the Hāna land got underway and the thick jungle brush was moved out to actually create a road where one could walk, the county ordered the work on Grandma's property to stop.

Recalling that event years later, sitting in his Nānākuli home, Grandpa still felt the raw anger, frustration, and sadness from that moment that he could never claw back.

"Some haole went and complained, said we need some kind of survey done. Can you believe it?" Grandpa said, his voice rising and the anger building up in his voice.

"Can you believe it? They wanted some archae-o-logical survey done! Would have cost us another ten thousand dollars. You know *why*?! Because they said the property was near the heiau, an important archae-o-logical site!"

The irony was cruel. In 1972, Grandma's mother, Mileka, and her siblings had, along with the Hāna Ranch, donated the heiau and sixty-one acres of surrounding lands to the National Tropical Botanical Garden, a nonprofit organization, with the promise that the heiau would be preserved, restored and forever protected. The heiau was designated a National Historic Landmark. Now the bureaucracy of that protection was a reason blocking Grandma's return to that ancestral land because her land was down the road from the heiau.

"We sat there with the lawyer, him telling us this," Dad remembered. "And when your grandma heard that, her face just fell. It was like it was over. It's like she knew she wasn't going to see that house built. Ever."

When Grandpa and Dad told me the story, I just sat in silence, stunned. I joined in my father's and grandfather's anger, regret, frustration, and more. Why were the forces so hard to overcome? Who were these people preventing Grandma from doing what she wanted with the land that she owned? Why were there so many barriers to a Native Hawaiian woman who just wanted to return to the land of her ancestors after all the miracles it had taken for the land to remain with her—and our family—at all? In her mind, the money, the faceless bureaucracy, the powers that be must have just felt insurmountable. It seemed impossible. After a few minutes, Grandpa went on; this time, his voice was more subdued.

"The whole point of moving back to Hawai'i was that we could someday build a house in Hāna," Grandpa said ruefully, sitting across from me at the kitchen table, gazing down at Grandma's plastic-coated tablecloth. His narrow eyes were watery. His mind was remembering her and how close they had come. He was confessing to me that he had somehow let her down, too.

"It was like the air left her. Her dream had been wiped out," Dad later told me, remembering that news. "She kind of gave up. She said, 'Oh, well. I guess that's it.' It's like she knew her time was short."

Six months after the county stopped Grandma's efforts to build a house, she died of a sudden stroke. And by that time, the jungle forest that had been cleared from the Hāna land had grown back. The pandanus trees, the wild papayas, and the brush reclaimed their space, without a trace of Grandma's home site and the road visible at all. It was as if the jungle swooped in and swallowed it all away.

"There's something about, between the bureaucracy stopping her or Grandpa, who was ultraconservative financially, everybody telling her she can't do this, you can't do this because you don't have enough money . . . she resigned," Dad said. "The Hāna property never came up again. She had said all she was going to say about it. She expressed her wishes. It was like, you have heard it all. The rest is up to you."

PART TWO

SEARCHING

4

UA MAU KE EA O KA 'ĀINA I KA PONO

"The Life of the Land Is Perpetuated in Righteousness"

After striking out with our legal review, it was time for plan B.

Dad called me one afternoon to tell me about his new plan to reduce the taxes on the Hāna land: we were going to make a farm. Or, at least, make it look like one.

When he first explained it to me, I thought he was crazy.

Dad's idea was to convert Grandma's land—which was currently a wild, rocky, overgrown rainforest in a remote part of Maui—into acres of tropical plants. Here's how it would work: First, we'd have to somehow get heavy equipment out to the land to clear away the jungle trees and brush to make space for our new crops. This would require us to find a bulldozer to rent and then find a truck driver willing to haul it on the two-and-a-half-hour drive along the narrow road that hugs enormous cliffs along the Maui coast, across at least fifty-nine bridges, to Hāna, most likely traveling in the middle of the night. Then we'd have to assemble a crew of family members to fly to Maui and help cut down the existing trees in a one-acre space, using machetes and shovels in Hāna's alternating hot sun and rainy downpours. This would most likely require several of my uncles and family members to take time off work to fly in from California, Massachusetts, Virginia, and Maryland. Then we'd plant something in the cleared space that would resemble a farm. The final step would be about documentation: we'd take photos of our new agricultural use to send to the county as evidence of our farming activities.

In a way, we didn't have a choice. Our taxes had gone up more than fivefold in one year because Maui County decided that Grandma's property no longer could qualify as being used for agricultural purposes. For raw and undeveloped land, the county had one of the highest property tax rates. So the most straightforward way to lower our taxes back to the original amount would be to try to get our "ag status" back.

Our goal was to complete the farm before the end of the year so we could submit for a property use change to the County of Maui. If we succeeded, the county would approve our ag status for next year's taxes—thereby lowering our taxes to what they were before.

In other words, this would be an enormous task that would require time, money, logistics, and a bit of luck. Or as Dad said, "Challenging, but doable."

Dad activated the "coconut wireless" system in our family and got to work. He found out that his cousin Bobbie and her two siblings, who own the land parcel next to ours, also saw an enormous tax hike for the same reason we did. Like us, she had panicked when she got her property tax bill in the mail and saw the taxes had gone up several times over. Like our land, hers is also wild and uncleared. As a retired widow and cancer survivor living on a fixed income on the neighboring island of O'ahu, she confided in Dad that she was considering selling her land because she wasn't sure she could afford to pay the taxes. The latest bill was causing a lot of family angst: not only did she face a higher tax bill, she'd have to foot the bill on her own. Her sister had never been involved or interested in the property. And her brother, who had been helping with the tax bill, now said he wouldn't help anymore and encouraged her to sell.

"He doesn't have the same interest or connection to the land. He doesn't care," she said of her brother. "He doesn't understand why we are holding on to it just to pay more and more taxes."

In a way, I totally understood the practical argument from Auntie Bobbie's brother. In recent years, living in Hawai'i has become challenging for all local residents who struggle just to pay their own rent or mortgage. Hawai'i's housing costs are 2.7 times higher than the national average. Over the past decade on Maui, four in ten homes are owned by people who live in another state—driving up prices and more competition for locals who need housing for their families. In 2023, the governor declared a "state of housing emergency" because the housing problem had become a people problem—local residents were leaving because housing costs were too high. So I could see how paying higher taxes on land your family doesn't live on—or can't ever afford to build on—wouldn't be the biggest priority even if you could afford it. If we or Auntie Bobbie or any other members of our family sold the land on the open market, we 100 percent know where it would go—to a wealthy US mainlander or foreigner looking for a vacation home or investment. We knew this because our family's land is next door to land long owned by the actor Jim Nabors and in the same town as Kris Kristofferson's and down the road from Oprah Winfrey's property.

Unlike other celebrities, Hāna tends to attract wealthy people who want to live in the more secluded parts of Hawai'i.

But the bigger picture is that Hāna is one of the few parts of Hawai'i where a large portion of Native Hawaiians still live and work. If all the members of the Kahanu family sold our land, we'd just be another property sale on Maui fetching top dollar, which would just exacerbate the existing problem: less land available for locals, higher land values and taxes for everyone else, driving up the cost of living for everyone still struggling to make ends meet in Hāna. Moreover, we'd lose our connection to a place that has been sacred for nearly two centuries.

The decision was up to Auntie Bobbie—and it was not an easy financial one. She was on the fence. Auntie Bobbie's two adult daughters don't have any children. But they urged her to hold on to the land. "My girls grew up listening to stories of how our kūpuna got the land, so they want to do something, but you need money, yeah?" Auntie said. "You can't just do things and not live there. If we clear it, it's going to be overgrown again. I'm hoping somebody comes up with an idea. I'm at the point where sometimes I tell my daughter Joni I'd like to lease it because I'm getting older; I can't go over there to Hāna and keep digging and weeding."

The decision was stressing Auntie Bobbie out. Dad walked through his "farm" idea with her and made her an offer: If our family was going to go to the trouble to clear our land, why don't we share the cost and clear her land, too, since it's an adjacent property? We could design the farm in a way that we could plant crops on one acre that would cover both properties. 'Ohana helping 'ohana.

Auntie Bobbie talked it over with her daughters. She came back, and they'd all agreed.

Joni, who was particularly close with her late grandfather—my grandma's brother, Juinchi "Clarence" Matsuda—volunteered to fly to Maui from Honolulu to help clear the land, too. Our little "farm" in Hāna would now be larger, stretching across Grandma's property and including Auntie Bobbie's, too.

Next, it was time to find the equipment to clear the land and round up the volunteer brigade. Dad's next call was to Uncle Keith and Auntie Gizelle, who live in Kula, Maui, and whose family also has nearby plots of land adjacent to ours from our shared Kahanu ancestor. Gizelle is Dad's cousin—one of Uncle Take's daughters—who seems to know everyone on the island. She quickly became our family's guide to how to navigate the local system, trying to back-channel with people she knew who worked for the county about how other Maui property owners were also trying to get their taxes lowered. Although Gizelle's family hadn't seen a spike on their Hāna property taxes, Auntie Gizelle and Uncle Keith knew that they could be next.

Since they already live on Maui, Keith and Gizelle visit their property regularly and they had already cleared their own land parcel, which sits on the slope of a hill on the other side of the dirt road that divides our extended family's land. Years ago, they had put a small converted trailer to camp on, with a large deck that provides a beautiful ocean view.

Dad asked Uncle Keith how to go about hiring a bulldozer. "Eh, bruddah, no need," Uncle Keith said in his thick pidgin. Uncle Keith had a construction business on Maui and explained that he had access to bulldozers that he could transport to Hāna, which he'd done dozens of times on the hairpin turns along that road in the middle of the night—avoiding the tourist traffic.

Uncle Keith is the person in our family whom we jokingly call the "real Hawaiian." He's a tall, broad-shouldered man with dark, tan skin; long, graying brown hair down the middle of his back; and is quick to give a smile and the shaka sign to anyone. Like Auntie Gizelle, he also grew up in remote Hāna, but his big Native Hawaiian family—he's one of nine children—had a large farm. He loves spending time on their family's plot of land with their two adult sons, hunting and fishing and taking care of the land, surrounded by the quiet beauty of it. And as someone who was raised on a farm, he also knew best about how to tame the land in the rainy, jungly climate.

"We say I married the city girl," Uncle Keith likes to joke about Auntie Gizelle, who grew up in Hāna, a town of 731 people that doesn't even have a stoplight.[1]

With a few text messages to his network, Uncle Keith got us a low price to rent a bulldozer and generously offered to transport it on his own dime and help us by driving it to clear the land himself with his sons.

"Do dem all da time," he told Dad.

"You sure, Keith?" Dad asked.

"It's 'ohana!" Uncle Keith said, exclaiming the Hawaiian word for "family." Now, Uncle Keith and Auntie Gizelle not only provided our family with local knowledge about the best way to go about it but also volunteered to help us themselves.

It was 'ohana. It was true aloha.

Next, Dad called around to assemble a crew to fly out to Hāna for about a week's worth of backbreaking labor to help create the farm. Dad started with his brothers and brothers-in-law to see whom he could round up. His younger brother, Uncle Duane, who lives in Massachusetts, was in. His older brother, Uncle Darrell, and his brother-in-law Uncle Tim, who live in the Santa Barbara area of California, also said yes. And my brother, Ben, who lives in Richmond, Virginia, also was in.

I'd like to say that I attended this trip, but I didn't. The trip was scheduled quickly, based around when Uncle Keith could reserve the equipment and drive it out, so I was unable to leave work and kids behind on short notice. But after settling on a date, they flew out to Maui where they met up with Uncle Keith, his son Luka, and Joni, who took the hopper flight over from her home on Oʻahu. Dad's crazy farm plan was now taking shape, and we had an extended family crew that was now activated to save the ʻāina.

The taxman had forced us to scramble, and we were ready.

Just as planned, Uncle Keith and Luka left before everyone else, on the road to Hāna in the dark of night, to get there faster and not cause a traffic jam. Uncle Keith is such a local that normally he could drive the Hāna Highway in half the time it takes me— passing slower drivers along the way with just inches of space between the car and the cliff. I can only imagine how he navigated his way hauling heavy equipment on a flatbed truck at a record pace in the middle of the night. The rest of the crew followed them up to Hāna the next morning, ready to go.

Ben said they had a system: Uncle Keith would drive the heavy equipment to clear the land, and the rest of the crew would fan out behind him on each side, wielding machetes and chain saws, whacking away the brush and cutting down the spindly bushes, whose leaves are like long, sharp knives.

"It was a lot of fun, actually, like *FernGully*," Ben said, referencing the animated movie set in an Australian rainforest.

Somehow, they found the original road that Grandma had cleared back in 2004, before she died. Although many plants, vines, and young trees had quickly filled in the space, they could still make out the path of flattened rocks that led to the ocean. Ben, my dad, Uncle Darrell, and Uncle Tim, along with my cousins Luka and

Joni, took turns using machetes and chain saws. For lunch, Uncle Keith parked his truck in the hot sun, put Hot Pockets and microwave burritos on the dash, and after a short time sitting in the searing heat, they were ready to eat. The crew outlined a one-acre square across the two properties—it was really hard to tell where ours started and Auntie Bobbie's ended except for a few small, old markers—and used a jackhammer to break down large rocks. Once the space was cleared, the crew planted ti leaves, coconut trees, and heliconias donated by Kahanu Garden and whatever else they could find. When work was pau (pahoh) for the day, they celebrated with some well-earned cold beers and then collapsed into bed to do it all again the next morning, starting early before the sun got too hot. After a week of sweating, bulldozing, and hard labor, they managed to create something that truly looked like a farm—or at least a very large garden of various plants. Dad joked that it's not really how one thinks of using vacation time off work to spend a week in Hawai'i, but they declared the mission accomplished!

To wrap things up, Uncle Tim used a drone to take aerial photos of the land to show how Grandma and Auntie Bobbie's land was now being used for agricultural purposes again. With crossed fingers, we hoped this entire effort would get us and Auntie Bobbie qualified for a lower tax rate the following year.

I wasn't sure that this farm effort would work, but it showed how one decision—one stroke of the pen on one document by one government agency—had the power to throw our family into a crisis and threaten our kuleana to take care of this land. It demonstrated just how precarious it all was and how, with short notice, we'd have to act or face losing our land.

What we didn't want to happen was to become the latest Native Hawaiian family to lose their land to sell to a wealthy haole who would own it, maybe develop it into a fancy vacation retreat, maybe visit it once a year. We didn't want to become the literal end of the generational line who had held that land in our family as a testament to our promise as native people to maintain our ties to it. It was not about losing the economic value of the property or benefiting from it. It was that it was our only lasting physical existence and tie to the Hawaiian kingdom, to a way of life, to Old Hawai'i.

While it was awesome to see my family come together, across generations, uncles and aunties and cousins, on the mainland, on Maui, put literal skin in the game to help keep our 'ohana lands in 'ohana hands, we also knew it was just a Band-Aid. We knew, of course, that spending thousands of dollars on airline tickets and renting bulldozers or backhoes every year was not going to really be feasible, nor did it make sense. The idea of creating a farm sounded crazy because it was crazy. We needed something more permanent—or at least more lasting that would provide us with greater certainty that we could afford to hold on to the land.

Oddly enough, we learned that the county's tax system is such that we'd pay a lower rate for having land for agricultural use rather than land that was raw, wild, and undeveloped for no use. And we'd pay an *even lower rate* if we developed our land, such as by building a small cottage. That reality forced us to think about whether we should build something on it as a long-term plan. After all, that was Grandma's dream that was never fulfilled. Building a small cottage would give us a foothold in Hāna that, as a family now largely living on the mainland, would make it easier for us and future generations to come to Hāna. Flying from the mainland to Hawai'i was already expensive. But getting to Hāna and being able to afford to stay in Hāna is also tough, given that there's only one hotel, which offers rooms at more than $600 per night, and only a handful of other, more affordable inns with limited capacity. Building something for our 'ohana would encourage us all, and our kids and our kids' kids, to "come Hāna," as Uncle Take would say. For that reason, I—and Dad and other family members—liked the idea that if we built a small cottage, it would serve as an investment in keeping that connection to our family roots.

But there were just as many—if not more—reasons to not do that and to keep the land undeveloped. First, it would be incredibly expensive to figure out how to pay for bringing electricity and water pipes and construction materials to the remote site. Grandma's land is literally not connected to the grid or anywhere close. To just break ground would cost us tens of thousands of dollars—the electricity alone would require us to install electric poles, at $5,000 each, and we'd need a lot of electric poles to get down to our property from the main road. Fresh in my dad's memories and mine were brutal fights among Grandma's siblings over getting easement rights to bring costly water lines across one another's properties. One branch of our family basically stopped talking to another over a water pipe decades ago. And finally, there were big, uncomfortable questions we'd need to answer for ourselves: What if no one used the house if we built it? Who would pay for it? Who would maintain it or pay for maintenance? The logistics of building, the enormous cost, and time investment seemed daunting and fraught for potential conflict within our family. The reality of getting it done without enormous headache and cost gave me a lot of pause.

The remoteness of Hāna is what makes it so special. But it's also what makes it so hard to build there. Hāna's constant rain, sun, and junglelike environment would eat alive any wooden building. Anything that we built would need constant maintenance and care. Not to mention, my local cousins warned me that trespassers commonly came onto our property to hunt or fish. My cousin Gabe had recently paid $1,000 for a large storage unit and put it up on his nearby property only to find out it was stolen two weeks later—including the pallets he put it on. He lives on Maui, but not in Hāna. Whatever we built would need protection, and that would be challenging unless we had a family member living there or someone who could keep eyes on it.

I could argue both sides, even if deep in my heart I could envision a small cottage there and deeply wanted to have a small home to visit. But truthfully, it wasn't even my call. It wasn't even Dad's call. This was a conversation that Dad would need to lead among his brothers and sisters first. Their generation—now in their sixties and seventies—was in charge of the family trust that controlled Grandma's land. It was their turn. Now *they are the kūpuna*. It was their call to make a decision—or worse, they could decide not to do anything and we'd face the possibility of losing the land if we could not keep up with taxes.

If history is our guide, our family seems to move, with each generation, to the same conclusion: it's too costly and too much trouble to do anything but the status quo. "I used to be more optimistic about building something on the land, just because I was younger and I didn't see all the complicated family dynamics," Ben said after he got back. "But as I've gotten older and seen different interactions between family members, it's been a starker reality. The number one reason properties are distressed and go into foreclosure is because of this exact [family] issue. Parents own a large property, pass it on to their kids, and kids can't agree to distribute it equally. And in deciding to do nothing, nobody wants to fix up the house and nobody wants to sell it."

He sees an apt parallel with our land and more potential drama once it's not just land but also a house. Over the next few months, Dad created a long email chain to brainstorm ideas with the families involved in the decision. *Here's a company that will modify a shipping container into a tiny house, which will look cool on Instagram and have a tiny kitchen and bed. Best of all, you don't have to build much, just transport it to the land. Or what about a nicer version, a kind of glamping approach to install a nice trailer on the property—an easy rental and family use with no commitment to build?* This first step was certainly easier than asking each family branch to come up with a few hundred thousand dollars each to try to construct something.

With a variety of ideas on the table, Dad also finally decided to have more direct conversations one-on-one with each of his siblings to declare if they were in or out. They needed to get serious about having a plan—whether that plan was to keep paying the taxes or to build a house or something in between. They would need to start making some decisions and commit time and money to decide what to do with Grandma's land. Although normally the eldest son would take on a leadership role, that task had always been held by my father, the third-born child of eight children. He's the doer. He was once again back in his get-shit-done role.

Four out of the eight Goo siblings—Darrell, Duane, Maureen, and Dad—decided to be in and pledged funds and time toward figuring out a solution. Perhaps not coincidentally, the four *in* siblings all had children and some had grandchildren. The four *out* siblings did not. Now, Dad had a working group. Auntie Maureen volunteered to serve as the secretary of the group, who kept correspondence with us all and the county tax office and kept track of our collective budget and funds. Dad began to arrange for the four of them to meet regularly, and Auntie Maureen shared updates on our request for the new ag status.

Next, this new family leadership group began to bring in what we called Gen 2, which consisted of all the four siblings' children. For the first time, my extended family of aunties, uncles, and cousins from across the country gathered together online to discuss the future of the land. We held regular Zoom calls—held at an ideal time for folks from Massachusetts to California—to deliberate. From the first meeting, it was clear that some of my cousins—ranging in age from high school to early forties—knew more than others about the land or its significance to our family. Only about half of us had actually seen it. But all of them were really interested now. Dad and my brother and uncles shared photos from the Hāna labor trip to show what they had done and what it was like. For the first time, we began to have a dialogue about our shared history, our shared stakes in our future. It was inspiring at these gatherings to see each of my cousins show up to ask questions, to bring ideas, and want to have a seat at the table. Vincent asked about our genealogy; Ben shared his ideas for returning native trees such as koa and sandalwood to the property. Shannon began planning her first trip to Hawai'i and to see the land in Hāna. Vincent decided to spend a semester studying at the University of Hawai'i. A group of my younger cousins, led by Stevie and my brother, Ben, began planning a family reunion, since it'd been a long time since we'd gotten together. And I began to hold online calls to talk about the history of the heiau, our family's genealogy, and all the other information I'd found that was now not mine but theirs to know, to keep, and to have forever.

We were starting down this path as a generation of siblings and cousins and 'ohana. Before we could decide what to do with the land, we needed to build a foundation of shared understanding and commitment for ourselves.

———

In 2007, we became pregnant. From the moment I saw those two blue lines on the home test, I knew that I wanted to give our child a Hawaiian middle name, keeping with tradition in my family. But Grandma had been the one to pick out all the grandchildren's middle names. Grandma had helped my parents pick out my middle name, Kehaulani, which means "snow of heaven." My sister Haley's name is Kanani, which means "the beautiful one." My brother's middle name, Malulani, means "under the protection of heaven." And my youngest sister Emily's middle name is the same as Grandma's—Kekauililani, which means "riding the clouds of heaven." My aunties and uncles and cousins also have Hawaiian middle names. I knew that giving my child a Hawaiian name would be part of marking his identity and maintaining the generational tradition that had continued for centuries in our family. Without Grandma, what would I do?

Searching for the right Hawaiian name brought me right back to the memories of my wedding day, where I felt those twin feelings of joy and loss. I yearned for Grandma to be here to help me. I wished to hear her voice and talk through her ideas. I yearned to call her and tell her that her first great-grandson was about to be born. I could just imagine her delight—her sweet giggle—in hearing the news. Instead, I found myself talking to her in my head. *Grandma, I wish you could see this sonogram. Grandma, how did you ever have eight children and go through this pregnancy thing so many times? Grandma, please give me some guidance on Silas's Hawaiian name. I wish you were here to tell me what it should be.*

The truth is that I worried about the responsibility of giving our son a Hawaiian middle name. Even if it felt right in my gut, it brought up lingering feelings of uncertainty about my own Native Hawaiian identity. I felt the honor of carrying on the tradition because I wanted our son to feel that part of his own lineage. But I also worried about the weight of that responsibility and what it would require of me as a parent. I thought about that term I'd heard— *banana*. I didn't want my son to be Hawaiian in name only. I didn't want myself to be Hawaiian in name only. *What's in a name, after all? It would be my first imprint on my child's identity. It's a reflection of the aspirations I have for my child. It's honoring the past in my child's name forever.* I hadn't truly thought about any of this until this baby was growing inside me. Sure, picking out a crib, making a baby room, and buying diapers felt like a long list of tasks that expecting parents need to do. But the name choice weighed on me most in those months before Silas's birth.

Before I met Michael, when I was living my busy single life as a news reporter in Washington, I often doubted that I'd find a partner who would ever truly understand my cultural background. I had a boyfriend once who, whenever I talked about Hawai'i, would make a hand motion like he was fake hula dancing. When I told would-be suitors that I was part Native Hawaiian, more than once I'd hear some version of "Mooka aka hiki, come on you wanna lei me!" More so, I was puzzled by just a total lack of any cultural curiosity. There was no interest beyond the surface of a desire to visit Hawai'i as an exotic vacation. Right or wrong, I had judged a lot of potential partners about that because I saw that as a sign of how they thought of me, too. In some white men in particular, I found it odd that they just didn't seem to have a culture of their own in their family. When it came to family traditions, stories, history that grounded them, it was just a void. I don't know how to describe it other than to say that I felt sadness about that. It made me want to cling to my own family and our history even more.

But Michael was different. He was not only curious about my family's culture, he wanted to understand it and become part of it. Michael worked with Native American tribes early in his career to help run public health programs that would expand health care access on reservations. On his first trip to Hawai'i with me, about a year after we started dating, I loved how he wanted to understand the traditions and language as much as I did. I delighted in taking him to my grandparents' favorite hole in the wall to eat a hot bowl of saimin, a thick noodle soup with egg and strips of pork. I introduced him to the local snack to go—Spam musubi, and he loved the salty pork taste mixed with rice wrapped in seaweed as much as I do. For breakfast, he tried—and devoured—loco moco, the local comfort food made with a heaping bowl of white rice covered with egg, hamburger meat, and gravy. We went on a quest to find the best shave ice on the island while perfecting our orders of the soft, sweet island dessert. For me, that meant coconut ice cream buried at the bottom of a soft mound of flaked ice soaked in lilikoi, or passion fruit, pineapple, and guava syrup, topped off with balls of chewy mochi.

On our honeymoon to the island of Kauai, Michael splurged on a beautiful 'ukulele and taught himself how to play it. As a self-taught guitar player, he instantly fell in love with the small instrument. We bought a Hawaiian music book, too. My memories of our honeymoon are dominated by us sitting on the floor of our honeymoon suite near Hanalei Bay, him strumming and me singing a famous song by Israel Kamakawiwo'ole:

Henehene kou aka.
Kou le 'ale 'a paha . . .
He mea ma'a mau ia,
for you and I.

That song, which is about the flirtation and courtship between two people, was the soundtrack of our honeymoon. We played it in our rental Jeep as we cruised around the island, and Michael played it on his new honeymoon uke every time he picked up the instrument. It brought me so much joy to know that this man I married was the right man for me, and he checked this box that I knew I needed all along in a partner for life—someone who would love my culture as much as I did and who knew how important it was to me. I also loved that he was the proud great-grandson of German immigrants who immigrated to Kentucky. Curious about his own roots, Michael studied German and lived with a family in Germany in high school and later spent a year in Vienna during college.

Through our marriage, I had the unexpected joy of gaining not just a husband but a daughter as well. To be honest, I wasn't sure how to be a stepmother at age twenty-nine, but I fell in love with Isabella as much as I did with Michael. She was a sweet, curious, creative kid who had her dad's beautiful blue eyes, long golden-brown hair, and adorable freckles. Isabella was just a few years old when Michael and I met. Thanks to his amicable arrangement with her mother, Michael's ex-wife, Isabella lived with us half the week and her mother the other half. To this day, she refers to me as one of her moms, and our relationship is an unexpected blessing that came with being married to Michael.

Two years after we got married, we knew we wanted to have a

child of our own. What no one taught us was how to blend our two families' cultures and histories as we became one.

Michael and I talked a lot about how we wanted to ensure that, when we had a child together, that child would have a great sibling relationship with Isabella. We wanted them to be siblings, not half siblings or part-time siblings. We wanted to combine our family unit from the start. Isabella was so excited when we told her the news that she'd be getting a baby brother. We took her with us to doctor's appointments when I was pregnant so she could hear the heartbeat and see the little baby growing inside me. We also knew that she had been at the center of our world as the only granddaughter for both of our parents. Now that center of attention would be expanded to include her little baby brother we named Silas.

Serious self-doubt began to creep in, and I realized that picking our son's Hawaiian name forced me to think about how, as his mother, I'd shape this baby boy's path in the years to come. How could I possibly raise a child on the East Coast of the United States and ensure that being Native Hawaiian was part of this identity? That now felt like an enormous weight on my shoulders. Michael and I had jobs and lives that were fully immersed in an East Coast city, and I did not see us moving to Hawai'i or even the West Coast anytime soon, as much as I missed California. I myself didn't feel equipped or confident in my own identity as a part–Native Hawaiian woman who grew up on the mainland. I still had so many questions I had yet to find answers to about the land in Hāna, the heiau, our family story. I thought about my baby's future, his life, and where it would take him. I envisioned that, as a family, I'd introduce him to the things and places that Grandma had introduced me to in Hawai'i. I knew that we'd visit Hawai'i often—or as often as we could afford it. I'd try to ensure that he'd have the same ties to our family land and our family story that I did. But would he feel the connection to the culture like I did? How could I ensure that he did?

I called Grandpa, who, after Grandma died, was living alone in Nānākuli at the time. He gave me two family names, both of which came from our ancestors in Hāna. One of them sounded perfect and perhaps was obvious: We named him Silas Kahanu. Kahanu was the name of the original ancestor who received the land from the king—the chief of the ahupuaʻa. It was a name I saw repeated among the men in our family tree. It would be a high honor for him to carry the name, and thus, in my mind, it was a lot to live up to.

When our daughter Chloe was born a few years after that, we made a simpler choice about her middle name. Seeing that our baby girl's due date was around the same time of year as my great-grandmother Mileka's birth month, I thought it was auspicious timing and fitting to honor both my great-grandmother and my grandmother by giving Chloe the middle name Mileka. Mileka is a Hawaiian version of the name Martha, Grandma's name; and my great-grandmother went by Mileka. As it would happen, Chloe Mileka was born on the same date as Mileka, on April 8, 2011—109 years apart.

I never told anyone about my self-doubt over giving our children Hawaiian names. Not even Michael, or my parents, or my siblings. It was an ongoing conversation I had with myself during my pregnancies. At times, I'd think about the irony of all the books I read to prepare me for giving birth or becoming a parent—what to buy, what to prepare for, what to feed a baby, how to feed a baby. Those are important things to know, for sure. But I wish I'd had more guidance about how a parent can carry on culture and heritage, especially in the United States, where so many couples are blending different family backgrounds and traditions. There was no book for that, no manual that gets passed down from one generation to the next. It all is unspoken, absorbed, understood. For me, at least, in the end, I had to dig down deep into myself and find some kind of confidence that the names I chose were the right ones and that I'd figure out the rest. Both children, I hoped, would be raised to feel part of this important heritage. Selecting their Hawaiian names and seeing them on their birth certificates gave me a clear task in the coming years to guide them and impress upon them what their names meant.

As a parent, I now felt a heavier responsibility I didn't have when it was just me, that Grandma's land was not just her land or my father and his siblings' land. It was a legacy that would come to me and to our children, too. How could I teach them and guide them so they'd feel connected to Hawai'i, a place I felt I was still searching to understand? I wasn't sure, but I was reassured that my kūpuna, my grandma and all those before, were still guiding me somehow.

We had a small, narrow window in the baby's room, where the moon—at certain times of the month—would shine directly down onto the rocking chair when I'd nurse baby Silas, and later, baby Chloe, back to sleep. Those were the quiet times I felt she could see us, and we could still hold hands through time. At those special moments, I felt her presence, like the moonlight, touch the angelic face of my children—Kahanu, Mileka, and me, Kehaulani. *See, Grandma? Your great-grandchildren are here, we see you, and we feel you.* These moments were mine and ours alone. I felt something deep in my bones—blessings—that told me that she knew we were all here. In those quiet moments, I felt a growing confidence that I was not alone in taking up this journey. Someday, I'd take them to Grandma's land in Hāna and tell them about Kahanu the chief, the king, and the heiau.

5

GETTING PONO

I got bit by the "journalism bug," as we say in the business, in high school. Once I realized that there were careers where people could write news stories every day and get paid for it, it sounded like a great gig. Neither of my parents were writers, but at an early age, I loved reading the newspaper and debating political issues. I loved that some news stories—of corrupt politicians, of street gang drama, of unlikely heroes—were more fascinating than fiction, and I loved that journalism felt purposeful.

History has always fascinated me, too. In high school, it was one of my favorite subjects, and in particular, I wanted to know more about the history I knew our country wasn't particularly proud of: the Trail of Tears, Japanese internment camps, slavery; these atrocities against large groups of people stuck with me. I always wondered: How could those awful things have gone on for so long and no one stopped them? Perhaps people didn't do anything about it because they didn't know or fully understand. Perhaps there was no reporting. Or perhaps *better* reporting that informed the world of what was going on might have made a difference.

Journalism seemed like an exciting way to somehow be part of history in the making. And I saw in it a civic good. A free press is key to a healthy democracy, and I wanted a career that served a greater cause. Growing up in Southern California meant that I observed a lot of people who liked to flaunt material items of success. Kids in high school drove BMWs upon their sixteenth birthdays and lived in oceanfront homes. It was the kind of place where people liked flashy evidence that they were living the good life. But I never bought into the desire to make money for money's sake. It felt empty. In high school, I showed up at the weekly community newspaper one summer and volunteered to write stories for free. I got a thrill out of interviewing people, telling their stories, and crafting just the right words to make a story memorable. With each article, it felt like a chance to empower readers with information—even if, at first, I was writing about the new court for drug offenders or a budget fight at the city council meeting.

In college, I decided that I would not only major in journalism but that I would train myself for it at every opportunity. I applied to dozens of newspapers for internships, offering to work for free at first, during my summers off from college and even during the school year. My first summer reporting internship, after my freshman year in college, was writing for the community weekly section of my hometown paper, *The Orange County Register*. They let me write stories, including one about a new British hairdresser who'd arrived in town and another about a new community garden. I'd cut my articles out of the newspaper, paste them onto sheets of paper, and send photocopies of my "clips" and résumé to newspapers I dreamed of working for, like the *Chicago Tribune* and the *San Francisco Chronicle*. I got turned down for most of these internships. I told my parents I'd never really make much money at writing news articles, but I loved it, and they supported me in chasing my dream.

One summer, while interning for the *St. Paul Pioneer Press* in Minnesota, I wrote about a teenage girl who was accidentally killed while handling a gun at home. During another summer internship, this time in Michigan, I interviewed auto workers who were on strike and concerned about their jobs as General Motors threatened to outsource their jobs at the plant in Flint to Mexico, under NAFTA. Another summer, in Cape Cod, Massachusetts, I wrote about the encroaching ocean threatening to wash away residents' homes. News gave me an escape to see more of the country, to get away from the hometown that I always suspected was just a little too comfortable and maybe a little boring. I loved being at the scene of the action; I loved the adrenaline rush of waking up not knowing what story I'd write that day but knowing it would be done by the first press run at 6:00 p.m. I loved starting over in a new community, where I knew no one but soon would. I loved the challenge of covering big stories that would somehow end up printed in newspapers that thousands of people would get delivered on their doorsteps every morning—even better if they were on the front page. I had, as those in the newspaper business would say, ink in my blood.

I hustled my way across the country—always moving farther east, away from California and Hawai'i, to find the next opportunity. The day after I received my college diploma, my mom and I loaded my tiny Toyota and drove across the country. I'd gotten an internship as a reporter at *The Wall Street Journal* that eventually became my first job in journalism. I felt like the luckiest girl in the world.

Looking back, I caught the tail end of some of the best years in the newspaper business. In the decade that was my twenties, the *Post was* my life, and I felt like DC was the perfect place for me. I made great friends with fellow reporters who worked in Metro and Sports, and I also worked with photographers and graphic artists. We were all young, new to the city and originally from all across the country, and we all had our own stories of small-town papers we'd worked for to get here. In Washington, I found a wider network of other journalists from other publications who were just like me—single, ambitious, eager to make it. I ended up spending so many hours in the *Post* newsroom on Fifteenth and L Streets NW, just north of the White House, that it became a big part of my identity. Early days turned into late evenings for the *Post*. I lived on Capitol Hill and made it my home because of the *Post*. I spent weekends with my friends who all worked for the *Post*. We called ourselves "Posties."

When I got promoted to editor, I loved the thrill of being part of the A1 meeting, when the top editors would try to make their case for why their stories—be it the uprising in Egypt or the oil spill along the Gulf Coast or the feature story of a local woman whose son was gunned down last night—should be on the front page. I loved glimpsing the presidential candidates, the top diplomats and government leaders, even the occasional movie star who would walk through the newsroom on occasion to meet with the editorial board. On special occasions, the paper's publisher, Don Graham, would invite certain reporters and editors upstairs to his fancy executive dining room, where we'd eat on blue-and-white china served by waiters and discuss the hot topics of the day. From time to time, if a reporter wrote a particularly good story and it made the front page, they'd be lucky to get a "Don gram"—a handwritten card from the publisher, thanking them for a "terrific story" or encouraging them to "keep it up,"—delivered to our mailbox cubby. We all loved Don.

I loved the bright lights in the makeshift live television setup in the front of the newsroom that stood ready to beam any reporter with a hot story onto CNN at any given moment. I loved the sweat and hustle of working with the page designers late at night when a big news story would break and they'd have to redraw the entire page again, rewrite all the headlines, complaining and loving it all the same. The newspaper business really was a small miracle of production done every single day, and later, as the internet became people's source of news, it was all the time.

But all that fun energy at the *Post* took a turn around 2008 as the financial crisis hit and the internet economy began to impact the newspaper's bottom line. The party, we could feel, was ending. In fact, the last four years I spent at the *Post* were downright discouraging. I'd watched the newsroom shrink from more than eight hundred journalists around the world to one half that size. The *Post* suffered from the same ills as the rest of the newspaper industry with the decline of home-delivery subscriptions and full-page ads in the newspaper, which paid the newsroom's salaries. The newspaper struggled to adapt to its readers' shifting online habits. Budgets shrank. Having fewer dollars meant that we couldn't cover the kinds of stories we used to pursue. At the time—just before billionaire Jeff Bezos bought *The Washington Post*—the storied institution I loved had been forced to downsize its ambition.

The financial stress of the newsroom and the constant churn of new managers and reorganization distracted me from my job and began to consume more of my thoughts outside work. It forced me to look up and, for the first time, worry about my own future and whether I'd be able to do what I'd dreamed of—which was to spend the rest of my life at the *Post*. Every month, it seemed, I counted another friend in the journalism business—a kick-ass reporter or tough editor who had made the government or big corporations accountable with their reporting, telling me that they were quitting the *Post* to work in a more stable profession. One left to work at a nonprofit. Another left for a lobbying firm. Another for a communications director job. As people left, no one was replaced, so the workload just piled on those who were still there.

One day, I sat down in the *Post's* much-derided cafeteria on the second floor, which served an abundance of heavy food like fried chicken and mashed potatoes and cooked carrots doused in butter. I picked up a Styrofoam cup to fill it with hot water to make tea later with a stash of tea bags I kept at my desk.

When I started to walk out with it, the *Post's* longtime cafeteria cashier stopped me. "That'll be a quarter, hon," she said in her Maryland accent.

"Can you believe it?" I told my reporter friends at the cafeteria table, sitting down for a rare moment away from my desk. I realized it had been weeks since I joined a regular crew of business reporters assembled at one of the long lunch tables next to the windows overlooking L Street. "They're charging me for water?!"

Our lunch table erupted in laughter. Even the cafeteria was pinching pennies.

"*The Washington Post* used to be a place where you put your feet up once you got there," one of my reporter friends from the Metro section said. "It was a 'destination newspaper.' Now, we just shrink and shrink. It's not what it used to be, but no one wants to admit it."

During these years of the shrinking newsroom, I failed to hear any new business ideas that would turn around the *Post*'s financial future. And we weren't alone. Dozens of news organizations had cut staff across the country—mostly at local newspapers and news magazines—because they couldn't find a way to adapt to the digital readership from their newspaper business model. From 2008 to 2019, newspaper jobs in the United States dropped by more than 50 percent.[1] It was not only a loss for a newspaper like *The Washington Post*, which became famous for its Watergate coverage; it was depressing for what this would mean for millions of Americans who would not have reporters keeping their community informed and state leaders accountable. It was alarming for democracy and the important role that journalists play in it.

One day, while I was eight months pregnant with Chloe, my boss called me into her office. I sat down in a chair across from her desk. She looked up at me with a dispassionate face. "We're going to be making some changes," she began. She explained that she decided to tap another manager—a male editor—to take over my responsibilities as news director, starting the following week.

I remember feeling completely betrayed. I had given the last ten years of my life to this place working fifty, sixty hours a week. I was trying to save it. I cared so much about this place and now . . . what was happening to me—and why now? I was stunned. I got up, mad as hell, and left her office and the *Post* that day with a deep pit in my stomach that my whole world had turned upside down. For the first time in my life, I wasn't sure where my career was going or that I had any control of my future. I just knew that I was free-falling.

Demoted, very pregnant, and free-falling.

A few weeks later, I gave birth. I told myself that I'd figure out my options while I was on maternity leave, and for the first time, I began to consider my entire relationship with the *Post*—and journalism. The problem was that the *Post* was not just where I worked, it was how I introduced myself. It had become me. I'd spent my entire independent life working there, making friends there, passing milestones like getting married and having kids. The *Post* was a big part of who I was. I'm Sara Kehaulani Goo, reporter and now editor at *The Washington Post*. To untangle the *Post* from me was scary. Who would I be if I was not that?

Those months at home nursing baby Chloe got me thinking about something that I knew deep down but couldn't allow myself time to confront. Off and on, since Grandma died—I had this nagging voice in my head. *"Find it,"* a voice kept telling me. *"Get there."* There was something distracting me, calling me—something far outside the walls of the *Post*'s building on Fifteenth and L Streets in downtown Washington, DC. I wanted to chase this story—my own family's story—but it seemed so elusive. I had left Hawai'i after the terrorist attacks of 2001 to chase that story—the nation's story— chase a career, and now I'd gone in way too deep. My life was out of whack. I needed to get pono (poh-no)—Hawaiian for "state of harmony" or "balance."

Grandma had died just before my wedding, but I felt her absence every day, not only as the matriarch of our family but as my closest tie to our Hawaiian roots. It's hard to describe, but I felt pulled in by that mysterious temple that I had first visited so long ago, as if it were calling to me, and that perhaps in going to answer it, I would feel more closure after losing Grandma. Maybe it was because I was at this stage where my grandparents were dying, my husband and I were having children. I began to think more and more about what I wanted to pass along to them. My family's Hawaiian history was important, but I never fully understood the story behind our ties to the heiau, its meaning, and the land that Grandma left behind. I felt Hawaiian in name only, yet I knew there was more that I yearned to connect to and to know.

This had been distracting me, eating away at me now and again for years. But it was too easy to shove aside those thoughts and instead focus on my day-to-day life in Washington and my never-ending to-do list. At work, there was always a news alert to put out, a deadline to meet, a story to edit for the next day's paper. And at home, there was another list: soccer cleats to buy, kids' doctor and haircut appointments to make, shopping for milk and broccoli. As a young mother working full-time, married to a spouse who also worked a busy, full-time Washington job, my needs—my items on the list—even simple ones like getting my own haircut, were always much lower. And getting answers to my family's history in Hawai'i was at the very bottom, until I realized it was stuck there for years like some ridiculous dream.

In my very little free time, I had started to conduct some interviews, collect documents to finally get a few clues about my family's roots in Hawai'i. I still didn't have clear answers about the heiau and our family's connection to it, but I knew that I'd never make any progress until I got back to Hawai'i. Nagging at me was the realization that some of my relatives in Hawai'i who could help me—like Uncle Take, Grandma's brother—were getting older. I recalled Grandma's words, whenever I'd ask her a question about the land or the heiau, and she didn't know the answer: "Ask Uncle Take—he knows." With every year that passed, I worried about how much time I had left.

A few months after my maternity leave was up, I did return to *The Washington Post*, though not for long. It so happened that I found out about a role at a nonpartisan think tank I admired that conducts public opinion polling and is well regarded by journalists and researchers. They offered me a role that would pay more than my *Post* salary, and I'd work regular, nine-to-five hours. Finally, I could see a clearing ahead to reset my life. I would take a little time off before starting the new job. I could book a flight to Hawai'i. It seemed like a no-brainer. Moreover, I felt overjoyed that I finally would be in control of my own destiny again.

I turned in my notice. The swoosh out the door was swift.

Suddenly, it was my last day at *The Washington Post*. My toes clenched over the edge. I stood up straight. I felt ready.

It was time for my "caking." That's the term Posties use to refer to the tradition of speech-giving that colleagues give to say goodbye to someone who is leaving the newspaper, delivered with good humor and a sheet cake. I remember the days when money was more flush, we had "cakings" for people who even moved from one section of the newspaper to another—say, Metro to Style. Some reporters and editors would even perform goofy songs and skits to roast and send off whomever was leaving. But—remember the twenty-five-cent cup of water? Times were different now. In the last round of buyouts, the newsroom managers sent out a memo to staff that they'd run out of money to fund all the cakes. So for mine, I suspect my colleagues scraped money together out of their own pockets for my chocolate confection, where in cursive it simply said, "We'll miss you, Sara." By this point, I had attended probably no fewer than one hundred "cakings" for others. I knew the drill. We all smiled at one another, and I tried not to let myself get choked up as I delivered my short goodbye speech.

Shit, despite it all, I was *really* going to miss this place. I scanned the scruffy newsroom that I'd spent more hours in than my own apartment. I'd miss the weird parts of the newsroom—the piles of disheveled papers everywhere; crumbs around the keyboards and the sign someone stole from some airport and hung from the ceiling of the Business news section that read "Economy Class." I'd miss "the trough"—a space on a file cabinet where people would put extra food that would inevitably get eaten by someone staying late on deadline no matter what it was—and I mean people put all kinds of nasty stuff there—like half-eaten sandwiches and hot-pink Sno Balls from the vending machine that came out by accident. I'd miss jumping in a cab from Capitol Hill to write my story with an hour to spare, crafting the top of the story in my head on the way back to the newsroom. I'd miss the thrill of working right up until the deadline and the panic of waiting for the critical callback—the key interview and the quote I needed to get the story and push the button on time.

I'd miss the days when budgets were more flush to cover the news, when I'd book a flight to cover a big story and my editor would push me out of the newsroom with an airline ticket, saying, "Go! Go! Go!" I'd miss the sweet days of seeing my name on the front page of the print newspaper—I used to keep track of every single one, if for nothing else than for my mother and my future children in mind to someday be proud. I started as a young, single reporter at age twenty-four, trying to figure out the news business and the enormously, powerful city of Washington, DC, and how it worked. Now I was leaving as an editor and mother and heartbroken about what happened to the newspaper I loved. I had thought it loved me back.

I held the tears. And yet I was smiling inside.

Now it felt right. I was happy—relieved, even—to leave. And I couldn't believe I'd ever feel that way—*relieved*—to be leaving a newsroom I once loved so much. I delivered the goodbye speech

I had prepared the night before while looking out at the room full of colleagues I admired—the fellow reporters, the editors, photographers, copy editors, and news assistants. In fact, I couldn't help but smile, perhaps because in the back of my mind I was thinking about my plane ticket to Hawai'i, where I was headed for my last reporting assignment. This time, it was for me.

Standing there on the thin blue newsroom carpet, I realized I had spent my entire career writing stories that people forgot about after they posted them on Facebook or threw away the next day into the recycling bin. I had somehow found myself so far removed from writing something that really mattered to *me*. I somehow lost that noble cause that once got my heart thumping about reporting. It got lost in the downturn of the entire news business—between the panting demand for online clicks and the third or perhaps fourth management reshuffle. *Forget it*, I finally realized. Stories were not just in newspapers. There was one more story in my life that I had yet to report on—one I realized I had spent my career training for. I wanted to finally get answers to my own family's story—and that story was five thousand miles away.

It was time for me to figure out who else I was. It was time to go back to the 'āina.

———

It was the kind of night I looked forward to in the middle of a busy week. After work one night in 2020, I met my younger sister Haley for dinner—just the two of us. My new job at the news start-up Axios was just a couple of miles from Haley's house in Arlington, Virginia. I was not only excited to be back in a newsroom in a new gig as executive editor, but the location meant that I now had an excuse to regularly see my sister, even though we both had busy lives. I had moved to DC to become a journalist. Haley had moved to the same city, some years after I had, to attend law school. Now, she had settled in and married her high school sweetheart, and they had just built a beautiful home in the suburbs of DC. We often joked how funny it was that two sisters raised in Southern California ended up raising our own kids in Washington, DC. She was a busy mom of twins working part-time as a litigation attorney—but nonetheless, we tried to find time to have dinner together. This time, we had a lot to discuss about the land.

I arrived at the Middle Eastern bistro and ordered us both a glass of wine at our table next to the window while I waited for her to arrive. I was early. After a long day, I looked forward to a rare midweek glass of wine and a chance to unwind over conversation. Somehow, red wine in a round, stemmed glass just tasted better in a restaurant like this, and it warmed me inside when I took the first sip. I looked outside at the chilly, wintry evening. The ground was wet from recent rain, and the wind was whipping at a flag outside—it was the kind of dark, bone-cold night that every winter I told myself I had to plod through one day at a time. By now, I'd lived on the East Coast long enough that I could deal with the cold. I just hated the lack of sunshine, and it sapped my energy every year like I was running on solar power.

"Sorry. I had to find parking," I heard Haley's voice behind me. I stood up to hug her, and she looked amazing as usual. Skinny jeans, heeled boots, a cashmere sweater, a new Louis Vuitton purse—my sister has always been more fashion-forward, more put together than me. Whenever I'm with her, I think I should spend a little more time keeping up with the clothing and makeup trends that she tends to be on top of. In high school, she was the football cheerleader and I was the yearbook editor. In college, she joined a sorority and I joined the student newspaper. And when it comes to tough problems—whether it be politics or relationships or our family land—my sister has always been the thoughtful, practical, logical one, whereas I tend to make the emotional or moral case.

We quickly caught up about our lives, our kids, and work. By now, Dad and our brother, Ben, had already flown out to Maui and cleared the land. Other than a few texts, Haley and I hadn't had a chance to talk about it. Among us four siblings, I felt closest to her, and we tended to share similar views. Now that the family's farm-building effort was completed, we were still waiting to hear back from the county to see if they'd accept our agricultural status.

"Okay, let's talk about the land," I said as she settled into her seat and removed her coat. She nodded and of course knew which land I was talking about. "What do you think of this whole farm thing?" I asked her. "What do you think we should do about the whole tax situation?"

"Well, to be honest, I'm a little annoyed with the back-and-forth," Haley said as we sipped our glasses of wine.

She saw the Hāna land as a responsibility that Dad's generation never resolved, and it would be a burden for them to pass that down to us and all our cousins. Build something on it, sell it, come up with a new structure to pay for the taxes. "They just need to decide what to do because they're in their sixties now, and they've been talking about what to do with the land for like fifty years," she said.

That was true. As kids, we were often sent out of the room after mealtime at holiday gatherings so that our grandparents could have adults-only meetings about "the land." That's when the tone got serious and heated discussions would ensue. We'd only learn later, when we became adults, what "the land" really was about. It was essentially the same conversation we were having now—should we build on it or not? And how could we collectively ensure it remained in family hands?

But over the course of our conversation and later ones, I was surprised that Haley did not feel as connected to Hawai'i as I did. Although Michael and I made trips to Hawai'i regularly and brought our kids, Haley had only been to Hāna three times in her life—twice as a kid and once when she and Brian, her now husband, came to our wedding on Maui. In fact, she hadn't taken her kids to Hawai'i yet. "If Dad built a house there in Hāna, I'd stay there. I'm not going to promise you we'd go every year. It's too far. As people who work, we only have so many vacations a year." Again, she was logical, practical.

Haley shared my view—and that of our other siblings—that the last thing she'd want to see is to have our family sell the land. But Dad and his siblings needed to do something with it. She didn't want that burden to be Gen 2's responsibility—hers or mine or our siblings' or cousins'. As we talked, she reminded me that our grandparents chose to leave Hawai'i to build a better life in California. And while the California dream paid off for them, it left a gaping disconnect between our branch of the family and the rest of the family still in Hawai'i. Our family was the mainland Hawaiian family. Our grandparents raised their children in California, and we were raised there, too. Even if Grandpa and Grandma returned to Hawai'i in their retirement years, culturally, we were more American than Hawaiian. Grandma didn't speak pidgin. Neither did Dad. Neither did we. On that cultural-connection continuum, Haley was farther toward the American side than I was. I *did* feel connected to my Hawaiian roots. Maybe I was more drawn to it than she was, but for whatever reason, even though we were raised in the same family, we had different experiences that informed that level of connection.

Haley told me how she had accompanied Mom and Dad to Hāna in 2000 to attend a big event at the Piʻilanihale heiau, along with Grandma and Grandpa. I must have been working in Boston at the time and unable to attend. They were there as part of a larger, extended Kahanu family gathering for a special ceremony—a crowning achievement for which the family had pushed for decades: the National Tropical Botanical Garden had finally completed a restoration of the heiau.

At the time, Haley was in high school and unaware of the backstory of how that big event was preceded by years of growing tensions—and the legal fight—between our family and the National Tropical Botanical Garden, which oversees the heiau. In 1972, our great-grandmother Mileka and her siblings donated acres of family land—which included the heiau, family grave sites, and a small cottage—to the Garden (which is what our family calls the NTBG), under the condition that the organization maintain the property and restore the heiau. But in the ensuing years, the Garden—which is chartered by Congress and operates two other gardens in Hawaiʻi and one in Florida—underwent various management changes, financial challenges, and priorities that lost the trust of the family. The heiau sat for decades, neglected. There was no action on the heiau's restoration.

In the early 1990s, after two decades of inaction, the Garden finally restored the heiau after a legal push from Uncle Take, Auntie Dolly, and all the Kahanu siblings. The big gathering that Haley attended was not only a celebration of that work finally done but a sort of hoʻoponopono (ho-oh-poh-no-poh-no)—Hawaiian for the practice of forgiveness and healing. The family and members of the Garden leadership and staff stood in a circle for the ceremony, near the base of the heiau, led by a Hawaiian spiritual leader. Later, they enjoyed food together under tents, and it served as a celebratory extended family reunion. The local newspaper was there to capture the moment.

Haley didn't know that context at the time. What Haley remembered was that the entire extended Kahanu family had matching T-shirts printed for the occasion. But there weren't enough for our branch of the family.

"I don't remember exactly, but it was some vibe between Grandma and her sister. Something like, 'We're the ones who are still here. You left [for the mainland]. You can't just be invited and last-minute wear your T-shirt over that.' I got the sense that you don't really live here," Haley told me. It was as if Grandma had moved to the mainland, so our side of the family didn't have equal standing. I had never heard this story.

"And I think a part of it filters down to me. When I go there, I feel like, what claim do I have? I think sometimes they look at me like, 'Who are you? You don't live here. You don't have ownership of this.' That's fair. I get that."

On another visit, Haley recalled driving to a local beach on Maui with Brian. They ran into locals who made it clear that the beach was not for tourists. "They looked at me like, 'You're a tourist. You're not in a tourist area.' It was intimidating," she said. "I'm part Hawaiian but not Hawaiian enough."

Ugh.

Haley was raising an uncomfortable truth that I also felt in my gut. Yes, I had felt that kind of vibe, too, at times. How Native Hawaiian could I really be if I didn't grow up there? Was I really Native Hawaiian if I didn't speak pidgin and got my Hawaiian words mixed up? Should this land belong to someone more Hawaiian than I was—than we were? Did our mainland upbringing disqualify us from truly being part of the tribe?

I remembered how, years earlier, I had written an article for *The Washington Post* about my efforts to learn more about the Pi'ilanihale heiau. After it was published, I shared the article with our extended family in Hawai'i and the mainland. Emails came flooding in from cousins, aunties, and uncles, thanking me for writing it. For some of them, it triggered a lot of emotion about our family's ties to the heiau and family memories. Others thanked me because they learned new information that they hadn't understood before. But one auntie, whom I think I met once as a kid, didn't respond well. She said that as kanaka maoli (Native Hawaiian), I should not speak or "boast" about sacred places such as the heiau. The article I wrote had included a photo from the top of the heiau, which she said was kapu (kah-pu) or forbidden. "Hewa" (heh-vah), she wrote, the Hawaiian word for "wrong." And she not only sent this message to me, but she copied everyone in our family on that email chain.

That reaction surprised me and stung. She was saying, "Shame on you. You're Native Hawaiian, but you're mainland and don't know all the rules, child." I wrote back to her immediately and asked if I could talk to her, but she never responded. Someone on the coconut wireless must have told Uncle Take about the email (since he didn't have an account), because a few weeks later, Uncle Take sent me a letter in the mail thanking me for the article. He also wrote, "Don't worry about all that stuff" with my auntie. "What you wrote was wonderful, and your grandma would be proud."

Because of that experience, I understood Haley's reticence about our shared heritage and that there was a difference between heritage and identity. Throughout our lives, we've had signals that we were outsiders looking in. We were mainlanders who had plane tickets, not Native Hawaiians with residency. We were neither kama'āina (kah-mah-aye-nah), or locals, nor malihini, visitors. We were 'ohana, but we didn't have T-shirts. There were cultural divides we'd never be able to bridge even if we were able to learn and translate as much as we could. I realized in that moment that we both shared this kind of uncertainty about how much we legitimately could claim. To non-Hawaiians, my appearance and my Hawaiian name made me Hawaiian. To Native Hawaiians who grew up in Hawai'i, I was a part of them, but also a step removed.

For Haley and me, as well as our siblings, Ben and Emily, our shared history with the land and the heiau is what linked us to that heritage. It was proof of our legitimacy, our Hawaiian blood in a genealogy and a connection to the king of Hawai'i that I could trace back to the mid-1800s. When I talked to my youngest sister, Emily, and my brother, Ben, I was relieved that we were all in agreement about our shared ties to the land. "There is a responsibility to the land, in a good way," Emily told me. "In the same way you want to be responsible for your children and the things your grandparents passed on to you. But it's also a source of frustration because you feel somewhat helpless, at least for me, in my ability to make changes to the situation, with regard to the taxes, with regard to developing the land." We were a continent and an ocean away, but, as I'd later learn about my cousins who lived in Hawai'i, we also had our own financial restrictions and our own busy lives to attend to with kids, work, and more pressing day-to-day priorities.

For me, whatever insecurity or self-doubt I had about my legitimate claim to "Hawaiianness" that I may have felt from time to time, I decided to ignore and focus on what my grandma taught me about the land, on what Uncle Take shared with me about the heiau. Being part Native Hawaiian was my birthright, but also something that I chose to embrace. I didn't choose to be born with the ancestry that I was born with. But I did choose to follow the path to understand what it meant for my family and me. My intention to embrace the history, the culture, my 'ohana—is what matters most. It didn't matter what some local guy thought about me on the local beach on Maui or if I had a Hawai'i driver's license to qualify for a kama'āina discount at the store. It doesn't even matter, frankly, if people liked what I wrote about the heiau. This was my journey, not theirs. Everyone had their own path, and who was I to judge? Who were others to judge me?

To be honest, I thought a lot about that email from my auntie for days and weeks and even years later. Perhaps she had good intentions in sending it, to try to instruct me. But if that were the case, then she would have followed up with a one-on-one conversation with me. There are, after all, certain spoken and unspoken rules about a culture. I was publicly scolded, like I had crossed some line that everyone else on the inside knew existed that had exposed me. But I recently reread the article I wrote. It's a story about a young adult trying to understand a place with an important history from her great-uncle. It's about me trying to find my way, to learn, at great effort, what kuleana is. It was my effort to share with the world about the heiau—the story that my great-grandma wanted to share with the world, too.

Dad needed to work together with his siblings and make a plan for the Hāna land. It was worth a shot to try to figure out a new agreement between the family and the Garden. But whatever that decision would be—especially if that result would be indecision—was ultimately ours as well. We would inherit decisions made about Grandma's land and the heiau at some point in our lives. Maybe not in five or ten years but maybe when *we* were in our sixties. It was coming for us. It was just a matter of time and a matter of who would take it on. I saw no reason why we should sit on the sidelines.

———

A few days after I said goodbye to *The Washington Post*, I was at the departure zone of Ronald Reagan Washington National Airport's terminal. "Is that it?" Michael looked down at my one carry-on black roller bag and then back at me.

"Yep." I smiled. "It's not a vacation, you know. It's research! I'm working!" I told my husband.

"Yeah, right," he joked, giving me a knowing look. I knew I was asking a lot of him. But when I brought up my crazy idea a month earlier to quit my job and leave him for a few weeks with the kids while I went off to Hawai'i, he understood and agreed right away. He knew that Hawai'i was consuming my thoughts; I had been talking about it for years. "Do it," he reassured me. "I can hold down the fort."

Now, on this sunny spring morning with a crisp chill in the air that felt about ready to give way to the day's heat, it was finally the day I'd been dreaming about. Michael pulled my bag onto the curb.

In many ways, we had fallen in love in Hawai'i. I had invited him on a trip to meet me there after I spent a few days with my grandparents. We had only been dating a few months, but for some reason, I knew even then that he was the kind of guy who would appreciate my culture. Grandma loved him and teased him. She liked his blue eyes, too.

"Just marry a tall one," was her advice to me. In her bare feet,

Grandma stood about five foot one—a few inches shorter than me, but my aunties were even smaller. "We need all the height we can get in our family," I remember her saying with her cackling laugh.

I looked up at Michael, who was nearly a foot taller than me. "You know how much this means to me. I love you. Will call when I get there."

He nodded and bent down to kiss my lips. "Yep. We'll be good."

I ran around to the back seat of the car to kiss the little ones goodbye. "Be good. Mommy will be back soon," I told Silas, not wanting to linger too long and run the risk that he would cry, and then I'd cry, too. I blew Michael another kiss and saw him wave as he walked to the driver's-side door to get in.

I walked quickly into the terminal. *Well*, I thought, *here goes nothing*.

I located my seat on the plane and sat down with a sense of disbelief. Out the plane's window, men were lifting luggage into the cargo hold. I sat alone, staring at my Starbucks coffee, looking down at my bag and the empty notebooks I packed at my feet. I realized how odd it was to be alone; it felt like I had left something behind. I felt slightly guilty about leaving my husband with three children for nearly two weeks. Yet I felt also liberated and a sense of excitement I hadn't felt since I was a teenager on my first trip overseas to Europe as a foreign exchange student. For the first time in years, I was traveling without small children, strollers, car seats, and backpacks filled with coloring books, portable DVD players, and other airplane entertainment. I had no one to feed, to entertain, to hold on my lap. It was just me, one roller bag—a carry-on, even—a package of three reporter's notebooks, a new tape recorder, and a laptop. (Okay, I threw in my bathing suit, too.) I rested my head on the seat and closed my eyes, letting it sink in.

Wow, I'm finally doing it. Is it crazy that I just spent $800 on an airline ticket and abandoned my family for the exercise of finding answers about our family land and the heiau? What if I don't find much? Doubt began to creep in.

This trip suddenly felt like a huge gamble of money and time. I had charged my flight on my credit card. Meanwhile, I was not working and would not get a paycheck this month. I began to worry that the trip would be a waste of time—that I'd come back with a tan and nothing else. Meanwhile, Michael would be wishing I were there to help with the workload of dropping off and taking the kids to day care and school, making dinner, and staying up after they went to bed to work from the kitchen counter on his laptop. I could just picture it.

Now here I was, eyes closed in 12C, my mind wrestling with itself and the conflict of these multiple emotions.

A few weeks earlier, I had calculated the six-hour time difference and nervously dialed Uncle Take's 808 area code, hoping he would remember my voice. I had also mailed a letter to his post office box telling him I wanted to visit and why.

"Uncle Take? Hi, it's Sara, Martha's granddaughter," I said.

"Ah, Sa-ra." His baritone voice seemed to ponder me slowly. I explained that I wanted to visit and learn more about the family, the land, the heiau. "Oh yeah, I got all dat family stuff. Come Hāna."

Once we nailed down a date, he hurried off the phone. "Okay, den. See you soon. *Alo-ha*," he said.

I said *aloha* back to him, trying to mirror the stronger "ah-lo" and a softer "ha" like he did.

"Ah-lo-hah," I said out loud, practicing. "Ah-lo-huh." Then I opened my eyes to see if any of my seatmates heard me.

More than thirteen groggy hours later, the Boeing 767 dipped suddenly, then the right wing bobbled as it turned a hard right, descending into Maui's tiny airport, finding its way against the island's trade winds. Out my oval window, I could see the glittering water along Maui's long patch of white sand in the distance, extending along the entire southern shore into eyelash-shaped curves. Maui is referred to in historical accounts as "the Bays of Pi'ilani"— referring to the famous chief Pi'ilani who once ruled here, long before Kamehameha. Whenever people ask me which island to visit in Hawai'i, I tell them what locals say: "Maui no ka oi." It means, "There's nothing better than Maui." Home to gorgeous beaches and warm, clear aqua water lapping the shore—Maui is what you see on all those Hawai'i postcards. As the plane made its bumpy descent into the valley between Maui's two volcanic craters, I wanted to pinch myself as my arrival back to Grandma's homeland began to sink in. Now, I could see the island's last sugarcane factory, billowing its smoke from an industrial rusted stack from afar; the straight rows of sugarcane with their long stalks blowing in the wind. On the right was the majestic Haleakala volcano rising up, just as tall as the plane now at ten thousand feet. And on the left were the steep green sides of the Iao Valley, with its picturesque streams flowing through and its famous "needle." Landing at this airport is like flying into the valley bosom of Maui.

"Aloha," said the flight attendant, through the intercom, once we touched down. "Welcome to Hawai'i! " I could feel the anxious rustle as the cabin took on an ebullient mood, as passengers forgot the rigid, cranky ways of the busy mainland we'd all just left behind. Vacations, adventures, and postcard selfies awaited on the other side of the Jetway—*let us out!* As I stood up, my body ached from the long journey, but the moment I stepped off the plane, I was greeted by the familiar warm, perfumed air that is like an *aloha* embrace. A little bird flew across the terminal, reminding me that there were no windows in this airport terminal, or any others in Hawai'i.

"No need," as the locals say, when you've got eighty-degree perfect weather every day. I took a deep breath and could smell the ocean.

6

THE ROAD TO HĀNA

It was a Saturday afternoon, and the humidity was rising on the northwest side of Oʻahu when I knocked on Lilikalā's screen door. When I read her book about the Mahele, *Native Land and Foreign Desires: Pehea Lā E Pono Ai?*, I was delighted to find my ancestor's name in the index. I had been searching for more information about how Kahanu had received land from King Kamehameha III in 1848 and, after some online searching, had found her book and promptly devoured it.

Nowhere else could I find books in the popular press about one of the most historically significant events in Hawaiʻi's history, the Mahele, the law that allowed ownership of land on the islands and upended Native Hawaiians' traditional way of life. It also awarded my ancestor Kahanu Maui land—of which about ninety acres are still in our family's hands today. Before meeting Uncle Take in

Hāna, I first flew out to Oʻahu to meet this University of Hawaiʻi professor of Hawaiian studies and author of this book.

"Aloha, welcome," she greeted me at the door. Her voice was kind, but her presence was intimidating. Lilikalā Kameʻeleihiwa wore her long hair pulled into a bun on the top of her head. A large Hawaiian tattoo in the shape of a U-curve covered her chest from shoulder to shoulder, like an ornate, permanent necklace. I couldn't help but notice how regal her face looked; she reminded me of Frida Kahlo, with thick, dark eyebrows, a strong nose, and a rounded chin. Her body took up the full size of the door's opening, and she wore a muumuu, a long printed Hawaiian dress that draped over her body all the way to the floor. Her town house was nestled into the lush green valley with the backdrop of incredibly sharp green cliffs from the mountains behind. The neighborhood over-looks the blue waters of popular Kaneohe Bay. Inside, her elderly mother sat quietly not far from the television, watching a cooking show. "This is Mama," Lilikalā said, inviting me in. Her mother looked at me and smiled, and we walked past her, Lilikalā leading the way to the lānai in the back.

"So, what brings you from Washington?" she said while checking me out. I was a stranger who'd arrived on her doorstep after emailing her for help. "I'm free on Saturday," she'd replied. I was honored that she'd invited me to her home.

"Well, I've been trying to do some family research. You see, our family—my grandma—has land in Maui, and I've been able to find the award in the Mahele and trace through the generations to what we have now. My ancestor—Kahanu—is included in your book. I thought you might be able to help me understand it all a little better," I started.

As I talked, Lilikalā picked up some wet towels sitting in a plastic laundry bin, wrung them out, and began hanging them up to dry on a clothesline that ran across the lānai. The sun began to heat up; it was so bright that I was squinting to make eye contact.

"Uh-huh. So, what do you want to know about Kahanu?"

"Well, I want to know who he was—why he got this land in the first place. The story is that he was a chief who helped Kamehameha. And also this land included the Piʻilanihale heiau, the largest heiau in Maui. So why would our family receive this place with this very special historic heiau on it?"

Her eyebrows rose when I mentioned the heiau, and I could tell she was familiar with it. Of course she was. Few people I've met outside of Hāna or my family members know about it, even though it's now open to the public. But she's a Hawaiian historian, one of the most distinguished of her time.

She put down her wet laundry, looked at me very seriously, and spoke in a tone that sounded both like a teacher and a spiritual adviser.

"You are looking for your family genealogy."

I nodded.

"You should pray to them and ask them for permission, and they will open up doors for you. They will find you documents. They'll find all kinds of stuff for you, I promise. I tell my students that because that's what happens," she said.

I sat speechless. I was expecting an academic explanation, a suggestion about how I could better go about my research or stop at a particular Oʻahu library. What I didn't expect was spiritual advice.

Pray to my ancestors? I didn't know what to say. I just nodded.

Lilikalā smiled, and finished hanging up the wet towels. "Let's go inside and see what I can find for you on Kahanu."

She gestured for me to take a seat at her kitchen table, and I laid out some fruit I had picked up on the way for us to share as we talked. I found a knife and cut some papaya and removed the seeds, providing a slice for each of us. Lilikalā brought over two large binders, then laid them out on the table as she took a seat across from me and put on her glasses.

"Let's see . . . Kahanu, Kahanu," she said, flipping through pages in one of her binders. "Ah yes, here he is."

Lilikalā had spent years researching the Mahele awards of land that King Kamehameha III had doled out in 1848. I was fascinated by her incredible encyclopedic knowledge of the various chiefly lineages going back several centuries. I'm embarrassed to admit that I had tried reading other accounts of who's who in the Maui chiefly line and the Big Island line, but after a while, the list of names that began with *K* and then went on forever became very hard to follow. Eventually, my eyes would glaze over or I'd get really confused. It was like reading the Old Testament of who begat whom.

But she knew these Hawaiian ancestries like the back of her hand. Inside the binders, she had categorized name records and flipped to a Kahanu page immediately.

"Ah, okay, Kahanu in Maui is on a list of authorized *'awa* sellers—this is off the name files in 1848," she said, referring to the medicinal crop.

"'Awa. Really? Okay." I wondered what she was looking up.

"Oh, and here's an 1881 obituary for Henry Kahanu. It says he was on the House of Nobles and Privy Council, so his father is Kahanu. Mother is Kaweka."

Lilikalā continued, "On his mother's side, Kaweka goes to Kalauhea, whose father is Kauilike—so Maui chiefs—that's the Pi'ilani line. This Kahanu's wife is part of the genealogy that is related to Kamehameha. Because for ten generations, the Maui chiefs intermarried with them."

She looked at me like, *Well, there you go. Mystery solved.*

"Wow, really?" I said, floored that this woman was so quickly and matter-of-factly answering questions about my family that I had found so difficult.

"And the fact that he's in the House of Nobles and Privy Council means that there must be some priestly connection. They would not have given that [heiau] land to him otherwise," she said. She smiled. "Actually, my family is from the Pi'ilani line. When we were growing up, my mom would say, 'Now don't you go acting like that—you're from a chiefly family.' And I always wondered, 'Well, where's the chiefly money?'" Lilikalā said, laughing.

"I assume that whoever had the land that Pi'ilanihale was built on, not only is that the priestly side of the family, but it would have been priests of the temple, since the temple was built by Kiha Pi'ilani. So we're cousins. Welcome, cousin!"

We both laughed. Small world, these Hawaiians. I felt the warmth of her smiling eyes as we laughed across the table. I had arrived a stranger and, it turned out, I was a distant relative whose ancestral lines crossed with hers somewhere in the past.

"Well, wow. I've come all this way!"

Suddenly, Lilikalā was not a stranger who had volunteered to help. I felt her warm up to me even if, at first, she was probably wondering why this lost journalist who had blown in from the mainland was taking up her time on a Saturday. Now she was like my wise teacher—a kumu—in more ways than one.

I peppered her with questions like a student in one of her classes and took notes, my tape recorder in front of her. "Why do you think the Mahele had been so disastrous for Hawaiians?"

"Hawaiians—we're bad at capitalism," she said. "I don't think fundamentally that anybody in the world should own land. I think land is like an ancestor, so when we buy and sell land, it's like selling our grandmother. What's happened is—as we can see in America— people have made huge, vast fortunes off of taking and selling native land, basically, everywhere across America. And those who are extremely rich today keep making themselves richer by charging for land that everyone else lives on, whether it's rent or mortgage. We can't afford to live on our own land.

"We're ocean people. We're lucky if one percent of us can afford to live on the ocean. So capitalism is really bad for everybody, but it's especially bad for Hawaiians because we believe in sharing resources, in feeding people; 'āina is that which provides and feeds."

As someone who grew up on the US mainland with capitalism ingrained into them, I wasn't sure I'd ever met anyone like Lilikalā. She didn't believe in owning land? But I could see her point. I could see how spending years tracking the loss of land and the riches of Hawai'i's resources and who owns and controls them, the rising cost of living in Hawai'i today—where owning a home is out of reach for most locals and especially Native Hawaiians—would result in her concluding that it all began with the Mahele.

"By the way, did you know one of the Kahanus married Prince Kuhio?" she added as an aside. She was talking about one of the last royal family members of Hawai'i. After the overthrow, Kuhio ended up becoming the first delegate to the United States Congress, and he married Elizabeth Kahanu Ka'auwai of Maui. I had come across their names in newspaper searches and found the couple cited in the society pages in Washington newspapers of the time—around the early part of the 1900s.

"Yeah," I told Lilikalā. "I have seen that. But we're not related to her."

"Why would you not be?"

"I don't think . . . I mean, you think all Kahanus are related?" I asked.

"I think they are. Kahanu, it means 'the breath.' Names are kapu [forbidden]. You take the name from the family," she said. It wasn't like today, where people just select any name they want. Names were a way of tracking genealogy, and in Native Hawaiian society the bloodline was essential to one's identity and role, she explained.

I looked at my watch; it had been nearly three hours since I'd been taking notes and asking her questions at her kitchen table. Lilikalā glanced at her mama, who was starting to fall asleep. It was time for me to go.

But there was one more thing, she said. "You also need to know it comes with a certain responsibility," she added with a nod, referring to the answers I was seeking, the research I was doing, the journey she understood I was on. "You need to share what you learn with your cousins, with your family. It's theirs, too. When we give our children those Hawaiian names, that ancestral spirit lives within the child and guides the child."

Wait, hold on.

It was like a lightning bolt. A record scratch. A freeze-frame.

Her words felt like she'd truly seen me and what I'd been wrestling with: the ancestral spirit lives within the child and guides the child.

I felt a chill down my spine. It gave me "chicken skin," as the Hawaiians say.

"Yes," I said. "We gave my son the middle name Kahanu. I felt that was important to carry on. And our youngest daughter's middle name is Mileka. She shares the same birth date as my great-grandma Mileka."

She nodded, and we walked toward the front door. I gave her a hug goodbye, my heart full of gratitude. I walked to Grandpa's station wagon that I'd borrowed and just sat in the driver's seat for a moment, trying to let it all sink in. I thought I was going to conduct an interview with an expert, and instead, I felt like I'd had an encounter with a woman who could see through me. Yes, at first, I'd thought she was a little bit too woo-woo with the "praying to my ancestors" bit. I pictured myself kneeling down, hands clasped together: *Now I lay me down to sleep, I pray . . . to my ancestors?*

But no, that's not what she meant. The more I thought about it, I *had* prayed to my ancestors. At least, I'd asked for their guidance. I'd been collecting breadcrumbs from my ancestors' paper trails, our genealogy, and stories about land and the heiau. Grandma's hand guided me, the child, on my wedding day. I'd felt that again—that reassurance and guidance—for me, my babies, late at night in the moonlight. I'd been lost and seeking answers, seeking her blessing and guidance.

Lilikalā was right. I had asked for guidance. I had been seeking answers. I had prayed to my ancestors. And doors had opened.

And what she was saying about sharing information made a lot of sense. I had involved many relatives for help in my quest for answers about our family, our land, the heiau. Grandma, Grandpa, Uncle Take, Dad, my aunties and uncles. But it never occurred to me that part of my responsibility was to share what I learn to pass on to others. But yes, of course, it made sense. The answers that I would find would be for all the family members who ever wondered the same questions I did. The answers would be for not just my children but my sisters' and brother's children, my cousins' children, and the entire next generation. Perhaps this journey—digging up documents, piecing together the family tree—was not just to satisfy my own personal curiosity. Perhaps what I learn could also be a gift.

———

To get to Hāna, I'd have to take that long, undulating, infamous road that had me nearly puking from the back seat. This time, I was in the driver's seat.

I always get carsick, but I hoped that my stomach would forget if I could keep my brain focused on getting there. I hoped to make it by dark because Uncle Take would be expecting me by the next morning.

The road to Hāna is advertised by the local tourism companies as an adventure not to be missed while visiting Maui. The tourist guidebooks, which sell shuttle bus adventures with a catered lunch at the end, advertise the road's breathtaking views from the end of the cliffs, the waterfalls that you can stop and hike to, and the picturesque single-lane bridges that you can count along the way. But truthfully, I really pity people who sign up for these tours or buy the hokey CD "tour guide" that narrates the drive along the way. No doubt, the road to Hāna is amazing, majestic, and earns all those superlatives. For me, it's a beautiful, challenging road but a necessary path I must take to get to the even better reward—my destination in Hāna. Sadly, I think most people just blow by the tiny village, missing a chance to experience one of Hawai'i's remote natural beauties.

Small shuttle buses ferry people from their hotels all along the tiny highway, and without fail, I see these poor tourists sick to their

stomachs by the side of the road. Last time I was in Hāna, I stopped
at one of my favorite places to eat—a little snack take-out place by
the horse stables—and sat next to a couple visiting from Germany
who just stared into the horizon, their colorless faces telling me
that they had endured a painful trek.

"Carsick?" I asked.

"That was awful," the German man told me, sitting next to his
uneaten lunch of a turkey sandwich and a side of pineapple.

"We were in the back of the bus. I didn't think I was going to
make it. Now we have to turn back," the woman said. She looked as
though she were going to cry.

I felt for them. I really did. They'd not only wasted an entire day
traveling a road that would become one of the worst memories of
their vacation, but they'd never get to enjoy Hāna—the black sand
beach, the wild waves crashing into the black lava shores, the miles
of coastline uninterrupted by hotel resorts.

Before I hit the road, I pulled my red Ford Focus rental into a
natural food store in Pa'ia, a hippie town with surf clothing shops
and funky restaurants. It's the last place to buy anything before the
long trip. The narrow road to Hāna has very few places to pull off
and stop once you get going and no reliably open stores along the
three-hour drive. Plus, there's only one small grocery store in Hāna,
so it's always good to stock up before the journey to isolation. I put
an apple, a package of dried mango, a bottle of water, and some
nori—seaweed—crackers into the grocery basket. In the dairy aisle,
I looked longingly at the rows of yogurt with Hawaiian flavors I
can't get anywhere else—guava, lilikoi, and haupia. I wanted to take
several cups of each with me, but I didn't think it would be good
for my stomach.

In the car, I loaded some of my favorite Hawaiian slack-key

guitar CDs into the player. The 'ukulele and the fast picking of the guitar on the slack-key tuning always transported me to Hawai'i, even on the coldest winter days in Washington. For this road trip, I started with a classic: some Iz to get me into the mood. His 'ukulele strummed the tune that's been heard a million times in movies and commercials—the modified "Over the Rainbow" of *Wizard of Oz* fame. The song never fails to inspire and take me to Hawai'i. Iz, a large Hawaiian man who easily weighed more than seven hundred pounds, had the lightest falsetto voice, and as it began, "Oooh oooh, ooh ooh ooh," I put the car in gear, rolled out of Pa'ia and out to Highway 36, otherwise known as the Hāna Highway. I looked up and smiled at the sign along the side of the road warning of what lay ahead; it looked like a black, wiggly snake with an arrow pointing straight ahead.

Driving the Hāna Highway takes nerves, patience, and, I learned, some cool. It started out easily enough with some turns interrupted by a few straight patches of road. But by about the second mile, the topsy-turvies began. Here, I could still drive on the slim shoulder to let the fast-driving locals, in their beat-up pickup trucks with friends sitting in the back, pass me by. I gave them the shaka—the "hang loose" sign—with my arm out the window to let them know it was cool. No need to hold anyone up who knew these roads better than I did. *Beep beep.* They passed. I got the shaka back.

I reassured myself that there was less reason to worry driving *into* Hāna, on the interior side of the road hugging the mountain, which is less precarious than on the way back, when on the cliff side. At times, my car came within inches of the foreboding boulders and rock side of the mountain, whose edges have been shaved down to make room for the road, but there's less risk here I'd somehow miss a turn and end up falling off the edge. Still, I could feel the pinch of my shoulders and tension in my arms, locked onto the steering wheel as if this tiny economy-size rental and I were tempting fate together.

Relax, I told myself. *Focus on the strum of the uke coming through my speakers. Try to enjoy one of the most beautiful drives in the world.*

The first section of the road wove through a misty rainforest, where ferns cover the ground and tall bamboo shields the ocean view at times. If I dared to look down, I could glimpse little black rock coves here and there that looked inviting. But I couldn't even entertain stopping to pull over because there was no shoulder and nowhere to park. The road pushed me through its middle intestine.

I whipped around my first blind curve while also punching the gas up at an incline and just prayed that there wasn't a big truck or shuttle bus coming the other way. *Henk*. My little rental gave out a pathetic "excuse me" as I tried to warn other drivers who might be around the corner on what narrowed to a single lane. An hour into these turns like this, one after another, I'd forgotten that I wasn't getting carsick. I was too focused on congratulating myself for having made it around one sharp bend in the road and then bracing myself for the next driving judo move I'd have to make. *Where did that truck come from, and why is it riding my ass? How am I supposed to go any faster around this S curve when it says fifteen miles an hour? Is this guy really going to pass me around a blind corner?*

The road is largely a mental game of skill and, I realized, letting go of your driver ego. I hated that I was driving a rental car, which was obvious because it was clean, a sedan, and screamed, "I'm a haole." The locals were much easier to spot: they had pickup trucks, or cars with MAUI BUILT bumper stickers, and they were zooming around curves of this road like they were used to driving with one wheel over the edge of the cliff. Whenever I got frustrated,

I'd inhale deeply and remember my useful driving signal—not the blinker, not the brake—the shaka sign.

Go ahead and pass me, brah. Shaka.

So it went like this: bendy curve, bendy curve, shaka. Bendy curve, bendy curve, shaka. A little stretch in the road and da local guy pass? Pull over and shaka. Sometimes I'd get a little beep and see a shaka out the passenger window back at me.

Eventually, I was able to find a rhythm and even steal a peek at a waterfall spewing down from an unknown spout high beyond the trees. I could tell I was getting close to Hāna when the fern-covered rainforest along steep cliffs gave way to slightly flatter, agricultural land. It had stopped drizzling, and the sun began sinking lower in the sky. The curves became a little less hairpin and more like regular, weaving U-turn rollers. My stomach even felt stable enough for me to pull a dried mango out from my grocery sack and bite into the leathery sweetness. The road was becoming more familiar now. I tried to let my shoulders drop from their locked-in, hunched position over the wheel. This damn road has its own way of getting me there.

Relax. I've made it. Inhale. Hāna.

I spotted cows grazing on the bright green grass in the distance and rolled down my window to smell the ocean and the recent rain on the pavement. The air smelled sweet from the grass and blooming flowers, and a light breeze cooled my face. The undulating road finally settled into a straight line. I made it. I pulled the Focus into the driveway of a little inn by the bay where I'd rented a room for a few nights. It wasn't until I was out of the car that I realized how all that tension I'd been holding in needed to be let go. Now my body wanted to release all the muscles in my back, arms, neck, and shoulders. I wanted to plop myself down and crash. I don't even remember pulling my suitcase out of the car. I just remember I was desperate to close my eyes and never have to drive again. This had been a journey, in more ways than one, just to get here.

I was ready for it, but not until the morning.

———

Hāna faces east, so when the sun rises, so must everyone else. On my first morning in Hāna, I woke suddenly to a room so brightly filled with light that, at first, I thought someone snuck in and turned on every light in my little bed-and-breakfast suite. It took a moment before I realized it was natural light—the intensity of the sun rising along the Pacific horizon straight into my bedroom window, bursting open the day. And I didn't mind. It felt appropriate for my first day in Hāna, as if the sun were bracing me by the shoulders, commanding me to get up and get started. *Not a moment to waste!*

With a direct view of Hāna Bay, I opened the sliding glass door of the lānai and saw evidence of a morning shower that had already passed by. The bamboo floor of the lānai was wet, and I could smell the water drying on the palm trees' leaves. Every morning, Hāna is greeted by a swift and powerful rain, as if she must take a shower to get ready before the day begins. The tourists hate this, because they worry that the Hāna rain is like the mainland rain, and it foretells a day ruined by cold clouds and dreary grayness. It fills tourists with regret about their vacation choice, and they ask the hotels for their money back. And indeed, there are some days like that in Hāna where it rains and rains and feels like a wet, green mossy place. But most days, it's just the Hāna "good morning" rain.

Indeed, the Hawaiians who lived their lives dependent on the elements devoted so many words of their language to describing the weather. I counted nine words just to describe different kinds of rain. Ukiu rain is a fine rain with wind from the mountains; 'awa rain is dark, cloudy rain that falls all day long; koko rain spreads "over the surface of the sea with a rainbow. It is a sign of trouble of some importance when seen."[1] The Hawaiians were precise and poetic about the weather that came and went across their islands. There's an old Native Hawaiian story that refers to the "rain of the low sky of Hāna." The story goes that a warrior chief ran to a banana grove to escape a sudden Hāna squall. As he stood safe and dry under the tree, he lifted his spear through the leaves and a trickle of water fell down. He said that the sky was so low in Hāna that he had pierced it.[2]

In my small kitchenette, I brewed a pot of coffee and then sat outside on the lānai to take in the view of the rocky bay below. *Maybe I should call Michael and the kids*, I thought. But then—*wait*—with the time difference, he was six hours ahead and probably at work. I wondered how he was managing it all with the kids while I was here, packing all the lunches and checking to see that all the little teeth got brushed and little bodies got bathed. I tried to wipe away the guilty feelings about this moment of luxury, sitting on a faraway tropical island, alone, without children calling my name simultaneously, asking for me to make breakfast, demanding my attention. My mind began to wander: *What am I doing here? Why have I always felt Hawai'i calling to me?*

Ever since Grandma died, I'd set out to try to find more answers about the heiau, to do research here or there to better understand why our family of all families had this responsibility for the heiau. And how is it that a structure that was so old—centuries old—had no written or oral history explanation that could be found? Its sheer size spoke of grandeur and purpose. How could the stories of it, and the indigenous people from here—simply not exist or not be found? As a journalist, I simply didn't accept that it was possible. It felt like my toughest assignment—an investigation that was going to be a particularly tough story to crack. I needed to be patient and think creatively about how to get to the bottom of the story, and I knew that I eventually would. As my grandmother's daughter, I felt a sense of outrage at the fact that it just couldn't be found. It was as if the people I was from didn't exist or had been wiped out. We didn't matter. It was as if Native Hawaiian people, their story and their existence, weren't worth writing down or putting into a book. It was as if our history wasn't worth knowing and passing along. It was as if the world had moved on, deciding it was not significant enough to take note of. I refused to let that be the case.

But there was another reason I had returned to Hāna. Part of my soul just feels drawn to this place and made whole in a way I can't really describe. Hawaiian music, with its soothing 'ukulele strums and falsetto voices, makes me feel alive. The music seems to reach right inside my heart and light it up. Although I only know some basics of the hula, the practice of it feels so natural to my body, with my bare feet on the ground and arms and hands telling the stories that generations of dancers have done before. When I dance, I think of my aunties and how they beautifully synchronized their foot move- ments, their hands, their eyes, to tell stories of Hawaiian people and places. Even the Hawaiian language has a rhythm, when spoken, that sounds more beautiful and natural than any other language to my ear. I love hearing my own voice pronounce each vowel and 'okina. Though imperfect in my mainland tongue, every word I learn carries a meaning that I innately understand. I love hearing Hawaiian children speak the language, and I'm so envious about their knowledge, at a young age, to understand it. Every Native Hawaiian word I hear, spoken by me or anyone else, honors and keeps alive an ancient language that nearly became extinct. This culture is a part of me, even as I'm still discovering it. The deeper I go, the more I want to know and the more whole I feel. Yet I feel like I am still at the edges of what I need to understand and I still feel so far away.

From my perch on the lānai, I could take in the black rock Hāna shoreline. The air was fragrant, wet, and salty. Delicious. My hot ceramic coffee mug sat on my lap, and I felt the warm sun on my face, and I could smell the bamboo-framed porch drying in its rays. This is why Hāna feels so cleansing to my soul.

Up close, watching the waves in Hāna Bay lulled me into a quiet Zen state. The violent surf crashed again and again against the tough, giant, unmoving boulders lying in its path. The shore felt like it was fighting between the power of land—created hundreds of years ago by cooled volcanic lava—matched up against the titans of the sea, roaring with anger and sustained by a wild momentum. After watching for a few minutes, I closed my eyes, and the crashes transformed into something else. They became softer and lulling—a peaceful reassurance. There was a rhythm to it. The sun warmed my shoulders, and I just sat and listened. Every few seconds, the crest came in to meet the shore, pulling handfuls of loose pebbles, like scratching an itch. Or like a scrubbing, a cleansing. Repeat and repeat. It seemed to reach inside me and cleanse me, too. Each pull of the wave on the rocky beach scrubbed the city away; the cold East Coast where I'd come from. It scrubbed my pale skin with thick, salty air; wave by wave, it washed Washington away. I could breathe. And my lungs filled with the kind of oxygen that I could not inhale anywhere else but a place surrounded entirely by ocean. There is nowhere else where my body feels more rested than Hāna, hearing and smelling the wild shore outside my window.

Grandma, I am close to you again. How blessed are you to have grown up with this sound of peace outside your front door.

My moment of meditation was disrupted by my own new thoughts of my busy day. This morning, I planned to accompany Uncle Take to Saint Mary's Catholic Church up on the hill in Hāna town. Uncle Take and his wife, my auntie Lei, attended morning Mass every day of the week and volunteered with the church. I decided to be a good reporter and a good grandniece and begin my day just as Uncle Take does—at sunrise service.

I'm not Catholic, but Grandma was devout and took pride in sending all eight of her children to Catholic private school. I had attended Mass often enough with her as a child to generally be familiar with the routine. And even though it had been years, I was curious to see what the local church was like. Although it was close enough to walk, I drove around the block to Uncle's house in case he wanted me to give him a lift. I pulled into an open spot on his lawn, next to his pickup truck, where the grass had been rubbed off on the right side because so many cars have pulled up here. Uncle was waiting for me inside his small wooden house.

"Uncle!" I said, happy to take him in full view. It had been a few years, but he looked the same as ever, wearing a faded yellow polo shirt and black sweatpants. I noticed his shoulders seemed more hunched over as he walked, but his body was still slim and indicated that he was still active for a man in his mideighties.

"Eyyyy!" He walked over to embrace me and planted a kiss on my cheek. "Alo-ha. Welcome to heavenly Hāna." He looked me over, too.

"You drive Hāna last night?"

"Yeah, Uncle, I'm getting better at it." I smiled. "Where's Auntie?"

"Oh, the school call her early dis morning. She go help out with dem," he explained.

"I thought she doesn't work at the school anymore."

"Yeah, dey call her when someone call in sick. So she go. She already go. You ready?" he asked. Before I could remove my shoes and enter the house, he walked over to put on his "slippas" (flip-flops), and we were ready for Mass.

We drove a block up the road and turned left onto the Hāna Highway, passing the old Hotel Hāna-Maui, which had been recently purchased by a Texas company. Uncle spent decades working there as the resort's bookkeeper, and it had recently undergone a series of new owners. The latest owner has renamed the hotel Travaasa and replaced the sign that had been there for years announcing the hotel's entrance.

"That name, ugh, it's so awful," I said, waiting to see if Uncle would join in my disparagement of the new hotel owner, who chose to ignore decades of tradition and give the Hawaiian hotel a name that wasn't even Hawaiian. "I think it's Indian," I said.

Uncle joined in quickly. "Why dey have to do dat?" I looked at him and appreciated how much older he looked now, his hair completely white. But his quick wit was still the same, and he still wore the same thick, brown-framed glasses.

"Gabe still working dere?" I asked about my cousin, Uncle Take's grandson, who had lived with him and Auntie on and off. It'd only been a few minutes with Uncle, and already I had just tried on some pidgin. My mainland way of talking automatically made me sound like an outsider when I visited Hawai'i, but within a couple of days, I found myself adopting some pidgin words and phrases, particularly with my family who lived here.

I remembered once Uncle Take explained to me that locals in Hawai'i used pidgin to communicate not because they were unintelligent but because they preferred a shorthand way of speaking.

"It's a shortcut," Uncle Take explained. "Save words. So we don't say, 'Are you going to the store today?' We say, 'You go store?'" Indeed, a lot of pidgin is spoken in short, declarative sentences with an uptalk intonation that so many sentences, even if they aren't questions, sound like questions.

My favorite pidgin example I hear when I visit Hawai'i is people often ask, "You go stay, or you stay go?" That is a way of asking, "Did you just arrive in Hawai'i, or are you about to go back?" Or better yet, how far along are you on this visit? It's an inside joke between my dad and me that whenever one of us is planning a trip to Hawai'i, we ask each other, "You go stay or you stay go?" just for fun. "No, I go stay," one of us will answer. It's a way to warm up our mainland attempts at pidgin, which I find charming, though I also know I can't just fully code switch into it.

Uncle Take instructed me to turn right soon after we passed the hotel, and the white stuccoed church looked out over the highway, its classic steeple and lawn sprawled out as if ready for a church picnic. When we walked in, there were only two other parishioners seated in the church, which was decorated with Easter lilies from the holiday two weeks earlier. The lilies sat in pots, fronting the altar. Tall, colorful displays of tropical flowers in pink, yellow, bright green, and red—locally grown from someone's backyard, I'm sure—flanked the pews on either side. The arrangements of pink-fleshed heliconias, bursting toward the ceiling with their trademark staircase petals, reminded me of my wedding in Maui—sheez, now, when was it? Seven years earlier.

Michael and I got married on the other side of the island, but my cousins had brought similar arrangements of heliconias from Hāna for the occasion. I can't help but smile seeing them again. It's one of the things about Hāna that is easily part of the everyday but so unique to the rest of the world to have these gorgeous, wild beauties growing easily and in abundance here.

Uncle dipped his fingers into the holy water and crossed himself, and I followed him to the fourth row, behind a woman who looked to be in her sixties, kneeling in front of us and leading a prayer. The other parishioner, a woman about the same age, sat across from us, echoing the homily. Uncle's baritone voice joined in, and he pointed to the book where I was supposed to follow along. Uncle introduced me to the woman sitting across the aisle. We bid each other aloha and then noticed another man who had come in and sat behind us. More warm alohas. There were no more than a half dozen people in the church, and I'd now met all of them.

On the mainland, Catholic churches I attended always felt so formal and stiff, like everyone in the room was following a polite script with God. But in Hawai'i, it felt different. I remembered a visit when Grandma and Grandpa had taken me to their local Catholic church in Nānākuli, where the priest delivered his message while barefoot, and parishioners welcomed every visitor with a shell lei and a song—touches that brought a warmth and humility that I instantly loved even if the rituals of Mass felt foreign.

After the service, Uncle headed over to the candles at the back of the chapel and motioned me to follow.

"We go light a candle for Grandma," he told me. I nodded. Yes, Grandma was Catholic, too, and she would have liked the idea of me lighting a candle for her at Saint Mary's in Hāna. First, Uncle instructed me to help with some of his duties and removed the remains of other candles that had burned down to the metal square of the wick, and cleaned up the candleholders, which contained several rows for candle pots. He handed me a box of new candles, and I carefully placed them inside, thinking about all the prayers that would be made with them.

I lit the match for Grandma's candle. Then Uncle Take took my hand and closed his eyes.

"Alo-ha, Martha. It's Take and Sara here," Uncle said. "We pray for you. We are thinking of you. We send you alo-ha."

I closed my eyes and felt zapped by emotion as he said those final words. Did that tingly flood that just washed over my body mean that she saw us or God saw us? From church, I remembered a verse about God being present every time two or more were gathered in prayer. Uncle squeezed my hand, and I looked down at Grandma's candle, alongside all the other candles representing prayers for other people who needed them. As Uncle Take prayed, I thought about what led me here, all the way from Washington. I yearned to be closer to her and find answers that I didn't have time to get from her while she was still with us. I opened my eyes. The church was empty. I followed Uncle Take outside to take in the view of the bright sun, which had now lifted itself from the horizon above the ocean and burned away any evidence of the morning shower. The air was clean and green, and we could see the ocean in the distance.

I'm here, Grandma. I'm so glad I'm here. Just being in Hāna made me feel closer to her.

Grandma had led me back here. And I thought about Lilikalā's words of wisdom to me, to pray to my ancestors and they would open doors for me. What I didn't know was just how much more was about to be revealed.

PART THREE

FINDING ANSWERS, FINDING MYSELF

7

THE MAHELE

The next day, after visiting Uncle Take's church, I walked up the small wooden steps to his single-story home alongside the town's main road and pulled open the creaky screen door. The bright sun always made it appear dark inside. Keeping with tradition in Hawaiian homes, I took off my slippas before I walked in and left them on the front stoop.

"Aloha! Uncle?" I called.

I was here to reconnect with Uncle Take, who had served as our family's collector of documents and genealogy. I told him I wanted to better understand the story about our family and the Hāna land and the heiau. I wanted a simple answer: How did land that extended from "the mountain to the sea" turn out, 150 years later, to be Grandma's ten acres in a very off-the-beaten-path part of Hawai'i? If I could find this, I thought perhaps I could better understand my own connection to the land and the legacy of it. Grandma had provided me with a few answers before she died. But I remembered that when she didn't know an answer to a question I'd ask, she'd suggest I talk to her brother: "Ask Take. He's got all that information in Hāna."

Uncle Take had been retired for some time; he had worked for years as the bookkeeper at the Hotel Hāna-Maui, the high-end boutique hotel in town that remains the small town's biggest employer. His wife, my auntie Lei, also retired recently after working for years in the cafeteria at the Hāna School, which is home to more than three hundred kids from kindergarten through high school. She still helped out there, and she borrowed the school's kitchen on occasion to make her famous Hawaiian shortbread cookies with the school kitchen's enormous trays.

"Come, come," I heard Auntie Lei's grandmotherly voice. "You want eat?" Auntie Lei, whose full name is Leialoha, also spoke in thick pidgin. While Uncle Take was the man-about-town who liked to chat up everyone and pull over his truck on the side of the road, Auntie Lei was the quieter of the pair. She observed everything and always had a warm smile.

I walked over to give her soft, wrinkled cheek a kiss and to give her a hug. She was sitting on the couch, wearing an oversize T-shirt that said EAST MAUI TARO FESTIVAL and shorts with bare feet. She moved to get up when she saw me through her thick glasses.

"Ah, no, Auntie, I'm fine. Thanks, no."

She gestured for me to sit at their kitchen table, which was just a few paces from the front door. Then I saw her reach behind the table for a tin cylinder. I smiled because I knew what it was—a canister full of her shortbread.

"Oh, shortbread?" I asked, intoning my voice in the local style without realizing. My eyes lit up, and we exchanged a knowing smile. "Ah, okay, yes, Auntie, thank you!" I couldn't resist.

She pulled off the round top to reveal an array of blond short-bread cookies stacked inside, each piece cut into a rectangular shape with extremely straight edges, separated by wax paper.

She placed one on a napkin as I sat down at their wooden kitchen table next to the boxy microwave perched on top. The shortbread was an edge slice that was crispy from being baked on the side of the pan, which toasted it brown on one side. My favorite kind. I bit into it and felt the buttery crumbles scatter across my tongue with lovely familiarity.

Auntie Lei's shortbread is flaky, solid, with a middle ground of sweetness from its simple ingredients. It's the homemade-ness and the tin and the butter that served as my reward for making the long drive to Hāna every time I visit. Each shortbread piece was cut large enough to be filling, but not too big so that you couldn't have more than one in a sitting. In other words, they're the perfect size to eat without too much guilt—until it's too late to realize how many you've eaten.

Auntie also heated up some coffee in the microwave, which made a perfect pairing, as the bitter taste from the coffee cut through the buttery crumbs from the shortbread. As I was finishing off my sec-ond piece, Uncle Take came through the back sliding glass door, carrying a large cardboard box.

"Alo-ha," Uncle said, and I got up to greet him with a kiss on the cheek.

His hunched back curved over even more than I remembered as he moved to set the box on the floor next to me. Then he cleared off the kitchen table and sat down. He looked around and found his thick-framed glasses and slid them back up his nose with his finger.

"You see," he said, beginning to riffle through the documents, "I spent many, many years doing dis."

"Ah, you got the box for her?" Auntie said. "Ah, Sa-ra, you be busy!" She laughed.

Uncle Take's white cardboard box was the size of any office moving box with a lid slightly flattened out of shape. But inside was a treasure trove of documents, organized into dozens of worn manila folders: legal papers, family letters, family documents, and newspaper articles. Many documents were handwritten or type-written in the Hawaiian language. Some papers had handwritten English translations to the side of the Hawaiian text.

In a few cases, they were so old that the thin onionskin papers had begun to wear at the corners. Small holes, which appeared to be made by insects of some kind, created tiny pores through bottom corners. Luckily, the holes did not ruin the text.

Of all his brothers and sisters, Uncle Take had lived in Hāna the longest. Except for when he moved to Oʻahu to attend high school, Uncle Take had spent his whole life in the town of fewer than one thousand people. He and Auntie Lei raised their family of four children in Hāna. Their home was the central gathering spot for generations, as my dad and my uncles and their cousins remember gathering there on summer visits. My cousins, who lived elsewhere on the islands, made many summer memories piled into Uncle Take's modest three-bedroom home and playing at the beach and going fishing every day.

So when it came to sorting through the family's land, Uncle Take did most of the handling of the family documents and dealing with the Kahanu Garden. He played a pivotal role in the 1960s and '70s when my great-grandmother Mileka and her siblings, with the Hāna Ranch, donated the Piʻilanihale heiau and sixty-one acres of surrounding land. Although that arrangement between the family and the nonprofit organization would later become a source of family and legal friction, at the time, it made sense for Uncle Take to play this role because he also worked for the Hotel Hāna-Maui, which originally had the same owners as the Hāna Ranch. He knew everyone.

The owners of the ranch also helped Uncle Take and my great-grandmother connect with Honolulu's Bishop Museum, the pre-eminent museum of Native Hawaiian and Polynesian artifacts and culture. In 1964, the National Park Service designated the Pi'ilani-hale heiau as a National Historic Landmark, in an event made official with a big event and plaque commemoration at the heiau, with many of my family members in attendance.

With all this activity, Uncle Take had spent years, with the help of others, researching land titles, gathering family wills, and attending court proceedings. The white box contained the fruit of decades' worth of his effort. He removed the lid and started to show me how the information was organized, pointing out certain papers and reading some things aloud. I felt honored to be allowed to even peek inside. With every page, there was a new discovery or a clue of an answer to my long list of questions.

And then, as my thighs began to stick to the plastic-coated kitchen chair, Uncle Take stood up and announced he was leaving me with his box of documents for the rest of the day.

"Auntie and I, we go town to-day and be back afta-noon," Uncle said, and by "town," he meant that they were taking the Hāna Highway out of Hāna to Kahului, Maui's biggest metro center and home to the international airport. "What you want. You see some-ting, you take or let me know. I make copy." He smiled.

"You be busy," Auntie Lei repeated, grinning.

And just like that, the screen door creaked shut. Uncle Take's truck engine started. I peeked inside the white box, my hands giddy with excitement, unsure where to start. It was just me, this box, and half a day to ourselves!

I pushed my napkin full of shortbread crumbs to the side, washed my hands so as not to soil any of Uncle's old papers, and began sifting through the worn tabs of the manila folders. The small house was still and dark, shaded from the bright sun outside by the glass-shutter jalousie windows in the kitchen and living room.

Outside, it was a perfect beach day, and I thought of all the mainland tourists who were probably walking down to Hāna's famous black-sand beach right now. The Hawaiian birds cooed outside. I couldn't have imagined a better morning than me and my pale skin and this white box full of family revelations.

And then, after about a half hour of poking around, thumbing through the folders and carefully placing documents back where I found them as I went, I found it. I found the Mahele.

Or, rather, I found a single, photocopied page of the Mahele. It was handwritten in Hawaiian, in small, neat cursive. At the top, it said, "Kamehameha III."

I couldn't believe what it was at first. I had read about it in Hawaiian history books and from my meeting with Lilikalā Kame'eleihiwa. But here it was—at least, one page of it.

The *Mahele*, which means "division" in Hawaiian, is considered the most significant order issued by a Hawaiian royal. Even if I knew our family land was from the Mahele, seeing the actual award itself gave me "chicken skin." The paper was sectioned off into four parts with double horizontal lines. In each section, it listed an area of land and a name of the person who was awarded the land.

I read over the foreign language in the document, and suddenly, my eyes fixed on the second of four sections. There it was, in perfect cursive penmanship, my family's name: Kahanu. I could not make out all of it, but it clearly said "1/2 'āina," or "1/2 land," and "ahupua'a" and Hāna, Maui. The name *Kahanu* was written, at an angle, in slightly larger script.

It was dated "Februari 2, 1848," and it also said "Hale Ali'i." Translated, *hale* (hah-lay) means "house," and *ali'i* (Ah-lee-ee) refers to a royal, noble, or elite ruling class in Hawaiian society. But more formally, this phrase referred to an actual place: it was the name for King Kamehameha III's seat of government in Honolulu.

Wow.

There it was. An official government document that proved my family—Mr. Kahanu—*did* receive land from the king himself! I felt like I was reaching back through time and had found the golden treasure that had been sitting in Uncle Take's storage shed all along. For years leading up to this point, I had searched federal databases and online genealogy sites, scouring for clues. I had casually been hunting around to see what I could find in my spare time.

But in my hands, I found not just pieces of paper but confirmation of history and my family's role in it. I now understood why so many people love genealogy as a hobby. It was like I was playing detective and the reward was, string by string, finding a personal link to history. Forget covering Washington at *The Washington Post*. This was the most satisfying reporting I had ever done.

I noticed the Mahele document also mentioned another word I recognized: *ahupua'a*. One surveyor in 1875 described how the land boundaries were marked with an altar: stacked rocks, "an image of a hog, a pua'a, carved of kukui wood and stained with red ocre [*sic*]." Thus, the name ahupua'a combined the word ahu (ah-hoo), or pile, and pua'a (poo-ah-hah), pig. The ahupua'a fulfilled all of life's necessities: "From *uka*, mountain, whence came wood, *kapa*, for clothing, *olona*, for fish-line, ti-leaf for wrapping paper, *ie* for rattan lashing, wild birds for food, to the *kai*, sea, whence came *ia*, fish and all connected therewith."[1]

From *uka*, mountain, to *kai*, sea. *From mountain to sea. Ahupua'a. Aha!*

So it made sense that when the king decided to dole out land for the first time, he did so not in terms of surveyed acreage but in ahupua'a. The Mahele page that Uncle Take had in his files not only listed Kahanu's name; it made clear the 'āina, or land granted to him, was the "1/2" the ahupua'a called Honomā'ele near Hāna, Maui.

Grandma's "mountain to the sea" inheritance, when she first told me, at first seemed too vague a description. Originally, I was skeptical of the notion because "mountain to the sea" described pretty much any section of any part of the Hawaiian Islands. After all, the islands were built by lava that had burst through the ocean floor, creating enormous volcanoes—the mountains. Pretty much anywhere you stand in Hawai'i you can look up and see a mountain behind you and a sea in front of you. The islands are a chain of volcanic mountains.

But now it made sense. *From the mountain to the sea.* My family's story checked out. Previously, I just didn't know enough to understand what she meant. Grandma was talking about the ahupua'a in the Hāna region. And it was right there in the Mahele all this time.

Amazingly, that wasn't the only centuries-old document in Uncle Take's white cardboard box. It also contained handwritten and typed copies of Kahanu's will, from 1856. Upon his death, Kahanu directed that his 990 acres of land in Hāna be divided among three people: his two brothers and his aunt. (To his wife, he left "one horse, one cow, one calabash, 2 boxes of trunks, 2 pigs.")

I read that again. Nine hundred ninety acres?! Wow, an ahupua'a sounded like a lot of land, but 990 acres—which was just half of it—floored me. It was exciting to see the puzzle pieces starting to fit together. From family records, I also recognized Kahanu's aunt's name—Naki. I knew our family line descended from Kahanu's aunt, so his will confirmed some of the genealogy that I knew. In earlier times, Hawaiians went by just a single name, so Naki did not have a last name. Other land records showed that Kahanu's two brothers who inherited his land sold their portions. So the will explained how Kahanu's original 990 acres very quickly became the 330 acres that Naki—our family's line—inherited.

What happened to all that land? Uncle Take's painstaking recordkeeping laid it all out: the sugar plantation.

On legal-size paper, Uncle had typed out four single-spaced pages listing every land transaction he was able to find and record. In capital letters and in chronological order, it started with the Mahele in 1848, and every decade, land was leased or sold.

The document itself was a little hard to follow, given all the family members and long Hawaiian names involved. I wasn't quite sure how I was related to all these people. Certain dates and documents were underlined two or three times. And each line included the words *lease*, *deed*, or *mortgage*.

Primarily, the land went to one of the first sugar company owners, Dutch immigrant August Unna, whose name appears as the lessee.

Here's a sampling of what it said. (Note: Not all family records had all details of agreements.)

1865, Nov. 10—Lease to Unna, 10 years, for $50.00 a year

1867, Feb. 20—Lease to A. Unna, 10 years

1875, April 22—Lease to A. Unna, 10 years

1886, March 10—Lease to Marie Unna, 10 years for $30.00 a year

1895, March 9—Mortgage to William O. Smith, trustee

1897 (undated)—Lease to Hāna Plantation, 15 years

1897, May 28—Lease to Albert Trask

1906, Sept. 5—Deed A. Trask to M. S. Grinbaum

1906, Sept. 6—Deed M. S. Grinbaum to Ka'eleku Sugar Co.

1910, Oct. 14—Lease to Ka'eleku Sugar Plantation Co., 15 years

1924, Oct. 16—Lease to Ka'eleku Sugar Plantation Co., 15 years

1933, June 14—Sale to Ka'eleku Sugar Plantation Co.

1942, Sept. 28—Lease to Ka'eleku Sugar Plantation Co., 15 years, 137.5 acres for $200 per year

It was simply stunning to see the paper trail of a centuries-old relationship between my family and the sugar business laid out like this. Not every transaction on Uncle Take's land document list had a price, but for the ones that did, I was taken aback by what I saw. Fifty bucks a year? Thirty dollars a year? Two hundred dollars a year? These dollar figures might have been a significant amount of money to my ancestors at the time, but it certainly seemed like pennies on the dollar to me. Especially given the price of Hawai'i's real estate today.

I envisioned this fertile rainforest shrinking and shrinking from its natural habitat, and year by year, cleared to make way for rows and rows of sugarcane stalks. I pictured my ancestors as dark-skinned natives, signing papers generation after generation, for whatever reason, giving up the land to the big plantation in town owned by the white foreigners.

Picturing this shrinking pie and seeing these transactions made me a little heartbroken. It also made me angry. It made me wonder whether the prices to my family over the years were fair and negotiated in good faith. I also wanted to know what was not on the documents: Why did my family members decide to lease and sell their land year after year? Were they cheated? Did they know what they were doing? Did they benefit from these transactions? Certainly, I know that none of them became rich. Many of them left Hāna and left Maui.

I did know that in creating the Mahele, King Kamehameha III intended for commoners, or makaʻāinana, to lay claim to their lands that they had been stewarding under the previous system of caring for their section of the ahupuaʻa. And once it became law, soon there was a bureaucracy related to land that Hawaiians had to understand as a concept and then had to navigate. The king's advisers had set up a land commission to issue land titles and resolve disputes. Hawaiʻi had only a handful of surveyors who suddenly needed to catalog each of the islands and the boundaries of the ahupuaʻa. Once Hawaiʻi had landownership, there were quickly fights over who was a true owner of various parcels of land, which gave room for fraudsters and schemes to displace people from their land and their land rights—especially those Native Hawaiians who didn't understand the new system.

Because Hawaiians had no real understanding of landownership, many did not make such claims for their land after the Mahele. And they did not understand the system by which to make a claim nor had the money to pay a surveyor. So it laid open an opportunity for foreigners and particularly the sugar businessmen to lay claim to it. And if they were successful in claiming their land, they did not understand a new property tax system that had been created with it.

Records show that only 14,000 Hawaiian applications were made to the newly created land commission, which was empowered to officially dole these out. And of them, only 8,421 were actually awarded.[2] Many of these land plots were small, and all together, they totaled only 28,600 acres of land, or less than 1 percent of Hawai'i's total acreage.[3] "If the road to hell is paved with good intentions, then the road to a completely Americanized Hawai'i was paved with the Great Mahele," wrote historian James L. Haley.[4] The Mahele "had the net effect of evicting thousands of native Hawaiians from the countryside and leaving them worse off than they were before."

Within fifty years of the Mahele becoming law, the landholdings by haoles far outnumbered the Native Hawaiians' so that they quickly became landless in their own kingdom. As historian Gavan Daws put it: "The great division became the great dispossession. By the end of the 19th century white men owned four acres of land for every one owned by a native, and this included chiefs' lands."[5] Many of the king's advisers and missionaries (or sons of missionaries) suddenly became quite enriched with land under the new system. The king's minister of interior, Gerrit P. Judd, ended up with about 5,300 acres in the Mahele; he, his wife, and offspring in subsequent decades were involved in 1,212 property transactions on O'ahu.[6] Within four years of the Mahele, sixteen prominent members of the Congregational Mission acquired more than 7,800 acres. Later, Judd pushed for a new law that enabled missionaries to buy land at a reduced rate.[7] "There is no record of a missionary speaking out regarding the hypocrisy of preaching moral values to Hawaiians on Sunday and then acquiring their land during the rest of the week," wrote Michael Dougherty in his book *To Steal a Kingdom*.

According to other Mahele research, some Hawaiian royal family members were heavily in debt and sold land to solidify their finances or received large awards but did not have heirs to leave them to. One rare exception was Princess Bernice Pauahi Bishop, a member of the Kamehameha family who became one of the largest landowners by combining her own land award with inherited lands from her cousin and parents. When she died of cancer, her haole husband, Charles Bishop, abided by her wishes to create the Kamehameha Schools for Native Hawaiian schoolchildren, which still exists today and sits on that original Mahele award grant.[8] After her death, her husband also established the Bernice Pauahi Bishop Museum of Honolulu.

As I held our family land records in my hands and thought about the bigger context of the land dispossession, I remembered all the conversations I'd had in the past with family members about what happened to our family's land over the years.

Da family was poor, you know? one auntie told me. *Some of dem, dey need to sell the land.*

I heard that one of the uncles—I forget which one?—okay, one night, dey was gambling, yeah? And dey lost it dat way, a great-uncle told me.

Da Hawaiians, dey didn't unda-stand dat, what-you-call-it, haole way. As soon as da Hawaiians learn the rules of the game, the haoles go change the rules, a cousin told me.

In our own family records, I kept following the paper trail—just like I was reporting a story for the *Post*. I examined the dates of the various land transactions from the 1800s and noticed two things. First, most of Kahanu's land got sold to the sugar plantation within twenty years of the Mahele. Second, few of my ancestors who inherited the land lived for very long after inheriting the land.

For example, Kahanu himself died in 1856, just a decade after the Mahele law. One of my aunties said he died while on a trip to O'ahu to sign land commission paperwork that would officially grant him the land. The remaining 330-some acres that were not sold to the sugar plantation by Kahanu's brothers were held by my branch of the family, in the hands of Kahanu's aunt Naki. But she died just eleven years after she received the land from Kahanu. According to probate records, in 1867, Naki left her 330-acre land to her two children, Pūnana and David Uaiwa Kikaha, my great-great-great-grandfather. Pūnana sold his land, leaving Kikaha with the remaining acreage.

In 1910, records show that my great-great-great-grandfather received land title from the land commission, which should have been 175 acres but is later listed as 130 acres. And then I found something curious. Paperwork shows that David Uaiwa Kikaha made his petition with the land commission with a cosigner whose name was listed on other family records: M. S. Grinbaum. I recognized that name from Uncle Take's list of family land transactions, but I didn't know who he was.

The land commission document notes that $331 in taxes was paid at the time (today, that works out to be about $8,000—hardly a small expense for my great-great-great-grandfather, who was listed as a carpenter in the 1900 census). Who was this person, M. S. Grinbaum? He certainly wasn't a family member. I looked him up in Hawaiian newspaper archives and . . . bingo. I found that

"M. S. Grinbaum & Co." bought the Kaʻeleku Sugar Plantation in Hāna in 1905. Lo and behold, according to Uncle Take's records, my kupuna Kikaha signed a fifteen-year lease with the plantation to enable Mr. Grinbaum's company to grow sugarcane on the family land the same year that Mr. Grinbaum and Kikaha successfully petitioned to receive the land award. (However, I later found an obituary of Mr. Grinbaum, who apparently died two years into the contract while en route to Germany.)[9]

Seeing records like these filled in the story of my family and our land. But for every answer, I had even more questions. For example, it looked like these two men—my great-great-great-grandfather and this European plantation owner—partnered together to take care of taxes and establish formal ownership of our ancestral land. But it's hard to know if this land commission document represented a mutually beneficial arrangement for both men or if it was a situation where the white man knew the rules and the native got the deal that was offered because he didn't. I was left to read between the lines.

Perhaps those land leases and land sales were decisions that financially benefited my ancestors as new landowners in the new capitalist system. Perhaps some of my ancestors who sold their land wanted to make a better living and did so by leaving Hāna and selling their land to start a new life elsewhere on Maui, on another Hawaiian island, or overseas. I don't know. But I do know that the Kahanu land story represented what the historians say was a rapid displacement of land of Native Hawaiian people. Through newspaper archives and land records, census records and family wills, the only story that was crystal clear was one of land loss. The Kahanu land shrank with each generation, hundreds of acres at a time and then tens of acres at a time. Sold, sold, leased, taxed, sold. For more than 175 years.

There's an old saying that Native Hawaiians are "land rich and cash poor." Although I'm not sure the "land rich" part is still true, it is true that many Hawaiians have part ownership of—or "undivided interests" in—land parcels that have never been formally divided among owners. For example, if an owner leaves her property to her five children in a will and the children don't divide their interest into smaller parcels, they each have an undivided interest in the whole of the property left to them. In the days of the sugar plantations in the late 1800s and early 1900s, when ranching expanded, many families sold their undivided interests—or were pressured to sell—under so-called quiet land title actions.

In our family, early survey maps show that the Kahanu family had undivided interest in dozens of acres with the Hāna Ranch, probably from the days when our family members leased and sold land to the Kaʻeleku Sugar Plantation, which was later acquired by the Hāna Ranch. But our family formally divided our land parcels with the ranch in the 1970s through an agreement.

Native Hawaiian families have lost their undivided interests in land where ownership was never formally divided or never clarified in family wills or probate courts. These undivided interests have been lost or threatened by quiet land title actions in which a partial owner or owners go to court and claim full ownership. For example, a co-owner could make a case to the court that they are the only owner living on the property or paying taxes, so the land should belong to them. Quiet-title claims are a way for the court to decide ownership among multiple parties with an interest in the land, to clear liens, or settle boundary disputes.

What often happens for Hawaiian families with ancestral lands is that their undivided interests get passed down and spread out among more children and grandchildren and great-grandchildren.

Most Native Hawaiians don't have enough money to develop property that they have an interest in. And if one party buys out the others or, for example, one co-owner sells their portion to a developer, the developer could use quiet-title to convince the court that they are the rightful owner. In that situation, landownership is co-owned by so many parties that any profit from the land sale to the original Native Hawaiian families has historically been a pittance.

One recent example is when billionaire Mark Zuckerberg bought hundreds of acres of land on Kauai on which, it turned out, several Native Hawaiian families had undivided interests.[10] His shell company tried to quiet-title the land in court, which outraged Native Hawaiian co-owners. Zuckerberg later reversed course.

As an American, I understand real estate. Of course, people have good reasons to sell or lease land; it's a transaction of supply and demand. But there's another value to land that's hard to put a price on. Anyone who has bought a home or owned property knows it can be an emotional decision, too. One's life experience and memories are closely tied to it. And in the bigger sense, of course, property ownership is also about power.

As a woman who is part Native Hawaiian, I also understand that there was more to land than the monetary value of the land. In Hawaiian, 'āina doesn't mean acreage or square footage or even dirt. This isolated chain of islands whose people once sustained themselves on what they harvested from the land and the sea now imports more than three-quarters of its food by airplane or ship. The ahupua'a allotment was documented in the Mahele award, but for all intents and purposes, the ahupua'a system ceased to exist with that document, too. Today in Hawai'i, the price of land is so high that few farms can afford to grow crops for the local people. Not only were most Native Hawaiians displaced by the Mahele, but it forever changed Hawai'i's landscape—the 'āina and the people—to become what it is today.

To me, the land transactions of my family told a bigger story about Native Hawaiians that was not too different from other Native American groups whose land had been lost with the arrival of white men, who showed up unannounced, introduced landowner-ship and foreign rules, and then took homes and natural resources out from under the natives. I had read about those stories in history books in school about native tribes, but not about Hawai'i. Why didn't people know what happened to Hawai'i's native people, its old ahupua'a system of land tenure, and how its people lost their land once that got flipped upside down? Once again, I found my-self gobsmacked by discovering the truth about my family's land and how it connected to a larger story about the Native Hawaiian people. Why didn't our story exist? Why wasn't it part of our larger, collective history? Where was the outrage?

As for our family and the rest of the land transfer, it remained for a long time with my great-great-great-grandfather Kikaha, who by all accounts lived on the land near the Pi'ilanihale heiau located between the unpaved Ulaino Road and the ocean his entire life. He is buried there near the location of where our family hale once stood. Upon his death, he bequeathed the land to his eight mo'opuna (moh-oh-pu-nah) or grandchildren. One of those grand-children was Mileka, my great-grandmother.

In a document dated May 15, 1920, D. U. Kikaha wrote a "bill of sale" that recorded a sale of his property in the ahupua'a of Honomā'ele for one dollar to his "mo'opuna": Keou (Ella); Mileka (Martha); Iokepa (Joseph); Kaupena (Julia); Hanale (Henry); Ane (Annie); Keoni (John); and Ulunahele (David). Translated to English, the document states that upon his death, the land, "my interest is 130 acres, more or less," will go to his grandchildren "and their heirs, Forever, and they cannot Sell, Mortgage or do anything which will involve this land under the law, but it is agreed they may sell to their heirs." (Capital letters original to document.)

That last line was a generational promise written down from my great-great-great-grandfather, that still lives today. No matter what, we would commit to hold on to this land and keep it in the family. As Kikaha's eight grandchildren, who included my great-grandma Mileka, grew older, they kept that promise. Several of those grandchildren sold land to one another or within the family, especially those who did not have heirs. Of the land that exists today, all is now owned by just two of the original eight mo'opuna—my great-grandma Mileka and her brother, my late great-uncle Henry. Great-grandma Mileka then left her land to her six children, including Uncle Take, my grandma Martha, Uncles Juinchi and Jusuke, and Aunties Dolly and Ane. Uncle Henry left his land to his seven children, and one of his sons lives on the land today.

Collectively, our 'ohana still has about ninety acres of land from the 1848 Mahele. And while a few family members have built homes on their property, the land today remains pretty much as it was when Kahanu lived here—a wild, vibrant green full of tropical trees, flowers, and bushes from the lower slopes of the volcano down to the wild, rocky coast.

As I sat there, hours later, at the same spot at Uncle Take's kitchen table, I was overcome with a mixture of emotions that I never expected to feel from holding a bunch of folders and papers in my hands. The documents confirmed my family's nearly two-centuries-old connection to the kingdom of Hawai'i. But the more I learned about the Mahele, the more I realized that my family was both typical and atypical in our experience.

The same documents that provided proof of my own family's land grant from the king had actually resulted in the rapid land loss for the vast majority of Native Hawaiians. Private ownership not only ushered in the rapid expansion of the sugarcane business, it upended Hawaiian societal structure, and the power structure shifted rapidly to the landholders, who very quickly became the haole ruling class.

The journalist in me was thrilled to find that my family had kept records like these that dated back more than a century and a half. Finding answers to a very big question that explained what happened to those 990 acres had not been easy. But I never knew that discovery could come with a gut punch. That land eroded, generation by generation, bit by bit, uncle by uncle by auntie by cousin, to the demands of capitalism and, likely, the confusion of navigating an entirely new system with rules and costs and deals along the way. The drama of this story that I could see in the paper trail, record after record—lease after deed and story—is the slow burn of how it played out, generation by generation. And it's still playing out today.

On the other hand, my family seemed to be able to keep some of their land simply by virtue of being good record keepers. They must have understood the basics of the legal system so that they knew there needed to be written wills, lease agreements, bills of sale. And they were proactive enough to keep all their documents. The fact that we still had land was not only rare but, considering we had no royal blood (as far as I knew), it seemed actually a miracle.

The intentions of my kūpuna was more than a story, more than a promise from one generation to the next. It seemed to be speaking to me. It seemed to be calling to me—saying, "Here! Hello!"—it's all here. It wasn't in the box, but as I sat there surrounded by all those documents, I realized that the long line of my family's kuleana for this land—from Kahanu all the way to me—was part of the discovery, too.

———

"Did you hear about Uncle Larry?"

I don't remember who sent it to me, texted it to me, or emailed it to me. But as we were trying to figure out an answer to our tax problems on the Hāna land in 2023, Uncle Larry died, and his house on our family ancestral land, along with his Hāna property, was for sale.

We saw it on Zillow: asking price, $1 million. My cousins, especially those who live on Maui, freaked out.

I don't remember meeting Uncle Larry, Grandma's nephew, but he had built a small home on his plot of land down the road from Grandma, which he inherited from his father's part of the Kahanu lands. During Uncle Larry's final years living alone, my cousin Gabe would take care of his lawn and run errands for him. When Uncle Larry died suddenly, he didn't have any children or a will, even though he told Gabe that he'd like to leave his land to him. Uncle Larry didn't have any kids, so his land went to his next of kin, who the family learned were maybe his nieces who lived in Las Vegas. No one knew for sure. Soon after his death, word from the coconut wireless was that some of these cousins flew out to Hāna to see the land, and soon enough, the property was listed for sale. My Maui cousins frantically tried to reach these distant relatives whom no one had met—nor were we sure they were even blood-related—to try to talk some sense into them, to try to convince them to reconsider.

From my cousin Mark, I got the phone number of one of these distant cousins named Deanna. I texted her, figuring I'd give it a shot, too.

"Aloha, Deanna. My name is Sara, and I'm a member of the Matsuda/Kahanu family. I see that Uncle Larry's land is for sale, and I'm interested in talking to you about it. Do you have time today?"

Deanna said she didn't have time to talk today and texted me a screenshot of the property listing on Zillow. She referred me to her real estate agent.

I told her I wasn't interested in speaking to her real estate agent. I wanted to talk some sense into her. "Before you sell, there are some things you should know," I wrote.

I wondered if I should try to fly out to Vegas and confront Deanna in person. I wondered if she knew that the Kahanu family lands were originally granted by King Kamehameha III. Or if she knew about the family agreement that our kupuna had to offer the lands to sell to family before selling to anyone else.

She texted back. "I understand there's a lot . . . there's a whole history," she wrote. "In all honesty, we (the cousins) appreciate the history, but we are doing what we can now to live our lives."

That was it. They were just Americans trying to "live our lives." They were just heirs who had gotten a sudden windfall to sell land that they thought they could get $1 million for. To them, it was a lucky day in Vegas. That whole history was just another story. The better story, I imagined that they texted with each other about, was, holy shit, some long-lost uncle of theirs had just died and left them land in Maui!

The whole thing made me so angry and sad. News of Uncle Larry's land for sale quickly lit up the text chains and email threads

The Mahele land grant from King Kamehameha III was half of the ahu-pua'a of Honoma'ele, Maui—990 acres "from the mountain to the sea" that included the Pi'ilanihale heiau, a structure originally built around 1200 AD. *(Mike Opgenorth, Kahanu Garden)*

King Kamehameha III's handwritten Mahele award no. 42 to Kahanu, dated February 2, 1848. It grants "1/2 Honoma'ele," lands near Hāna, Maui. *(Hawai'i State Archive)*

Five of the eight Kahanu moʻopuna, or grandchildren, who received land from their grandfather in 1920, and spouses. *From left:* Julia Kumaewa, John Louis Kahanu Mileka Kahanu Matsuda (my great-grandmother), Joe Kahanu, Jennie Louis (wife of John), and Lei and Henry Kahanu. Of the eight grandchildren, two still own Kahanu land: descendants of Mileka and Henry. Date unknown. *(Sara Kehaulani Goo)*

Great-grandma Mileka Kekauililani Kahanu Matsuda in Hawaiʻi, 1962. Born in Hāna, Maui, her first language was Hawaiian and she later moved to Honolulu. *(Sara Kehaulani Goo)*

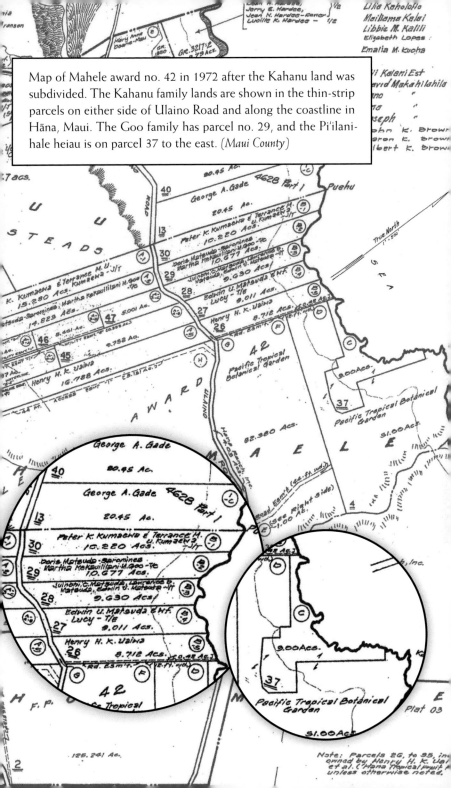

Map of Mahele award no. 42 in 1972 after the Kahanu land was subdivided. The Kahanu family lands are shown in the thin-strip parcels on either side of Ulaino Road and along the coastline in Hāna, Maui. The Goo family has parcel no. 29, and the Pi'ilanihale heiau is on parcel 37 to the east. (*Maui County*)

The Kahanu family land today is largely wild growth and undeveloped, except for a few family members' homes, and runs from the Hāna Highway to the shore in Hāna, Maui. (*Sara Kehaulani Goo*)

My grandma Martha Kekauililani Goo at a beach in Honolulu when she was dating my grandpa, 1940s. (*Sara Kehaulani Goo*)

My grandparents Richard and Martha Goo moved to Southern California after World War II, when Grandpa was hired to work at Norton Air Force Base in San Bernardino. They would raise eight children there. Date unknown. (*Sara Kehaulani Goo*)

My family's land along the shore in Hāna, Maui. *(Sara Kehaulani Goo)*

Me and Uncle Take Matsuda at the Piʻilanihale heiau, 2010. He was well known in Hāna and would frequently give tours of the heiau and Kahanu Garden. *(Ron Dahlquist)*

Dad, *third from left in back row,* is one of eight Goo children. In sorting out the Maui land, they agreed on a plan to try and return it to its original "agriculture" tax status. When it came to matters of the land, Dad called them "Gen 1." *Left to right:* Darrell Goo, Kathy Goo, Duane Goo, Doreen Goo, Dennis Goo, Maureen Gaasch, and Ross Goo. *Not pictured:* Richard "Rick" Goo. *(Sara Kehaulani Goo)*

Me and several of my Gen 2 cousins in Carpinteria, California, 2016. We gathered at Auntie Maureen's house shortly after Grandpa Goo died. *From left:* Shannon Goo, Vincent Goo, me, Jonathan Gaasch, Haley Pfeifer, Stevie Goo, Samantha Gaasch, and Jordan Goo. *(Sara Kehaulani Goo)*

The Goo family reunion in Virginia, 2023. *(Sara Kehaulani Goo)*

Michael and me with our kids, *from left*, Isabella Silas, and Chloe, on a visit to Kahanu Garden near the base of the Pi'ilanihale heiau in 2016. *(Sara Kehaulani Goo)*

of our family, this time from Maui and O'ahu to California to the
East Coast. I thought about that bill of sale and the land records for
our family's land. About how my great-great-great-grandfather had
bequeathed his land for one dollar to his eight mo'opuna, including
our great-grandmother, under the condition that they only sell to
one another and keep the land in the family. So much for family
promises. So much for family connections. So much for history.
Land is money.

Moreover, all this brought up another painful chapter in our
family's more recent land history. There had been other members
of our family who sold their land—for example, Uncle Joe sold
his land to Uncle Take decades ago. But no one had sold land to
haoles since the early 1990s, when my uncle Terry sold his parcel—
which is located along the shore just next to Grandma's—for more
than $400,000. Uncle Terry, who lives in Honolulu, is an only
child, an adopted son of Auntie Julia, my great-grandma's sister.
After his mother died, he told me that his father asked him if he saw
himself ever moving to Hāna on the family land.

"Dad was getting on in life. He was in his eighties, I think, and
he asked me, he said, 'Boy, you plan on moving to Hāna?'

"And I said, 'No, Dad. You know, I'm a city boy. I was born and
raised in the city. My family is here.' So I asked, 'Why? Why do
you ask?'

"And he said, 'Well, you know Daddy doesn't drive. Daddy is
getting older. If I move to Hāna, who is going to take care of me if I
need to go to the doctor? How am I going to get to the doctor? If I
need to go by kau kau, how am I going to do all that?'

"So I says, 'Well, why are you bringing this all about?'

"He said, 'Well, why don't you look into selling mama's land in

Hāna?' And I looked at him. and he said, 'Please.' He said, 'If we can find someone to buy the land, sell the land, we'll build a new house here,' he said, 'for my grandchildren.' So I said okay. I said, 'You sure that's what you want?' He said yes.

"The money we got from selling the land we used to build this home," Uncle Terry told me, sitting in his house with a breathtaking view of the Honolulu coastline. Uncle Terry's dad, Uncle Peter, died before the house was built, but he did get to see the foundation laid, and Uncle Terry recalls seeing him smile in satisfaction.

But the land sale created a lot of family pain. Other family members were upset that Uncle Terry sold the land and that they did not have a chance to buy it from him first. Uncle Terry was upset that family members got angry with him about the sale and accused him of manipulating his father about the decision and, even worse, saying he was somehow unworthy of the decision or illegitimate because, as an adopted son, he did not carry on the Kahanu bloodline.

"And Daddy was hurt, too, big-time, because a few of them called here and they swore at him over the phone, accusing him of doing something that their auntie—my mom—would not do. And you know, it hurt him because he and my mom opened up their home to them, some of their nieces and you know. But I went about it the legal way, the way they wanted, the pono way."

Decades after Uncle Terry's land sale, when he told me his story, the wounds still felt fresh. So when Uncle Larry's land went up for sale, it reopened that wound. It was a marker of another generation where yet more land was about to be lost at the same time that rising taxes threatened several other Kahanu lands. Modern-day realities were colliding further with Kahanu kuleana promises. More Native Hawaiian land gone from Native Hawaiian hands. Another decade, another parcel erased from the map. Economic reality was winning.

We hadn't had a family member sell land since Uncle Terry, thirty years earlier. Now Uncle Larry's land was about to be gone. Through the coconut wireless, I learned that I wasn't the only family member who had tried to reach out to this distant cousin Deanna and their Las Vegas family. Dad questioned whether legally they could claim the land. Uncle Larry hadn't kept up with the taxes he owed on his land, so these new heirs had to pay out several thousand dollars of back taxes before they could take title. They were in a hurry now to sell the property to get their money back, and then some. One of my cousins on Maui said she cried on the phone talking to the Vegas relatives, trying to get them to understand and to at least consider selling to another family member. Uncle Larry's property is right next to Uncle Take's family's property, where some of my cousins would very much like to live in Hāna or stay in Hāna, but building a house is too expensive. One of my cousins who grew up in Hāna has a successful food truck business but was struggling to find a way to afford to live in town. If they could start with Uncle Larry's house (which needed a lot of work), it would not only preserve the family compact but enable more of our family to live in Hāna.

Instead, they were—like me—directed to make an offer through the real estate agent. These Vegas relatives, whoever they were, had the distance of an ocean between themselves and Maui. But they had an even bigger distance between themselves and the culture, the land, the stewardship. They were living in a different world, an American world, a real estate transaction world. It was all logical and practical to them. A deal's a deal.

Hewa.

8

CLUES IN THE ROCKS

On my 2011 trip to Hāna, I was eager to return to the heiau. I had two goals: to better understand its purpose during ancient times and to know more details about how our family was linked to it. Through my own research, I'd found academic papers about heiau in the years since my visit with Grandma, digging around from time to time to, as journalists say, follow an anthropological paper trail as I was trying to also understand our family's land paper trail. For example, there were a few documents from the US National Park Service—the original files from the 1970s, when this heiau in Hāna was designated a National Historic Landmark. I also found an old anthropological survey conducted on the site from 1960 in Grandma's old files that Dad had kept. And when I searched online, I was surprised to find a few papers by anthropologists published more recently, in the 1990s. One of them was titled "Monumental

Grandeur and Political Florescence in Pre-Contact Hawai'i." No wonder this stuff was hard to find. Even though these papers were not written with the average culturally curious reader in mind, they provided some scientific answers to who built the heiau, what it was likely used for, and how long ago.

But more importantly, I was eager to see how this centuries-old structure had changed since I last saw it when we hiked through the jungle for the first time to see it with Uncle Take. Perhaps just by being there, walking the grounds, and hearing family stories, I would get more clues about its purpose. Maybe if I just closed my eyes and stood in its presence, I would get some kind of intuition about it, or some insight from its mana, or power within. It was a temple, after all.

I drove down Ulaino Road, which leads to both the heiau and our family's land. The paved road gives way to a dirt road, which is prone to flooding that creates deep holes and impassable mud at times. But today, by swerving my tires around the earthen potholes, I managed to find my way. The sign for Kahanu Garden was announced on a rock wall at the entrance, and it filled me with pride to see our family name at this spectacular place. A paved road lined by coconut trees led the way toward a small booth with a friendly lady ready to greet me and provide a brochure. *Wow*, I thought, *this place has really cleaned up nice*. No more hiking our way through the mosquito jungle. Now, the heiau grounds were a cultural tourist site, a community gathering place, and botanical garden. Where the jungle once thrived and sprawled, there was now an enormous expanse of golf course–like grass—acres and acres of it lined with breadfruit trees—that led to the foot of the heiau.

As I drove along the path inside the grounds, the "monumental grandeur" became apparent and breathtaking. The Pi'ilanihale heiau was now a scrubbed-up, taller, and prouder version of itself than when I saw it for the first time as a child. Its distinctive black shoulders stood up straight, and the tangled mess of trees and brush had been cleared away so you could see its full height, about four stories tall and emerging from the jungle green like a dark cruise ship rising from the earth. It had six clear terraces formed by rocks that locked into straight lines instead of the crumbling edges I saw years ago. In the bright sun, the temple peered down on people below, who looked like ants standing next to it. What hadn't changed was the bright green luminescence that remained in that Kodachrome color I remembered as a child: the papaya trees and the hala trees and the thick jungle all around glowed bright green against the heiau's black lava stones. A flat, neatly manicured grassy expanse now made a wide pathway leading to the bottom of the structure. Once in full view—*ahhh*—I can't really even describe what it's like to stand before the heiau, other than a hush.

The enormity and quiet of it felt like being in the presence of something sacred. My brain tried to process what I was looking at. Rows and rows of rocks stacked higher and higher into bigger rows and terraces filled the lenses of my eyes but didn't quite compute. It was like a Hawaiian version of the Mayan ruins or Egyptian pyramids—an ancient architectural feat that just makes you marvel at the ambition and determination of the people centuries before who commissioned and built it. I just couldn't believe that the mysterious structure I saw as a child was actually more spectacular now that it had been restored to its full glory.

Heiau is often translated as "temple," but heiau are not the kind of structures or buildings that you enter inside to pray. Hawaiian heiau take on many different shapes, designs, and sizes. And for the most part, they are solid stacks of lava rocks fitted together in such a way that they hold their shape without mortar, and they serve many different purposes. In most cases, certain kāhuna guided construction of the heiau. The kāhuna were revered people who served a role somewhere between a spiritual leader or priest and a skilled tradesman. Kāhuna were trained, often in the same family, to take up certain roles: there were medical healer kāhuna, kāhuna who oversaw chanting and religious rituals, and they all served the king, or moʻi (moh-ee). The architects of heiau, who decided where to build one and how it would be designed, were called *kāhuna kuhikui puʻuone*—which translates to "show" and "sand," because the kāhuna would first show how the construction plan would work in the sand.[1] And then there were many types of heiau. Kāhuna directed some heiau to be built to pray to before a fishing expedition, others to be used before battle, and yes, enormous ones came to symbolize power. Heiau in Hawaiʻi are similar to other large structures in other parts of Polynesia that symbolize both the power of gods and man—anthropologists have documented similar structures across Polynesia, called *marae*.

Anthropologists who studied heiau across Hawaiʻi found that the largest ones were constructed with rocks passed from person to person in a human chain, from far distances, such as the top of the mountain or volcano to the location designated by the kāhuna. The largest heiau, like Piʻilanihale, were thought to be symbols of the king's power, which is similar to man's desire to build "monumental architecture," or large edifices over time to symbolize power. The tallest skyscrapers in the world, for example, are also symbols of a country's aspirations or ability to reach to the highest, most impressive heights. Other enormous historic edifices, such as the Egyptian pyramids or Mayan temples, were also evidence of a sophisticated society and the prowess of their people. This monument located on our family's ancestral land was named for Pi'ilani, a famous chief of the island of Maui, who ruled in the 1600s and was known for uniting the island's east and west factions.

"Alo-ha, Sara," a young, handsome Native Hawaiian man with a shaved head named Kamaui Aiona greeted me when I got out of the car. A few weeks earlier, Kamaui and I had spoken over the phone, and it was nice to match a name with a voice. Hāna's morning rain had already passed through the area by the time we met up at mid-morning; the sun was beginning to burn, and the air began to feel heavy and humid. His forest-green polo shirt with the KAHANU GARDEN silk screen across the front was already wet with perspiration from his morning's chores at the garden.

"You want to go take a tour?" he asked with an inflection that blended pidgin and proper English. I could tell that he was the kind of local who could flip easily and fluently between the American English form and the local way of talking, depending on the situation.

Kamaui is a botanist by training. He grew up on the Big Island of Hawai'i and learned to speak Hawaiian fluently, thanks to a number of relatively new programs designed to revive the endangered language. Near the foot of the heiau, Kamaui had developed a "canoe garden" on the grounds to grow native plants that the original settlers of Hawai'i brought over in their canoes—as a way to educate visitors about how early Hawaiians subsisted on the land using the natural environment. He showed me the purplish stalks of dry taro, sweet potatoes, and kō, or sugarcane, which once dominated this land. He also showed me 'awa, an herb used to make a medicinal-tasting drink that the Hawaiians liked to imbibe for its mellowing effect, as well as 'awapuhi (ah-vah-poo-ee), a red flowering plant with a sticky sap that Hawaiian women used to make their long hair shiny. (It became more-well known to Americans in Paul Mitchell's shampoo.) Each crop had its own section which, Kamaui informed me with pride, had been planted by Hāna schoolchildren.

"Sara, have you seen the piko (pee-koh) stone?" Kamaui asked. He pointed to a large cylinder-shaped stone jutting out of the temple by a foot or two, which I'd never noticed. Unlike the other lava stones, the piko stone is smooth and rounded, as if it were sanded down. The odd, phallic shape of it looked so out of place that it made me giggle. "Wow, what is that? I can't believe I've never seen that before."

"*Piko* means 'belly button' in Hawaiian," Kamaui explained, smiling, too. "I guess you can see why they call it a *piko* stone."

Funny that this mysterious temple had so many odd features to figure out.

"Some people think that this is the stone that holds it all together and that it goes all the way back through the structure," Kamaui said. "That if you pull on it, the whole thing comes down."

I tried to picture the large stone reaching the size of a football field behind the belly button rock before me, and I raised my eyebrows at Kamaui.

"Nah," Kamaui said. "I don't believe it, either. But it must have some meaning. I just don't know what it is."

Many people ask whether there's an opening or a secret entrance to the heiau somewhere, perhaps on the back side that is hidden to the public. But this idea always seemed improbable to me because of its massive size and weight. I asked Kamaui if he had ever heard of anything like that or seen an entrance of any kind. He shook his head.

"There is an area on the back side where it looks like someone, at some point more recently, tried to remove a lot of rocks," Kamaui said, but it was not an entrance.

The heiau simply doesn't look like the kind of structure that would physically be able to contain an entrance or a hollowed-out space, purely by the looks of how the structure manages its weight. But if it were a temple, would it contain sacraments of some kind? Perhaps from Pi'ilani, Maui's famous chief from centuries ago, the namesake of the temple? That seemed possible.

The day before, I had found an old family letter in Uncle Take's box that left me wondering about that. It was handwritten in English by Auntie Julia, my great-grandmother Mileka's sister. Auntie Julia had written to Uncle Take all that she knew about the family's ties to the heiau.

"Whenever you come to this heiau or any heiau, don't disturb any rocks because most of the bodies are in the wall, many Hawaiians buried their dead in a sit position wrapped in a moena [mat] and rocks were piled around it until the whole body was covered with rock without it crushing him," she wrote. "It was neatly piled, somewhat like an igloo."

The letter did not provide detail on whether or not the Pi'ilanihale heiau had a person or persons buried inside it. But that concept of burial or bones as sacraments left behind in a heiau had been recorded in other locations in Hawai'i. And it might explain why, even as a child, Uncle Take and others had warned me to not take any of the stones. They believed it was bad luck, one of Hawaiians' many superstitions. Some of my cousins told me stories that Uncle Take regularly received mail from heiau visitors that contained stones or dirt that they had taken from the heiau. These people wrote that it had brought them bad luck and they wanted to return it. Many others left offerings of money, flower or ti leaf lei, coins, or prayers on a large rock at the base of the heiau. Uncle Take would say, "You feel the mana" of the place. So perhaps it was more than a superstition—perhaps it was also a cemetery of sorts?

Even in the official US National Park Service records, the Pi'ilanihale heiau's purpose is inconclusive. At first, when it was designated a US National Landmark in 1964, the Park Service seemed quite sure of its significance. "It was believed to be the largest prehistoric temple in Hawai'i and the largest intact example of a luakini or state level temple where human sacrifices were performed."[2]

The Park Service's report went on to cite other research that indicated several firepits were found on heiau on other Hawaiian islands, that were similar in size, some of which were used to fatally punish lawbreakers under the Native Hawaiians' kapu laws. It said academic research suggests that "these victims were interred within the temple platform" and "because the bones of dead chiefs and ali'i were believed to have special power (mana), desecration of graves to obtain bone for fishhooks and other implements was not uncommon. On occasion, burials were also disinterred after the flesh had fully decomposed and the bones (especially the skull and long bones) collected and placed in woven burial caskets for transport and burial in safer locations elsewhere."

But two decades later, in 1987, after conferring with Dr. Yoshi Sinoto, head of anthropology at the Bishop Museum in Honolulu, the Park Service seemed not as certain about its purpose. It suggested its purpose perhaps was much more benign.

"An alternative hypothesis was recently proposed by Sinoto who believes this structure may be the residential compound of a high chief, perhaps that of King Pi'ilani, a west Maui paramount chief who united the island of Maui," the Park Service document reads.

It continues: "Was it a heiau, a chiefly residential complex, or both? . . . Assuming that the structure is a heiau, however, even a residential compound that was later redesignated and dedicated as a luakini [human sacrifice] heiau, it is probable that various human burials representing various time periods are contained within the structure."

Still, the imagery of human sacrifices at luakini (loo-ah-kee-nee) heiau haunted me: the blackened human flesh and strangulations, the brutal fate that could have befallen any commoner for the slightest infraction of the kapu rules. I always imagined the beating drums, ceremonial chants around the fire, and the tattooed faces—or maybe that was just the images I had from reading the novel *Hawaii* by James Michener years ago. I had difficulty reckoning that brutal purpose of this place with my own feelings about the heiau linked to our family because, in the presence of Pi'ilanihale heiau, I always felt awestruck and humbled. Its towering height and impressive construction speak to a kind of grandiosity to visitors that makes one want to whisper and step lightly. Its aura—I don't know how else to express it—is present, omniscient, and quiet. It is not one of evil or wickedness or death. I remembered how, on the first visit as a child to see the heiau, Uncle Take was the first to mention and then cast doubt on that "human sacrifices" idea. Both the brutality of the human sacrifices concept and the native cliché it presented didn't sit well with me. Maybe even part of me didn't want it to be true.

I had learned from reading texts of Native Hawaiian historians like Samuel Kamakau that most heiau were destroyed after King Liholiho ended the kapu in 1819—a system of rules and order guided by religious beliefs by which Hawaiian society had been organized for decades, if not centuries. Under the system, it was kapu, or forbidden, for example, for men and women to eat meals together; women were not allowed to eat certain foods; it dictated when certain fish could be taken from the sea or when crops could be harvested; it also dictated behavior around aliʻi, or elite members of society. When King Liholiho ended the kapu system—with the simple act of eating at a table of men and women—all of Hawaiians' rules and religious practices also were declared over. Heiau, as central to the system, were ordered destroyed.

A century later, haole historians and anthropologists became curious about heiau and discovered remnants of these structures dotted around the islands, in various sizes and conditions of disrepair. Scanning through the microfiche at the University of Hawaiʻi's Manoa campus on a research trip, I found an old newspaper article describing an effort to find a rumored enormous temple said to be hidden in east Maui, near Hāna. The front-page article of the August 14, 1919, *Honolulu Star* reported, "Thomas G. Thrum, a well known antiquary of Honolulu," returned after a two-week visit to east Maui to try to document heiau that he had not seen before.[3] "Mr. Thrum relates meeting a very old Hawaiian who evidently knew [a] considerable [amount] considering the location of some of the antiquarian structures for which Mr. Thrum was searching," it said. But the Hawaiian man would not give up the location. The man "insisted that the subject was absolutely tabu that he was sworn to secrecy by his father." It made me chuckle because I remembered Uncle Take's story about being told *kuli kuli* and wondered if I was related to this "old Hawaiian."

Indeed, later, anthropologists who studied the Piʻilanihale heiau said the locals' effort to not talk about the heiau, especially to outsiders, likely resulted in it being the most well-preserved monument of its kind. Despite that, it was still in disrepair and needed to be restored with care and by people informed with cultural knowledge of how to do so.

In 1999, the crumbling walls of the heiau were carefully restored by the National Tropical Botanical Garden, after legal prodding from Uncle Take and other members of our family, who wanted to ensure that the folks who ran the Kahanu Garden fulfilled their promise to maintain the historical site. Before it was restored, the stones had begun to fall apart along the face of the temple. Rock by rock, a small team of Native Hawaiian stonemasons had carefully put each stone that had fallen back in its place as best they could. The process took an entire year and was overseen by Dr. Sinoto. Grandma and Uncle Take had always fondly talked about Dr. Sinoto because he worked closely with the Garden and the family and later became personally helpful to our family, accompanying them on a trip to Okinawa and serving as a translator and guide. Later, I'd meet Dr. Sinoto in person when he invited me to his office inside the museum, where he proudly displayed artifacts, bones, carved stones, and trinkets from his anthropological journeys across the Pacific.

I had learned that another anthropologist was allowed to conduct a small excavation of the site to determine how it was built and when, as well as look for clues to what the structure was used for. The excavation yielded clear evidence of numerous firepits on the top of the structure, with fish and pig bones. The site's oldest carbon dating put its birth at around AD 1200, but some parts dated to centuries later, creating the theory that it wasn't built all at once and sections had been added onto it over time. No human bones were found on the site, raising even more doubts that the site was used for human sacrifices. But the excavation was also limited to a small portion of the heiau.

When we talked by phone before my arrival, Kamaui shared with me that during the restoration a decade earlier, anthropologists and workers had found a lot of other artifacts as they went about their work. These artifacts provided clues about the purpose of the place, but no one had bothered to follow up or write them up and provide some interpretation about them, he said.

"So where are the artifacts, then?" I had asked Kamaui.

"They're still here," he said.

My jaw hit the floor. "You're kidding!" I said, picturing these centuries-old artifacts tucked away somewhere.

After we toured the heiau, I was hoping Kamaui would offer to let me see the artifacts.

"Come," Kamaui said, beckoning me to a dusty shed near the garden's entrance, not far from a chicken pen. He unlocked the wooden shed, where there were two large, deep shelves. He bent over the bottom shelf and pulled out several heavy cardboard boxes, some of which had the tops cut off, similar to the kind you see at the Costco checkout line. One of the boxes, I noticed, was a StarKist tuna can box. Inside, it was filled with items wrapped carefully in old newspapers. He pulled out something heavy and gingerly began to remove the paper. Inside were stones that had been smoothed and shaped into fine tools that could be used for cutting wood, for example, for a canoe or a hook for fishing. He unwrapped the newspaper comics page to reveal a round stone with a straight line cut along the middle of it, like a groove. It was used to hold the fishing line, which was wrapped around the center along the line, Kamaui explained. Inside another newspaper was a stone the size of my palm with a perfectly circular hole in the middle—a fishing weight, he said. Inside another newspaper, a figure with a top knob that rounded like a handle and had a wider, cylinder-like bottom that was almost soft from years of grinding—a large mortar. It was like Christmas as he pulled them out one by one. And I realized after a while that there were so many—several boxes, each filled with similar kinds of stone tools.

"Do you want to hold it?" Kamaui said, gesturing toward another smooth stone. At first, I hesitated, thinking maybe it was inappropriate—like taking an artifact out of its glass case. But as I looked down at it, it became too tempting to not see for myself. This might be my only chance, ever.

I smiled and crouched to get a closer look.

As soon as I picked it up, the rounded rock fit perfectly into the palm of my hand. No doubt it was used as some kind of scraping tool, perhaps to prepare food? Its surface was as smooth as skin, but porous and lightweight. I squeezed it in my hand and closed my eyes and thought about how lucky I was to feel something so old, so ordinary, yet so clearly linked to centuries past. I could feel how important this small tool must have been to daily life so long ago. *Was it a Hawaiian woman who once held this in her hand every day? And how many decades, generations, even centuries, have come between my hand and hers?*

"These should be on display!" I exclaimed to Kamaui. I looked at him with wide, serious eyes, and his gaze kind of grinned back at me in agreement. But he also slowly nodded at me, as if to sigh. And he was quiet. I noticed that small numbers had been painted onto the artifact—a sign that it had been cataloged. It's a shame, we both agreed, that they were hidden here in the newspaper, inside the Costco tuna fish box, for no one to see.

We spent a few hours together, and I thought perhaps we were one of only a handful of people in the world who knew about these treasures and could appreciate them together. There were more poi pounders, some softball-size and others soccer ball–size. He also showed me heavier, almost perfectly rounded stones that looked very similar to hockey pucks. These were stones from an ancient game that Hawaiian children played called *ulu maika* (ooh-loo my-kah). Similar to horseshoes, the Hawaiians would plant two sticks in the ground and then see if they could roll the stone in between the sticks, he explained. There were also several adzes, or slim, rectangular stones with blunt edges, used as tools to cut and sharpen objects. With all these objects, it became harder for me to imagine the heiau was a place of worship.

All these artifacts seemed to point to evidence of ordinary life with children playing, women and men working and doing daily household chores. Perhaps this was more of a residential community with the heiau as its center? These artifacts pointed to everyday life of families and a community, not tools of war or those terrible images of human sacrifices. For a thrilling moment, I felt as if I were the anthropologist, hot on the trail of evidence to unlock a centuries-old mystery.

The thrill, though, was followed by a settling sense of sadness. The evidence seemed to be here, in my hands, but there was no one to document it, to explain it, to write it down. I thought about how just the other day, I was on the paper trail for my ancestors' family land story, and now I was trying to interpret centuries-old artifacts without much expertise. There was no clear story here, no professional to help me and the rest of the world see and understand these artifacts. Seeing them here, unprotected in the box, wrapped in yesterday's newsprint, vulnerable and forgotten, felt wrong. I thought of the millions of precious artifacts sitting behind glass cases at the Smithsonian, back in Washington, DC, where I lived. I thought of the acres and acres of space in my city devoted to our nation's history, and yet barely any of it mentioned Hawai'i or this part of the globe. Instead, millions come to the National Mall to see Dorothy's slippers from *The Wizard of Oz* and fancy dresses worn by the First Ladies. Millions and millions of visitors come to Hawai'i every year, and yet how many understand the rich, centuries-old history of its native people? I could not help but be ashamed that these relics of history before me had been left behind, covered in dust for so long because no one bothered.

I couldn't help but wonder: *Does the world not care?*

No, I feared, it did not.

———

Sometime in 2021, a new email arrived from Dad. We were still waiting to hear back from the county about whether they would lower our taxes after we converted part of our land for agricultural use. Dad said that they'd assess the property at some point over the next year. Even if they changed our tax bracket back to ag, it would only apply going forward for future years, not the current year. We were in a bit of a holding pattern, and the taxes were eating into our reserves—about $15,000 left. If we had to keep paying $2,000 a year, we had seven or so years left, in theory.

But now a new issue arose: What about the heiau?

In talking with his cousins who all still owned land next to ours in Hāna, Dad realized that there was a lot of business that Grandma and her siblings never resolved about the heiau. For most of my life, I tried to avoid this dispute because it was hard to follow and seemed to stir up a lot of negative energy.

But the story goes like this: The various branches of the Kahanu family never came to an agreement with the new owner of the heiau grounds, the National Tropical Botanical Garden, before they died. In the 1960s, the heiau was "discovered" by tourists, and my great-grandmother and her siblings donated the heiau site in 1972 to the Garden, with certain conditions. One condition was that the family would continue to have access to the heiau grounds, the family burial sites, and the shore for fishing and traditional cultural practices, as well as to use the site for family gatherings. Another was that the Garden would restore the heiau, whose ancient stone walls were crumbling and falling into a further state of erosion from the encroaching jungle surrounding it. Moreover, artifacts found at the site were to be cataloged, interpreted, and protected. Bottom line: if the Garden didn't complete the heiau restoration as agreed to, the land could be reverted to our family.

Grandma, her siblings, and other branches of the Kahanu family formed an organization called Hoʻolina o Kahanu to represent the family's interests with the Garden. It gave them a formal means to maintain a relationship with the Garden and ensure that the heiau, and the family's agreement, would be honored. But nothing formal had ever been signed, despite more than twenty versions of an agreement going back and forth. Grandma, her siblings, and her cousins couldn't come to an agreement among themselves, and momentum stalled.

Since Grandma had died, other members of the group in Grandma's generation had also died, and the remaining elders were now in their eighties. Dad said it had been over a decade since the family organization had had a formal meeting. He realized that the organization's registration with the state of Hawaiʻi had expired because no one paid to renew it.

Should he renew it? Did I want to be part of it?

My first thought was, *Ugh*.

Dad was encouraged to settle this business by Chipper—a man

whose name I'd heard from family members over the course of my life and even met a few times on trips to Hawai'i. Chipper Wichman was the CEO of the National Tropical Botanical Garden, which oversees the Kahanu Garden and three others. He was about to retire after sixteen years, and he asked Dad if it was possible to try to get an agreement with the family as one final act. Perhaps, Chipper told Dad, the next generation would now be ready to take up this cause and come up with an agreement that works for them. In the email Dad forwarded to us, Dad said Chipper asked him and Auntie Maureen to help him reach out to the next generation of Kahanu family members and organize a big meeting.

"Oh boy," I said to Dad. "That won't be easy."

But Dad pointed out that he himself was retired now and he wanted to give it a shot for Grandma. "I think it's important for the next generation to become involved," he told me. "I'll go ahead and refile this family organization and get it started and reach out to my cousins and uncles and aunties. But we need your generation to help."

Groan. Okay. I had no idea what he wanted me to sign up for, but it sounded like a headache. But a part of it was also intriguing. I knew my cousin Brande, Uncle Take's granddaughter, was involved. So maybe I should be, too. Dad and my Auntie Maureen, who lives in California, were already working as a team to deal with Maui County about taxes. Dad wondered aloud if maybe the Garden staff, who had already had to deal with issues like building a visitors' center and adding water and electrical infrastructure, might be able to help our family if we wanted to eventually build something on our property, which was just down the road. Maybe restarting our family organization and getting to a permanent agreement about the family's rights to the land would be an opening for our family and the Garden to reset and resolve issues that were never resolved the generation before. Maybe.

If there was one thing I learned from poring over more than 175 years of our family history, it was that having written documents— contracts, wills, bills of sale, and leases—codifies agreements that must then be honored and upheld. Maybe I should meet with Chipper myself to get a better idea of what this is all about.

"Yeah," Dad said, "it's worth a shot."

On a trip to Maui in 2022, I asked Chipper if he'd meet me so that I could learn more about why he wanted to get this resolved once and for all. Of course, I'd met him before, on visits to the heiau with Grandma. For more than forty years, our family had a lot of back-and-forth with Chipper, and often it was hard not to have a conversation about the heiau or the Garden without hearing about Chipper. But I was a visitor then, eavesdropping on an adult conversation and not yet ready to understand the full scope of our family. Now, I wanted to know.

We met up at a local park on Maui and sat outside on the bleachers of the soccer field and talked while children kicked the ball around. Chipper is a tall, thin, haole-looking man with a gray mustache that runs into a goatee. In some ways, Chipper's family is similar to ours, in that his Native Hawaiian grandmother also was a large landowner on the island of Kaua'i—only his family had much more land. Their family also donated land to the organization that became the National Tropical Botanical Garden. Chipper, who talks in the local Hawaiian style, had been a Garden employee for many years, having started as an intern at the Kahanu Garden in the 1970s.

I immediately noticed from the way he talked that he was the kind of Hawaiian man who could code switch between the local, Native Hawaiian community and the wealthy mainland donor class that he'd had to court to keep the Garden in good financial shape. Looking at him, you would not think he was Hawaiian. But his accent was local, and he clearly had deep cultural knowledge. And he said he'd tried to infuse that sense of cultural and indigenous knowledge into the botanical and research approach of the Garden. It wasn't always this way, he said.

"The first time I saw Pi'ilanihale heiau was in 1976, when I first started at the Garden. I was an intern, and we came and lived there on the property for a month," Chipper said. "The heiau was still covered by vegetation. It was still a very incredibly impressive site, but very run-down because cattle from the ranch had been walking on it for probably a hundred years, and trees had grown up on the walls. It was a very impressive yet kind of a sad feeling because you look at what is an incredibly majestic site—it once was very powerful—and yet one that clearly was not cared for."

He explained how some powerful, influential haole families who had moved to Hāna in the 1960s discovered the heiau and felt that it should be designated as a World Heritage Site. They began the process to get the US National Park Service to designate the heiau as a National Historic Landmark, not realizing that the Kahanu family had an undivided interest in the land.

"When the [Kahanu] family got wind of that, all hell broke loose," Chipper said. "They were really upset that they had gone forward. They did not want the heiau cleared, and they did not want people going down there; they did not want the spotlight of the world brought onto this site. They wanted to keep it sleeping in the jungle.

"Part of it was they were very fearful that they, as [the Kahanu] family, would incur the negative consequences spiritually that could come from that if it were to happen. They felt responsible for it. The word they would use is *kuleana*. It was their kuleana or responsibility as the landowners to be the stewards of the site."

Chipper now was clear about the Garden's past misdeeds and how his life's work, as he saw it, was to overcome the sins of the past and be able to have a codified agreement with our family that would reset it on better footing.

He recalled how, during that time, Uncle Take stepped in and, working with his mother—great-grandma Mileka—agreed to donate the heiau to the Garden with the understanding that the Garden would restore the heiau and protect it for generations to come. The rest of the Kahanu land was then formally divided among surviving members of the family. "It was a very serious decision that had been made by your great-grandmother as to what to do. [She considered] we are the owners of the site, and yet we don't have the expertise or the money or the ability to deal with it in the right way. And so it's no longer an option to just say it's going to be covered with bushes. It was a decision they spent a lot of time thinking about. And in the end, they made a decision to give it to someone who would have that responsibility."

That leap of faith didn't last long. Just ten years after the Kahanu family donated the heiau site to the Garden, the leaders of the Garden tried to get our family to sign a document that confirmed they had completed the restoration, when in fact they hadn't. "That really stirred up a hornets' nest," Chipper told me, recalling those days. The family turned against the Garden, and suddenly, it was as if the mana of the heiau had come alive. The Garden was hit with a string of what one could call bad luck. Around that time, in 1982, the Garden was struck by a bad hurricane, which forced the

Garden to spend a lot of money to clean up and fix some massive areas; the financially strapped organization had to lay off almost all the Garden staff.

A few years later, the Garden's CEO unveiled a master plan to turn the heiau into a massive eco-resort, with high-end helicopter tours for high-paying visitors. Our family didn't like the plan, and neither did the heiau, it seemed. That CEO soon had a stroke that incapacitated him. The Garden replaced him with another CEO, who promised to fulfill the eco-resort idea of his predecessor. Then *that* man died of a sudden heart attack just months into the role. "Your Auntie Dolly had some strong conclusions about why both of those men died," Chipper told me with a rueful chuckle.

In short, the Garden learned the hard way not to mess with the mana of the heiau.

They also learned not to mess with the Kahanus. By then, our family had had enough. Grandma, Uncle Take, Auntie Dolly, and their three other siblings hired the Native Hawaiian Legal Corporation—the islands' nonprofit dedicated to fighting for indigenous legal rights on behalf of Native Hawaiians—to prepare a legal case against the Garden. As a teenager, I remember overhearing a lot of family discussions about this that were not intended for my ears about "getting the land back" from the Garden. I remember Grandma and Grandpa talking about the "reverter clause" and the Garden. Turns out, my great-grandmother and her siblings were quite clear about conditions by which they were donating family land to this new entity. The 1974 "indenture" between great-grandma Mileka, her sister Julia, and her brother Henry (the three were the only ones at the time who had not sold their Mahele land) at the Garden says clearly:

**Title to said Lots C and E shall revert to Family and their
respective heirs and assigns in the event that Grantee:**

Ceases to exist or ceases to carry out the functions mandated
in its Charter;

Ceases to use said land for the intended use; to wit: a
botanical garden for public view and/or for scientific study,
or;

Should attempt to dispose of any said lands for any reason.

Furthermore, the document states that the Garden must restore
the heiau "at its sole cost, all in accordance with good restoration
practices and accomplished as soon as practical. Said restoration
work must be performed by the Bishop Museum of Honolulu, Hawai'i, or under the supervision of an individual or organization of
similar professional stature within 10 (ten) years of the date hereof."

By 1984, ten years after that legal agreement, the heiau sat with
literally not a single rock moved. It was sitting quietly in the jungle,
with many of its rocks tumbling out of place. Our family's legal case
was strong, and the Garden knew it.

"That's when they asked me to be director of the Kahanu Garden," Chipper said. This time, I couldn't help but chuckle. To clean
up this mess, the Garden put the Hawaiian guy in charge.

When the Garden's leadership turned to him in the aftermath
of a disastrous first couple of decades, "I looked within our organization, and there was nobody who understood the cultural significance of what we had." Chipper said he agreed to take the job
under certain conditions, one of which was that "we will make good
on every promise we made to the donor family."

With Chipper at the helm, and our family's hiring of legal counsel, the Garden finally took action. Chipper hired a local anthropologist to conduct an ethnographic survey of the heiau and surrounding area, to research its historical significance and document any written or oral history. The Bishop Museum of Honolulu, which is the premier source of Native Hawaiian anthropology, once again got involved and began to catalog artifacts, such as stone-shaped poi pounders, fishhooks, adzes, and other man-made tools found on the site—the artifacts that I had held in my hands with Kamaui. Chipper hired Native Hawaiian stonemasons and led teams of locals and other experts in the painstaking work to restore the heiau's crumbling face, rock by rock. The culmination of this work was a celebration at the Kahanu Garden after the restoration in 1999, which many of our family members attended.

Grandma had a good relationship with Chipper, as did Uncle Take, most of the time. But the uncomfortable truth is that the rift between the family and the Garden also stirred up an internal sibling rivalry that never was resolved, primarily among Grandma, Uncle Take, and Auntie Dolly. I'm not privy to what went down among the three of them, but basically, they argued over small details about how the relationship between the family and the Garden should be codified and what rights the family would maintain to the land. Off and on, I also remember Grandma, Uncle Take, and Auntie Dolly fighting about water rights and easements that they tried to negotiate with one another over their own properties as well as the celebrity Jim Nabors, who owned property next to ours. And that lack of peace created an overall lingering sense that even if most members of our family liked Chipper and thought he was a good guy, some saw him as the Hawaiian man working for *the man* who then became *the man*.

To his credit, under his leadership, the NTBG did fulfill its promise to rebuild the heiau, and our family dropped the legal action. The Garden built a new visitors' center with a large new sign out front proclaiming KAHANU GARDEN, named after our family. The visitors' center now features a photograph of my great-grandma Mileka and the Kahanu family's history at the site.

Now was the time, Chipper said, to resolve this once and for all. "I always thought it was going to have to take the next generation to get this done," he said.

He asked for Dad's help, as well as help from my cousin Brande and other branches of the Kahanu family. His plea was: "We were so close. Can we give this a fresh start? A final shot to get an agreement in writing?" Or is it, as Chipper likes to say, stirring a hornets' nest from my grandma's generation?

Dad figured it was worth trying. He and Auntie Maureen fired up the coconut wireless one more time, trying to find phone numbers and email addresses for different branches of the Kahanu family. First, he'd try to locate them. Then he'd need to know if anyone cared to be involved. Then he'd try to organize us all on a call across six time zones.

One by one, Dad made his pitch to his extended relatives. He needed each branch of the Kahanu family—each of the original mo'opuna—to nominate a representative to the board of the revived Ho'olina o Kahanu. His pitch was: "There's no money in this and no power," Dad said. "It's all just kuleana."

9

HAWAIIAN RENAISSANCE

A few months after I got back from my visit to Maui in 2011 with Uncle Take and to see the heiau, I found myself rapidly sucked back into my Washington, DC, life. It was like a switch flipped. I turned my focus to my new job at the think tank and the small children that Michael and I were raising, plus winter on the East Coast was now approaching. Dark days with little sunlight. Freezing rain. Howling winds. Gray skies. One day merged into the next. It was the time of year that the pigment of my skin turned so light, so deprived of the sun, that I had to buy new makeup to match my winter complexion.

That escape to Hāna now seemed a world away, because it was. Now, my weekdays were so busy that I had a place to be and a thing to do every minute of every day, from 7:00 a.m. to the kids' bedtime at 8:30 p.m., and there was no time for rest or variation in between. Michael and I were in the grind, turning that wheel of daily life of getting bottles of breast milk for the baby filled multiple times a day, packing little lunches and snacks and extra pairs of clothes to school and day care. Every morning, we'd rush to the school drop-off line and pray for parking near the day care on the way to work to hopefully arrive at the parking lot near work downtown in time to snag the early-bird price of twelve dollars a day instead of nineteen dollars a day. Then one of us would rush out of the office by 5:00 p.m. so we could pick up Chloe at day care by 6:00 p.m. or face a late fee and disappointed looks by her teachers, Miss Gema and Miss Stacey, then drive over to pick up Silas from after-school care and pray he wasn't the last kid there. If Isabella was with us, which was every other week, we'd drop off at three different locations on the way to work and pick up at three different locations on the way home every day. We were living a special kind of insanity called *two working parents living in America.*

So on the weekend, especially cold autumn ones, I just wanted to enjoy doing nothing. It was one of those weekend days I didn't want to leave the house; I put on some soft pants and hoped I didn't have to interact with the outside world. I heard the clank of metal from our front door's mail slot followed by a whoosh of papers falling to the floor inside my foyer. I left the warmth of my blanket near the computer to go see what news, in the form of letters, had arrived from the outside world. I was pleasantly surprised to see a square envelope postmarked from Hawai'i.

I smiled. A welcome gift to take my mind off my winter mood. My thoughts turned to sunny Maui, picturing a January day on the island that looked perfectly sunny and just the same as one in August. I had a hunch that the padded envelope, about CD size, was from Kamaui Aiona, the director of the Kahanu Garden. Just a few months before, he had toured me around the Garden and the heiau and let me hold recovered artifacts found on the site. When

I interviewed him, he told me about a recording of Mileka, my great-grandmother, when she was interviewed by a local Hawaiʻi radio station. Family members had also mentioned this recording, but I'd never heard it myself. And when I left Maui, Kamaui said he'd send me a copy.

I ripped it open and popped it into the sleek opening on my Mac computer. The icon for iTunes bobbled up and down, and suddenly, under the line labeled "Artists," appeared the name of my great-grandmother, Martha Mileka Kahanu Matsuda.

A man's voice spoke first, through the crackle of what sounded like an old radio. His intonation asked a question that I could not understand because it was in Hawaiian. And then a woman's voice answered, slow and deep, like a lullaby.

The woman's voice belonged to my great-grandmother Mileka. The woman I had known only in weathered photographs—tall, with her long, dark hair pulled into a bun, wearing a flower-print muʻumuʻu, dark skin, and soft smile—had come alive. At least her voice had. As I sat at the desk near the kitchen in our home, it was like I'd opened a time capsule and she had arrived all the way from Honolulu in 1974, when it was recorded, into my brick colonial home in Washington, DC, thirty-six years later.

Ae. Yes, she said softly. That word, I knew.

The interviewer's hesitant voice asked long, awkward questions full of staccato pauses, like a journalist new to the job. She answered in a quiet, low voice, with short responses, like she was shy to go on too long. As a journalist, I knew the sound of two nervous people having a conversation they knew was being recorded, even if I couldn't understand the language they were speaking. The interview went back and forth like this a few times. It was not only the first time I'd heard my great-grandmother's voice, it was the first time I'd heard two people conversing in Hawaiian.

"'Ae, hānau 'ia au ma Honomā'ele." *Yes, I was born in Honomā'ele,* she said, using the name of the ahupua'a where she was from.

Since I never met my great-grandmother Mileka, hearing her speak in the rounded sounds and lyrical vowels that make up the Hawaiian language was like magic. The Hawaiian alphabet has only twelve letters, plus an 'okina, or glottal stop, written as a reversed apostrophe that's often placed between vowels to signal that the sound should be distinct. So Honomā'ele is pronounced with a pause between the "honoma" and "ele." The proper way to pronounce *Hawai'i* is to make the "ee" at the end distinct, so it's not "Ha-why" but "Ha-why-ee." Actually, the *w* is usually pronounced with a "v" sound, so you will also hear many locals say, "Ha-vhy-ee." The language makes full use of vowels, which is what gives Hawaiian its musical sound—oh-eh and uh-ee and ah-eh. When strung together into words and sentences, it's like hearing two people communicate in a kind of song with a round rhythm or a backbeat. At least, that's what it sounds like to my ear. Beautiful, special, lyrical.

I could make out a few words in the conversation that I understood, like *'ae,* and I yearned to understand more. To my surprise, the recorded radio conversation was about the Pi'ilanihale heiau. I could make out that part. Helpfully, Kamaui had sent a written transcript that he had translated himself. As I listened, I read his translation.

Radio host [translated]: Yes. Thank you for sharing. So, you really do have kuleana there and your song as well, because that's where this Pi'ilanihale is.
Mileka: 'Ae. [Yes.]

Host: It's a large heiau, isn't it?

Mileka: 'Ae. [Yes.]

Host: What's its story? Have you heard stories about this place?

Mileka: Regarding Pi'ilanihale? This was a heiau that was hidden by the families, the brothers, the siblings of this Kahanu family, their father. Therefore, when the white man came, it was noticed. It couldn't be hidden any longer, because it had been documented in the books. So it was gotten, they wanted to take all the important things from within it. But they were forbidden, they were forbidden to take these things. They should be left inside.

Host: Yes, and so your family, they are kahu [guardians] for that heiau?

Mileka: 'Ae. [Yes.] But, the heiau was turned over to the County of Maui. 'Ae. They are to clean it and take care of it now.

Then, a pause. An 'ukulele began to strum, and she sang a song—a song, it turns out, that she wrote about the heiau. She sang of its beauty, its power, its endurance through the years.

> *Aia ke ku ano ano nei i kai 'o Hale o Pi'ilani*
> *Ke pi'i nei ka la i ka lani i Kalahu*
> *Hu a'e ke aloha i ka mea kipa mai e*
> *E mai, e mai, e kipa mai ma loko nei o Kahanu*
>
> *Standing in reverence by the ocean is Hale o Pi'ilani*
> *Where the sun is rising to the heavens from Kalahu*

Our welcome overflows to you our visitor
Come, come and visit Kahanu Garden

Every strand of hair on my arms stood up. This beautiful record-ing brought alive the great-grandma I never knew, and here I was meeting her in the most unique way. I had been searching for her guidance, for what she wanted with the heiau and to know what role our family had to play. And finally, I could hear her voice and begin to match that voice with photographs I'd seen of her, with stories people told me about her. Here she was, not only speaking and singing in her native tongue, but sharing her story and her views about the heiau—something I had been seeking. What were the chances of that? It felt like the heavens had parted and this message in a bottle had been dropped from the sky and directly delivered to my home in Washington, DC.

Hearing her voice was more than a sentimental capsule of fam-ily history. She answered some of my deepest questions about our family and ties to the heiau with her simple answers. She confirmed what my grandma and Uncle Take—her children—had said about the family's efforts to keep the heiau "hidden" and our family's con-cerns for ensuring that the heiau was preserved. And again, she mentioned, as I had heard before, that people were trying to take "things" from it? What was inside? Perhaps the "things" she referred to were the artifacts that I had seen wrapped in newspaper, which I'd just held in my hands months before on my visit to Honomā'ele? This couldn't have just been a coincidence. I felt like I'd been hit by a bolt of lightning. I remembered Lilikalā's advice to me, which I had too easily brushed off.

Pray to your ancestors and ask them for permission, and they will open doors for you.

She also was clear, in her song, that now that the heiau was pro-tected, she wanted it to stand in reverence *ano ano*—for the world to see, for visitors to come and see the Kahanu Garden. Her wishes were that it would no longer be hidden but cared for, revered, and understood for the history it represented.

Reading the translation of her words also provided clarity and, in a way, relief that I could somehow, so many years later, help to carry on our family's responsibility by sharing the history of the heiau now that it had been "found." Her voice felt like a direct call to me. I needed to tell her story, our story, so that it would not die away. She is kahu (kah-hoo), a Hawaiian word meaning "protector" or "guardian." Our family is kahu. I am kahu. I carry the kuleana as a guardian, like my dozens of cousins who still live in Hawai'i, to ensure that this Hawaiian treasure—the heiau—is protected and honored forever. I understood that her words were not just her wishes for herself but for our entire family. And I heard her message loud and clear, even if I was now thousands of miles away, more than three decades later.

Mileka died in 1976, the year of my birth, in Honolulu. The radio interview occurred a few years before, when she met an en-terprising young graduate student named Larry Kimura from the University of Hawai'i, who had started the islands' first Hawaiian-language radio program in decades. Mileka's purpose for being on the show was pragmatic. She helped organize a local Hawaiian songwriting contest in O'ahu and went on the radio to encourage more participants. No one in my family recalls her writing or sing-ing any other songs, but other members of my family—namely, my great-uncles—were gifted singers and musicians who loved to jam together. And my cousins and aunties tell stories of them getting together at holidays, singing and playing Hawaiian songs, being in awe of their voices that told stories of special places and people of Hawai'i.

The three-minute recording changed my understanding of not only the woman about whom I'd known only from photographs and family stories. It also helped me better understand what happened to the Hawaiian language. I was always curious why my great-grandmother Mileka's first language was Hawaiian but my own grandmother Martha never spoke a word. And I, of course, growing up in California, learned only a few words and phrases from my grandparents and my grandma's sister Ane (pronounced as Ah-nay, but we called her Auntie Annie), who lived with us for a time when I was in elementary school. Auntie Ane was a character—she was a petite, round, and dark-skinned woman who wore big glasses and a straw hat with a beautiful band of feathers around it, called a *lei hulu*. On both of her arms, she wore several gold Hawaiian bracelets that clanked as she moved around. The bracelets were etched with her Hawaiian name in Old English script, a Hawaiian tradition, along with bracelets made entirely of green and white jade. My sister and I also remember she oddly wore the kind of pantyhose stockings that only went up to her knees, and she wore them with shorts! But she was a tough caretaker who was strict with us. I vividly remember Auntie Ane helping to potty train my younger sister Haley, and Auntie Ane would have her sit on the toilet until she was "all pau" or "all done." And we'd tell Auntie we were "all pau" with our dinner and she would point to the vegetables left on our plates and say, "No, you are not all pau."

I was exposed to small pieces of Hawaiian language but don't ever recall hearing people having a conversation in Hawaiian. Growing up, I don't think I was even aware that it was a language that people spoke to one another. Even Grandma didn't know

Hawaiian. One time while visiting Grandma's home in Nānākuli, I found a Hawaiian-English dictionary in the nightstand, with her own handwritten scribbles in the margin.

After listening to the interview recording, I wanted to learn more about how it came to be. I tracked down the nervous interviewer at the other end of the microphone and found Larry Kimura at the University of Hawai'i's Hilo campus on the Big Island. I reached out to him via email and explained who I was and that I was a journalist who wanted to interview him. He happily agreed, and we set up a time for me to call him one day late in the afternoon.

Now it was my turn to interview him. I asked if he remembered her.

"Oh, yes, of course," he said. He remembered her wearing a dark-colored mu'umu'u, long hair back in a bun. "I remember her as a stately Hawaiian woman."

Larry is now a professor of Hawaiian studies, and he, along with a group of other activist students and educators, is credited with helping to revive the Hawaiian language. It turned out that this radio interview was part of a larger project Larry started in the early 1970s to record all the living Native Hawaiian speakers. What I didn't realize is that when Larry recorded this interview with my great-grandmother, the Hawaiian language was near extinction. Only a few elders still spoke it. Larry, who grew up on the Big Island and who is part Native Hawaiian, didn't want to see the language die out. So he and a group of students set out to save it. First, they had to preserve what they had left.

"This was a population of people who were in their sixties and older, who were senior citizen age—a group that I knew from my own upbringing with my own grandparents that they would not be with us for a long time," Larry said. He conducted the interviews on

KCCN Radio (a station that no longer goes by that name) because, he said, "it would be very important for them to be heard."

Soon after the US government illegally overthrew the Hawaiian government in 1896 and imprisoned its queen, the provisional government banned the Hawaiian language from school instruction. From then on, in almost all public spaces, English quickly replaced Hawaiian. And by the time Larry Kimura's show was on the air, there weren't many places to formally learn the Hawaiian language, even as a second language. Larry had attended the prestigious Kamehameha Schools, the elite school for Native Hawaiian children endowed by the late Princess Pauahi Bishop. But at that time, even that school offered only a six-week instruction course, Larry said. After high school when he got back from serving in the military and touring Europe, he saw how important language was to a place and a culture. He saw its near extinction in Hawai'i and wanted to do something about it.

The idea of doing a radio show entirely in the Hawaiian language was radical at the time, and Larry said he had to convince station managers to let him do it. But once people heard it, they started calling into the station. They were listening, and they loved it. They wanted to understand what their elders were saying in Hawaiian. It became part of a larger movement in the 1970s for Native Hawaiians to begin to reclaim their culture.

"Language is the first aspect of a people to vanish," Larry said. He is now a faculty member at the University of Hawai'i's Ka Haka 'Ula O Ke'elikōlani College of Hawaiian Language on the Hilo campus. "People don't recognize that until it's almost gone, because they're hanging on to their typical culture identification tags such as their songs, their dancing, their foods, their religion maybe, or what they wear or how they look. But language is the one that is slipping away without them noticing it. And by the time it happens, it's in very dire straits."[1]

At the time that he started the radio program, Larry estimates there were only about 2,000 Hawaiians left on Earth who spoke the language. He interviewed about 320 of them over the course of nearly twenty years on his show. "If a person was a speaker of the language, you can automatically know that person was raised in a culturally Hawaiian way. That was a beautiful thing" about the interviews, he said. So his recordings were not just capturing the language, they were also recording aspects of the culture. "The [people I interviewed] were all from an older generation. Most of these people were from rural pockets that were isolated from the major impact of the rest of the world."

Isolated. Like Hāna, Maui. No wonder my great-grandma Mileka fit the bill.

Larry and other graduate students were influenced by other events at the time that is now known as the Hawaiian renaissance. In the 1970s, a group of Native Hawaiians had built a double-hulled canoe just like the ones that Native Hawaiians used when they arrived to first settle the archipelago centuries before, with a triangle-shaped red sail. Some of them had even learned the ancient form of wayfinding, or navigating the ocean by memorizing the constellations of stars, the tides of the oceans, and the birds of the sea to give them direction. They had set out to sail without modern navigational equipment—only wayfinding—from Hawai'i to Tahiti, and managed to prove to the world it could be done, just as their ancestors did.

Keiki Kawai'ae'a was also part of the movement to revitalize the Hawaiian language with Larry Kimura and was one of his students. She told me, "The '70s is really part of that whole Hawaiian renaissance. You know, we were part of the generation where women were burning their bras, and civil rights, and people were asking, 'How come I can't speak the language of my grandparents? How come they had this and I don't have that?'"

In 1970, the Native Hawaiian community was outraged when a group of pig farmer tenants were forcibly evicted from their lands by a wealthy developer in Kalama Valley, where the developer had plans to build a big resort. It sparked protests for tenants' rights and put a spotlight on not only the growing unaffordability of Hawai'i for local people but their rights to their land and way of life. A few years later, Native Hawaiians called for the US military to stop using the uninhabited island of Kaho'olawe for bombing practice, claiming it had rich cultural and historical significance, and later sued the federal government. All these moments, together, brought the public's attention to the fact that Native Hawaiians had a right to exist, for their culture to survive, and they were going to fight for their land and way of life. (The US military finally ended its live-fire training on Kaho'olawe in 1990 and began the process of turning it over to the state of Hawai'i, which made it a nature preserve in 1993.)

As for the language, Kimura, his students, and other activists decided that the solution was not just to push for Hawaiian to be taught in traditional schools. To revive the language, they wanted to start with young children—preschoolers—and build immersion schools where instruction was provided entirely in Hawaiian. Their goal was ambitious: to create an entirely new generation of Hawaiian-language speakers. "We knew we had to get to the babies to get [the language] back," he explained, because a new generation needed to learn it as a first or second language, from the beginning of their language development.

They pushed and eventually succeeded in getting Hawai'i's Department of Education to allow them to create Hawaiian "language immersion schools" in the mid-1980s.[2] They started their first Hawaiian school, called Pūnana Leo, which means "nest of voices." The state, however, did not offer any support or curriculum, Kimura said. So they created it on their own, starting with a handful of families in the first preschool, where kids could absorb the language from the start. And as those children grew older, they created a curriculum each year for kindergarten, then first grade, and so on.

Today, there are twenty-eight Hawaiian-language immersion schools[3] under the state school system and thirteen Pūnana Leo preschools.[4] And remarkably, more than eighteen thousand people now say they speak Hawaiian at home, according to the most recent US Census.[5] It was all because of Larry, his radio program, and the Native Hawaiian people who insisted that their culture not only survive their elders but charted a path for it to thrive into the next generation. Without his effort and this group of activists who demanded that their language not only be saved but revived, I realized that people like Kamaui, the young director of the Kahanu Garden, would not have learned how to speak Hawaiian.

"Language seems to be something subtle, and yet it is very powerful. That's how come it's so easy to lose a language—because people take it for granted. They don't realize when it's not around them anymore, because they feel they are still Hawaiian when they have other cultural references. But it's not just the music, it's not just the food that makes you who you are. It's your own language."

About 40 percent of the world's seven thousand languages[6] are said to be endangered—most of them indigenous. Hawaiian is still listed as "critically endangered."[7] When I return to Hawai'i, I now see and hear so many kids and young adults speaking Hawaiian to one another. My cousins have their kids enrolled in Hawaiian immersion programs, including one who is enrolled in a Pūnana Leo.

When I talked to Larry and shared how impressed I was with his success, and the entire effort that he and his fellow students had accomplished, he did not bask in that success. Instead, he said there was still so much work to be done. He looked at the bigger picture—today, more than six hundred thousand people claim to be at least part Native Hawaiian and so nearly twenty thousand language speakers are just a tiny fraction of where he wants to be. "We have made inroads, but we have a long way to go," he said.

I know that I missed out on the opportunity to learn the Hawaiian language in school, which is an incredible gap that I think will be hard to bridge. But it wasn't because my grandmother or great-grandmother didn't think it was important. It was because Grandma was not allowed to learn the language of her mother growing up in Hawai'i, at one of the most transformational periods of its history. Something about the language still connected with me, though, and it's hard for me to express. When I sound out a Hawaiian word, all those vowels roll off my tongue and naturally form on my lips. I'm at a preschool level, but I love soaking in new words, their meanings and double meanings that fill the Hawaiian understanding. I love learning that there are several dozen words for water, depending on where it is and what it's doing. And dozens of words for rain and wind depending on how fast it's moving and where it's going. As Larry told me his story, my heart was filled with gratitude for the greater context he brought to that old radio recording and for the gift he gave back in fighting for the Hawaiian people to hold on to their language. I was inspired that he and a group of others could make a difference and reverse the path that was leading toward extinction. More than anything, I was grateful that years ago, Larry interviewed my great-grandma Mileka. And a few decades later, I got to interview him.

Before we ended our conversation, Larry remembered that he had talked to my great-grandmother about the heiau, and I explained that I was recently there to try to learn more about it. After a moment, Larry got silent. "This whole [language] thing represents to me, of course, beyond the physical, it represents a bigger picture as language represents a whole change . . . I want to say replacement. You are replacing what was existing. You are being replaced by English.

"The human person has a lot to do with all this and also the mentality of the strongest person most negatively impacted, because if we lose the culture, the ones who have been impacted are the ones who lose. So what we are trying to do is we are trying to retrieve something, to bring to light a better understanding. In order to survive, you have to do that.

"In your interest, you are interested in this heiau, this physical structure. But there's more to it than this physical structure, of course. It connects to the bigger picture, of what happened in totality to the Hawaiian people."

Larry's kuleana was the Hawaiian language. And mine was the land and the heiau. I was inspired by his success and his commitment to see the bigger picture—the lineage from his grandparents' generation, to him, to his own kids and his grandkids—of how that kuleana was not declared "done" or over but that it was passed down. Each generation had a responsibility to keep it alive for the whole of the Hawaiian people and its culture to survive.

———

In the fifteen years since Grandma died, Dad had gotten his siblings to finally mobilize and make some decisions about Grandma's land. Not only did he organize the farm brigade, but he had gotten four of his eight siblings to agree to contribute funds each month to the family trust that would go toward paying the taxes and funding any project that they decided to do. But now it had been months without any action, and it seemed like things had stalled. He and most of his siblings were now retired, so it wasn't as if they were too busy to get started. I sensed there was something else going on.

Mom and Dad were going back and forth between Virginia, where they had moved to be closer to us kids and their grandkids, and Hawaiʻi. I sat down with Dad after one of our holiday gatherings and found some one-on-one time with him to see how things were going.

"We'll probably end up selling the Hāna land. I mean, whether it's my generation or yours, it's not sustainable," he told me.

I was shocked to hear him be so pessimistic, especially because he was leading the entire effort to save the land. I thought about my conversation with Haley and her desire for his generation to settle this.

"I don't understand. Why are you saying this? Dad, if you wanted to pay for the taxes yourself, you could afford to just do that. If you wanted to build a house there to fulfill Grandma's dreams, you could probably do that, too, even."

Born into a Hawaiian Catholic family as the third of eight kids, Dad, over the course of his life, saved and scrimped every penny.

As one of the first in his family to attend college at the University of California, Dad had worked hard to invest and live frugally to pay for our college educations and, over time, invest in real estate. He's the kind of guy you read about in books like *The Millionaire Next Door*, whom you'd never expect to have much money, because he doesn't look the part. He wears Costco jeans and fleece vests and has all kinds of financial rules like never buying a new car because it loses its value the minute you drive it off the lot. "It's the Chinese side of him," my mom jokes. She says that he's so determined never to get ripped off that he ends up buying the cheapest everything just to feel like he "won."

Even now, Dad still buys his toilet paper in bulk at Costco just to save a few extra bucks. As kids, my parents never let us order a soda at a restaurant—on the rare occasions we would go to a sit-down restaurant, we could only drink ice water—because Dad said the markup on soda was too high and it would end up being half of the bill if we all ordered drinks. He and Mom, to this day, annoy me by "sharing" a meal when they order at a restaurant. Mom gets into this, too. "Can I share your soup with you?" she will ask me or Haley, to our puzzlement. "Mom, who shares a soup? You get one spoon," I'll tell her, laughing. "I'll buy you your own." To this day, when I order anything but water from a restaurant, I have this Chinese daughter's guilt that I'm truly splurging on a three-dollar fountain soda because of Dad.

After Dad retired from the same tech company where he'd worked all his life, he and my mom became real estate investors who bought and fixed up homes and then sold them at a profit. He became a real-life house flipper. He even got my youngest sister, Emily, and my brother, Ben, involved. And now he was retired, and I saw that Grandma's land—and the decision of what to build, if anything on it—was his latest hobby-slash-income-slash-project to keep himself busy. He and Mom owned several properties that they were serving as landlords for or in the process of fixing up in Southern California, Maryland, and Virginia. This isn't to brag about him but to say that he knows something about real estate investing, and so it was really odd to me why he was indecisive about the Hāna land.

"That's not the point," Dad said.

He explained that family harmony was just as important as keeping the land. He didn't want to pay the taxes himself, because that would forever create a schism of resentment and claims to ownership of one branch of family over another. Grandma's dream was that all her children and grandchildren would feel this land was theirs, not one sibling over another.

"Look, I feel an obligation to honor my mom and her wishes. I think more important than that is that people remember her as a person. I guess I'm not as connected to Hāna as she was. I'm connected to her and my brothers and sisters. Land is an aspect of it, but it's not a living thing, and it moves in ownership no matter what you do," Dad told me.

He drew a contrast of our family land in Hāna with another property issue on Mom's side of the family. My mom's dad, Grandpa Champlin, had bought a cabin at Bass Lake in California, where we all used to spend many extended-family summer vacations with siblings and cousins and friends. For as long as I could remember as a kid, we'd always spend one week each summer vacationing there—waterskiing, boating, hiking, and hanging out at the "cove," where we'd spend hours jumping off a log or swinging off a rope and dropping into the lake. After many years of these annual trips, Grandpa Champlin bought the family a cabin to use that he told us grandchildren would be for us to take our own kids to someday. But as he got older, it was unclear about whom he'd leave the cabin to in his will, and it ended up leaving a major rift between Mom, her sister, and her brother that, to this day, hasn't been fully repaired. Eventually, my uncle inherited the cabin and later sold it. Now no one in the family visits the lake. It pains me to think my kids have never been. It pains me even more that my uncle and my mom—who were once so close that they lived in homes next door to each other—don't speak much anymore. That's the damaging power of landownership and family fights over inheritance.

That was, at least, the lesson that Dad took from it. And the long view, Dad said, was that the deck was stacked against us. As our family branches, with each generation, involving more stakeholders, it will become even harder to keep the peace among family, to align behind a common purpose, especially when it is something of value.

The raw, unused land, without a home, without a price tag, had the benefit of remaining just a concept. It was not yet—and never had been—an asset to be fought over. We didn't have fights over who last used it, who stayed there, who lived there, who rented it, who kept it up, who cleaned it after they were done, who maintained it, who repaired it, who was responsible for when it inevitably rotted and needed replacement. Dad did not want to put his thumb on the scale and pay for taxes alone or build a house with his funds alone, because that would make him feel—inevitably—that it belonged more to him than his siblings. And we—me and my brother and sisters—might feel that it belonged more to us and his grandkids than anyone else's. It would set us up, in other words, for disharmony. He didn't want the Hāna land to become the lake cabin.

More valuable than land, than a home, was family peace. That's what Grandma would want more than anything. And so, this land was not like his other real estate. It was a shared inheritance—not even an inheritance, actually, but stewardship. Kahu—guardians of land, not owners of land. He was thinking in the Hawaiian way, not the American way—and I respected that.

But even so, Dad was not optimistic that our stewardship would overcome the lack of control we would have, generation after generation, about the tax system or some other force that would ultimately result in us having to sell it or lose it. Somehow, we'd managed to hold on to it over generations in our family. But over time, that land had also shrunk to one-tenth of its original size. The odds, Dad concluded, were not in our favor.

Soon after we had this conversation, out of nowhere, right around Christmas 2021, the coconut wireless came alive again. Texts and emails came fast, first from Dad and then Auntie Maureen, sent around to relatives in chains with twenty or more family members looped in. "Did you see this?" Dad wrote, forwarding a local news article from Hawai'i. It was a news story about a new bill that seemed close to passing unanimously by the Maui County Council.

Keani Rawlins-Fernandez, a newly elected Maui County Council member and Native Hawaiian, successfully pushed for the passage of a new property tax relief bill. It was called the 'āina kūpuna bill—Hawaiian for "ancestor land."[8] It would allow families who had owned their property for more than three generations and at least ten years to qualify for tax relief, provided they did not sell it. It provided the first glimpse of hope in years.

Rawlins-Fernandez's own husband's family had been forced to sell their family land after years of rising property taxes. Armed with a law degree and voted in with a fresh crop of fellow Native Hawaiian county council members in Hawai'i's incredibly successful vote-by-mail effort, Rawlins-Fernandez pushed for the bill, and it passed the county council unanimously. Soon after, the mayor signed it into law. Auntie Maureen and my dad rushed to get our application filed, and they quickly organized meetings with Auntie Bobbie to walk her through how to submit her application, too.

It all seemed too good to be true.

I had so many questions about how, suddenly, this law passed that could potentially help not only our family but dozens or maybe hundreds of others in situations like ours.

I sent council member Rawlins-Fernandez an email to arrange a time to interview her. I was dying to know more about how this law came to be.

"I started hearing so many stories of Hawaiians losing their land," Rawlins-Fernandez told me. She grew up on the small island of Moloka'i. But her husband's family came to own land in Lahaina, Maui, in the 1800s, in what was considered at the time to be "rubbish land," she said. They raised pigs and grew alfalfa and other crops. Over the years, they had to sell off parts of their land to afford the rising property taxes. Then, in 2019, their property taxes went up to $70,000 a year. They started to rent out their property as a wedding venue, just to hang on to it. "They didn't want to get into the wedding business, but they had to do something," she explained. "The hoops that families have to jump through. They wanted to save their family property."

Sadly, she said, after his parents died, the family sold their land. But Rawlins-Fernandez said she worked on the bill for two years because she still wanted to see something done for the local people so they would stop losing their land, so that local people could afford to stay and live on Maui.

She said she didn't intend to become a politician. But she was inspired by the Hawaiian renaissance of the 1970s, for the Hawaiian people to see that they had a voice, and that it mattered, and that they could make a difference. The first graduates of Pūnana Leo, the Hawaiian immersion schools, are now adults, she noted.

"The rebirth of the '70s and '80s planted the seeds. And we are the seeds that were planted. That's why I went to law school. Partly what changed is our kūpuna made those investments in our generation in order to hui [hoo-ee, convene] the system, to protect our people and 'āina," she said, her voice getting emotional.

One unexpected benefit was Hawai'i's vote-by-mail system and automatic voter registration system through the state's Department of Motor Vehicles. "In order for change, people have to vote," and vote they did. For the first time in history, in 2020, the entire Maui County Council who were voted into office are part kanaka maoli, or Native Hawaiian. "Our lāhui [lah-hoo-ee, nation or race] is people, and culture is the heart of who we are. You can go anywhere and find white sand beaches. A lot of people want to help preserve that culture. We have a lot of allies here who believe in that."

The 'āina kupuna bill "would not have been possible" without voting access changes in the state, she said. "We ran as a slate— running with like-minded candidates that share a vision and a platform. We share the same values," she explained. And when it comes to land and taxes, she said, "we're the canary in the coal mine. What's good for our culture and 'aina will be good for everybody. There's history. It's about kuleana. Our land has a life of its own. We're just stewards."

When I interviewed Rawlins-Fernandez, the bill had just been passed, so she could not answer questions about how many properties would be approved and how much revenue this would mean that the county would have to give up. She said she had run the numbers with the mayor, and she wouldn't really know until the applications began to come in. It was all too new. The mayor, she said, was worried that the county would take too big of a revenue hit. But she was convinced it would be okay. It was exciting to hear that there was a new power center in Hawai'i—or at least in Maui County, which includes the islands of Maui and Moloka'i.

It seemed like a miracle dropped out of nowhere: this group of new leaders were elected to office, pushed forward with this bill, and it passed unanimously. Now we were hoping upon hope that the stars would align, and the last miracle would be for our application to get approved and to put this tax bill to rest. Without it, the tax policy of Maui threatened to kill our kuleana slowly, year by year.

PART FOUR

FINDING KULEANA

10

LEARNING TO HULA

Hula is the language of the heart. Therefore, the heartbeat of the Hawaiian people.

—King David Kalākaua

My research expeditions to Hawai'i yielded the answers I was searching for. But I also had to confront the fact that my life was, for now and the foreseeable future, settled on the East Coast. Michael and I were raising our children here. Both of our parents were nearby, our kids were young and growing fast, and as much as I yearned to be closer to Hawai'i, it wasn't enough to just visit. I needed to find some other way to connect with the culture—to fill the gap of distance between Washington and the islands.

As the years passed by, I realized two things: First, visiting Hawai'i every other year, which was when we could save enough money to afford to go for the whole family, was not really enough. I loved being immersed in the culture of Hawai'i to feel connected to it. But the practicality of getting there, along with the expense of flying our family of five, was a barrier that I just had to accept. Second, I realized this journey I was on was not just about me. It wasn't just about me finding answers for myself about the land, the heiau, the family story. I needed to think about how I'd pass them on in a meaningful way. I began to worry, in a way that I had heard my grandma and Uncle Take worry, that the next generation in our family would not uphold our kuleana. I wondered, at times, as I watched my children grow up in their circle of mostly white friends, whether they would ever identify as Hawaiian. At times, it nagged me and felt like an impossible problem. Genetically, they were less Hawaiian than I was. Culturally, would that be true, too? Would they feel any connection to the culture, to the creed, to the place beyond a beautiful vacation where we happened to have family living? It was truly uncomfortable. I had learned, through visiting my family in Hawai'i, about the land and the lineage. I was determined that my generation would not be the end of the line. I did not want my generation to be the one that lost the land or sold the land or gave up on the land—to close the book on 175 years of family history and roots. I did not want Honomā'ele to be the latest notch on the ledger of Native Hawaiian land to fall out of Native Hawaiian hands.

And yet, like my dad, I saw that the prospects of keeping that promise beyond me were nearly impossible. Even before the tax problem surfaced, it dawned on me that keeping the land in the family was not so much about financial means but about connection. It was the cultural responsibility, the stewardship, the kuleana that kept it alive, handed across generations. What did that next passing of the baton look like when it would inevitably get passed to me? Would my children pick it up when they were raised so far away from Hawai'i? Would my cousins' children pick it up?

I felt so lost about how to guide them, when I myself had spent many years searching for answers. I thought about how many hours

I'd spent as a young parent reading books to tell me so many other things about how to raise my children the "right" way. What to feed them to keep them healthy. What media was appropriate or helpful for them to consume—which books to read, which movies to see. What kind of electronic devices were appropriate. I even took classes on how to discipline them effectively. I worried about how much time to schedule them in sports. I stressed over summer camp registration every year. I worried about how much they weighed and what they ate too little or too much of. I stressed about getting them out the door and to school on time. I spent so many hours of my life on everything *but* how to raise them culturally. Like my search for books about heiau as a child, I found no books on how to be a good parent to raise my children in a way to pass on their culture. And I worried that if I did this part of parenting wrong, or in an incomplete or ineffective way, what would happen would be obvious. Their understanding or connection to Hawaiian culture would be a diluted version of mine. They wouldn't care about the land. It would become another piece of real estate that they had some small stake in that would happen to have some financial value attached to it.

I began to think of myself as a dead person. I knew that Grandma's land was now in a trust controlled by Dad and my aunties and uncles. Someday, that trust would be passed along to my cousins and me. If I played this out, once I died, the fate of Grandma's land was truly up to not only my children but also my cousins' children. God forbid my children would ever make a decision like this, would ever send a text like Uncle Larry's heirs, would ever feel so removed like theirs did. I'd just turn over in my grave. But how could I prevent that from happening? The reality is that I cannot, of course, control what my children do after I die. I realized that I needed to find some way to make sure they understood the family promise, that they understood the family responsibility. More importantly, I'd have to make sure that this was something they felt invested in, not "told" to do.

It made me think about what is missing in American culture that I felt so drawn to—called upon, really—in Hawaiian culture. What's missing is a sense of generational rootedness. In Hawaiian culture, I see myself in a line, where uphill I see and honor all the generations that have come before, and downhill I see all the generations yet to come. My life and time here is not just about where I stand but also how I stand. It is about the recognition that there is much in this life that I owe to those who have come before me and those who will come after me. It is not just what I do, what I accomplish, what I earn, what success I have, but what I honor. Once I realized this and saw myself in this line, it centered me. I was more balanced on that hill—I had found a steady foundation to understand my purpose beyond whatever career purpose I had set out for myself and spent years of my life striving toward. This purpose was entirely different and was about the important purpose as a daughter, as a granddaughter, as a mother, as a cousin and auntie and so on.

I have a connection to a place that is tied to my family. It called me back to Hawai'i. It called me back, very specifically, to the place of my grandma's birth, my great-grandma's birth. That call was loud and clear. I had been called back to the land to understand its story. Now my job was to figure out how to ensure that call endured for future generations beyond my life.

———

The community recreation center in Silver Spring, Maryland, carries a smell that mixes gym locker air from the pickup indoor basketball court with the Crock-Pot smell of simmering meatballs waiting to be shared by a group of seniors meeting down the hall. When I walked in the front door with my kids in tow, I felt the anxiety of spending the afternoon with a bunch of strangers rising up inside me. But on the outside, to the kids, I smiled and played it cool.

A few weeks before, I had decided to try something new— something that might possibly be the answer to my problem of being located so far away from Hawai'i and my desire to remain connected to it. The answer, perhaps, was to join a hālau (the "au" rhymes with "wow"). As luck would have it, the Washington, DC, area has a couple of hālau, or hula schools. Growing up in Southern California, I had never heard of them but really wish that I had. I reached out via email to one of the leaders of the group, who invited me to come to the next class. This group, called Hālau Nohona Hawai'i, met every Sunday in a suburban community center from noon until 4:00 p.m., with a potluck lunch. The woman I emailed with, Auntie Julie, said don't bring anything for the potluck the first time—and she welcomed me as a guest. Given that this group met about twenty-five minutes from our house, I knew that this would be a commitment. I decided I would not go alone, but if I were going to do this, I wanted my kids to do it, too.

I tried my best to put on a confident face because I'd dragged along Chloe and Silas, who were whining in the back seat on the drive to get there about how they'd rather have a playdate with a friend or do something other than this "hālau thing."

"Why are we going, Mom?" Chloe implored. She was seven years old, and Silas was now eleven. "Why can't I have a friend come over to our house instead?"

I grabbed Silas and Chloe by the hand and led them inside and asked a woman at the front desk where the hālau was meeting.

She pointed to an enormous open room, where a group of people wearing red outfits were beginning to form a circle. The women wore long red skirts, or pā'ū (pah-oo), with a black print along the edges, for practicing. The men wore red T-shirts and black shorts or pants. Little kids wore the same uniform; all together, they looked like a Hawaiian team. I immediately smiled because several of the older men and women, with their long, gray hair and caramel complexions and hapa roots, looked like my aunties and uncles. They greeted me with a smile and offered an aloha and a hug. "We have some visitors!" one of them announced, and I cringed at being singled out. My kids clutched onto my body, each taking an arm and squeezing it tightly.

We formed a circle, and I noticed we were the only ones not wearing the red-and-black uniform. The kumu, or hula teacher, a short Asian American man wearing a black baseball cap backward, smiled at us and said, "Let's welcome our guests. Tell us your names and where you're from."

All eyes went to us. God, I hated being the new kid, even as an adult. Chloe and Silas held my hands even tighter, and I could feel them trying to hide behind my legs.

"I'm Sara, and my family is from Hawai'i—from Hāna, Maui."

A few cheered when I mentioned Grandma's hometown. "All right!" one said.

I continued, "I grew up in Southern California. But I've lived here in DC for most of my adult life. And this here is Silas, he's eleven, and Chloe, she's seven."

They all clapped.

"Awesome, and we ask this of all our guests, just for fun: Did you go to public or private high school?"

I smiled, not sure why he asked this question of all questions. "Um, public high school."

"Woo-hoo! Yay!" There were cheers all around, and a few people shook their heads as if to say, "Too bad." What I learned quickly is that in Hawai'i, there's a big divide between locals who attend some of the elite private schools such as Kamehameha and Punahou, where former president Barack Obama attended, and public schools. More specifically in this hālau, there were people who had attended Kamehameha, which is a private school for people of Native Hawaiian ancestry, and those who attended their local public high school. But since I grew up in Southern California, the joke was over my head.

That first afternoon, the kids and I sat along the side of the room and watched as a group of musicians picked up 'ukulele and slack-key guitars to play familiar Hawaiian songs. The leader picked up a large ipu, or gourd, and tapped it on the floor to drum the staccato beat as the group practiced their basic hula moves.

I loved to see the women's red pā'ū sway with the swish of their hips. The men also stepped proud, with hands on their hips. Step together, step right; step together, step left. I felt like I was sitting on the floor, a kid again, watching my aunties dance hula at a family wedding, or in the church community center in Hāna, practicing for the "Maui Waltz." Part of me wanted to join in at that moment, retracing the basic vamp of the hula that my aunties had taught me when we gathered for Christmas and Thanksgiving in California. Only once, at my grandparents' fiftieth wedding anniversary party, did I attempt to dance with my sisters as we performed a very basic version of "Lahaina Luna." But I look back at that moment and kind of cringe because I didn't really know what I was doing. I didn't know how to hula. In comparison to the group I was watching now, it was clear I needed to really learn the fundamentals.

I longed to learn. For as far back as I could remember, the hula mesmerized me. I couldn't get enough of seeing my aunties and, on rare occasions, my grandma dance. Mostly at weddings, they would be encouraged to take a turn on the dance floor, and I'd fixate on their beautiful hands, the way their fingers gracefully curved and moved, with their gold and jade bracelets dangling from their wrists. I watched as their hips moved so gracefully, their feet moved so softly as they turned their bodies, their wrists, their sway, the way my aunties pinched their dresses at their hips, to tell a story. It was both the preciseness of their body movements and the bigger story their bodies were telling that pulled me in. And I loved that there were so many types of hula: traditional, fast-moving hula with no music but the beating of the gourd and chanting of dancers' voices; sweet, slow-moving, graceful hula often about love or beauty of a woman or a place; and fun, campy, kitschy hula, too. I loved watching my uncles—including Uncle Take—dance hula, too.

For the women, the hula is about grace, and also sometimes about strength, but always with emotions alongside their stories. To me, kāne (kah-nay) hula, or men's hula, oozes masculinity, power, duty, and sexuality. Actually, sex is a strong theme for both men and women. The sexy hip shaking is the dominant stereotype of hula for haoles, or foreigners, and in American culture who see hip movement in the hula for the first time. While hip shaking could not be more inaccurate, hip movement—such as the ami, or whirlpool movement—is an important part of Hawaiian hula. Indeed, there are many hula that are about or reference sex, procreation, and lovemaking. Most hula and Hawaiian songs actually have a double meaning. To witness hula is to have dancers sharing their aloha with you. Native Hawaiians, indeed, live a culture that embraces sexuality. But of course, not every ami, or hip turn, in hula is about sex or is a mating dance. The hula repertoire is much larger than that.

On our visit, Auntie Julie, a woman with long white hair and a deep voice, sat with the kids and me for a while and encouraged me to join the back row, just to practice and give it a try. But I declined when she first asked me to join. Inside me, though, instinctively, I wanted to be part of it. And I looked at my children's eyes: they, too, were mesmerized. I hoped they were like me, and inside, they couldn't wait to learn to dance hula.

Auntie Julie handed me the pā'ū, and urged me to put it on.

"Oh, no, no, no, no. I can't dance. I'm just here to watch this first visit," I said. I watched the members of the hālau as they lined up in rows facing a mirror and the kumu hula. *Boom, tap, boom, tap, tap.* The women and men began to move in unison, swaying their hips with steps to the right, then left, then back again. *Actually, it doesn't look that hard*, I thought. *Boom, tap, boom, tap, tap.*

"Do it, Mom!" my kids urged me. I smiled.

What the hell, I thought. *The worst that can happen is I make a fool of myself in front of my kids and all these strangers.* I had come to formally learn hula, so I might as well start now, I figured.

The beat drew me in. I put the skirt on, over my shorts. I slid my shoes off because you have to be barefoot to dance hula. The cold linoleum rec room floor felt like ice under my bare feet. I walked over to the group and found a place in line, in the back. A woman dancing next to me smiled and nodded. I would try to follow what she did with my feet and arms at the same time. I looked back at the kids, sitting along the side of the rec room.

Their eyes were eager and encouraging, as if to say, *Way to go, Mom!* Silas gave me a thumbs-up.

I turned my attention forward. *Boom, tap, boom, tap, tap.* I bent my knees to lower my body. I stepped to the right, remembering to keep my shoulders steady, not moving, so that my hips would sway. I kept my head level. One important secret to dancing hula is that you must dance with bent knees to get that hip movement. When you bend your knees halfway, it forces your hips to move from side to side when you step, making it look like you're swinging your hips when you are really stepping. But as I sank into my hips, I could feel them creak. As I kāholo'ed to the right, I turned my head to the right side of the room and aligned my arms at my chest, my right hand pointing to the right, my left arm up, bent at the elbow and fingertips also pointing right. I followed the group, trying to keep to the beat, and did the same thing to the left. *Boom, tap, boom, tap, tap.*

"Kāholo right!" the kumu called.

"Kāholo, 'ae," the group answered him.

I smiled and looked over at the kids, who were smiling, too. They were watching me literally put myself out there. I thought of how often I had pushed them to do the same—joining a new baseball or soccer team, or a Brownie troop. Joining a new group of people—of strangers—was hard. I had forgotten what that felt like until this moment. But here I was.

After a few times back and forth in that basic step, the kāholo, bending my knees and swaying my hips, the movement suddenly felt familiar. I remembered my aunties teaching me as a little girl the different steps in hula, how to softly roll my hands. Dancing hula was stirring these memories inside me. As I danced, I thought of Grandma. I thought of my aunties. It all felt so right inside my bones. *Yes*, I thought, *this is it. This is what I've been missing.* Suddenly, a switch inside me flipped. I went from being self-conscious to in the zone. The simple act of dancing these steps made me feel alive inside in a way that I had been yearning for. I knew at that moment that this hālau would become a much bigger part of my life and that we would join.

After the warm-up hula, the kids and I sat and watched some of the more advanced dancers practice their routines, and I wondered if I'd ever be able to dance the way they did. Some of them had danced since they were kids and performed for years. I was a woman who'd just turned forty-two, doing my first proper kāholo. I was just putting my bare feet on the floor for the first time. This, I thought, would be a long journey for me. All my life, I loved all kinds of dance, but I was never comfortable as a performer. I loved doing the steps and moving to music, but I always struggled to put on the smiling performer's face and make it look natural. I had a long way to go.

Hālau, I learned, was not just about hula. It was also about singing and chanting. On that first visit, we learned some new songs that, as a group, we sang together in Hawaiian. Even if I needed a translation to understand their meaning, they were catchy songs that I found easy to learn, and to my surprise, the kids picked them up easily.

On the drive home from hālau on that first visit, we sang the Hawaiian songs we'd just learned. And I smiled at the sound of my children's tiny voices singing, "'Uhola 'ia ka makaloa lā," in Hawaiian.

And so we began. Every weekend, for four hours on Sunday. It became our special thing that we did together, the kids and I. We began to practice hula together at home and started by learning the basic footwork. The kāholo represents the vastness of the Pacific.

Hela (hell-ah) is the name of the move where you tap your right foot forward, then return, then left foot forward, return, mimicking the forward-and-back motion of the waves on the beach. 'Uwehe (oo-way-hey) is a sharp "pop" out with both knees, like a raindrop. Maewa (mah-ev-ah) is like an anchored canoe shifting with the wave current; you keep your feet flat on the ground, but bend your knees and sway your hips from side to side. I loved learning how the hula was broken down into basic steps, each represented by your body's motion like something that was observed in nature; mauka, or toward the mountain, to makai, toward the sea. I could close my eyes, even in the dead of winter in DC, and in my living room, my body could make the motion of the waves on the sand or the raindrops from the waterfall in Hawai'i. The hula, with every step, transported me.

The kids and I spent hours learning the Hawaiian words that described each hula step, then what they meant, and that reminded us of how to move our bodies to emulate them. One week at hālau, they brought gourds for everyone so that we could learn how to turn the gourd into a musical instrument, an ipu (ee-poo), which is used to tap on the ground like a drum. The kids were so proud to have an ipu at home, and it made it fun for them to take turns making the drumbeat in our living room while we practiced our hula moves. We'd take turns lining up on the hardwood floor.

"E mākaukau?" I'd yell out, meaning, "Are you ready?"

"'Ae!" Yes, Chloe and Silas would respond.

"Kāholo pā," I'd call out.

"Kāholo, 'ae!" they'd respond.

Step, together, step, they'd sway to the right, then left.

"'Uwehe!" I'd call for another step.

"'Uwehe, 'ae!"

After a few of these practice steps, we'd take turns, and the kids loved pretending to be the kumu, tapping the ipu drum on the floor and calling out the names while I danced the basics.

"Mākaukau, Mom?" Silas would ask. *Tap, tap,* he hit the ipu on the floor. Pretty soon, we were all in. Every Sunday afternoon, I piled the kids into the minivan, and we drove to the community center for hālau, and during the week, I tried to find time for us to practice our hula. I was glad that my kids were getting a chance to learn hula at a young age. I wish I'd had that opportunity for more formal training when I was younger. Doing this together was a way for me to practice our culture, not just "visit" our culture in Hawai'i now and then. I loved that we were all learning together.

I printed out copies of the lyrics to the hula we were learning and songs we were learning to sing together, as well as chants we learned that were part of our weekly gatherings. Every week, I looked forward to those community center gatherings. I would think about my 'uwehe when I was in meetings at work and driving home on my commute. Hula songs began to play in my head all the time. *Boom, tap, boom-tap-whack, tap-tap-whack.* With every beat, every word, every song, every chant, I found a way to feel more connected to being Hawaiian.

It wasn't always easy. Despite the casual vibe at hālau, our kumu made it clear when he was unhappy that our group hadn't memorized a chant properly or practiced our hula in between classes. Even though by day, we were all accomplished adult professionals, at times we felt like we were scolded like children for falling short of the kumu's expectations.

"You should all know this chant by now. There are no excuses," Kumu would say. "It's not 'ah-pow' like *how*, it's 'ah-pow' like *bow*, okay? So let's get the pronunciation right."

Or he'd say, "This is a hula about love. I do not see any love in your faces. So if you're going to dance this hula, please do it right and express the aloha with your face as you dance. Otherwise, it's not worth dancing at all."

As a newcomer, it was a challenge just to dedicate four hours on a weekend to attend the class. As a working mother with kids, I did not have a lot of time to spend working on my chant pronunciation, and often, I was so stressed about doing the dances correctly—with proper foot and arm placement—that I knew I was one of the people not smiling.

"Sara, why do you look so stressed when you are dancing?" Kumu asked me once.

"Ugh, sorry. It's because I'm just concentrating so hard to get the right steps first," I said.

Part of joining the hālau meant that Chloe and I needed to wear the official red pā'ū skirt, which was made of fabric that has a thick gathering at the top and draped just a few inches from our ankles. (For Silas, all I had to do was order a red T-shirt and black shorts.) The hula skirt is important because it hides the legs and when you dance with bent knees, the skirt draws your eyes to the dancer's hips and her feet. The thickness of the skirt also sways beautifully when the dancer turns her body. Auntie Julie sat down with me and told me what kind of red fabric to buy and how much I needed. Since I didn't have a sewing machine, I enlisted my mom, who is an excellent seamstress, to help me out. She cut the fabric and made seams along the top and side edges. Then we spent hours trying to push elastic through the top of the pā'ū to create the thick gatherings at the top of the skirt. When we were done with mine, we had to do it again to make a smaller pā'ū for Chloe.

Mom has always embraced Hawaiian culture, and so she was

proud to help me make the pāʻū. As someone who loved to sew and who made my prom dress in high school on her sewing machine, she thought making the pāʻū was a fun challenge because we didn't have a pattern, just some handwritten instructions with some hand-drawn pictures. Mom knew, having watched my aunties and Grandma hula dance over the years, that it was something I always wanted to do. I'll never forget the moment we had just finished the painstaking process of pulling the final fifth elastic strip through the tiny wedge of material on the waist of the pāʻū. It was the third or fourth weekend in a row where Mom and I had spent buying materials for the skirts and trying to figure out how to make them. Finally, I was ready to put it on and see how it fit. When you put on the pāʻū, you're supposed to put it over your head so it brings aloha to your whole body, as opposed to stepping into it. So I lifted the thick, full skirt over my head and pulled it down to my waist. "It looks great!" Mom beamed. She took a photo of me wearing our creation (it was mostly her creation!). I couldn't wait for Chloe to put hers on, too.

But we weren't done yet. After the skirts were made, they had to get the final touches. One winter weekend, I drove Chloe out to Auntie Julie's house in suburban Maryland so that we could put the official hālau design on the pāʻū —to apply our hālau's black Native Hawaiian design along the bottom edge of the skirts. Together, carefully, I helped Chloe cover the foot-long stamp in black paint and then carefully press it down on the skirt. When we lifted the stamp carefully, we could see how it made a pattern of small triangles representing islands and a circle representing the sun. We repeated this all along the bottom edge of the skirt to make it look like one continuous pattern on my pāʻū. Working as a team, Chloe would apply the black paint to the stamp, and then we'd line it up and press it on the skirt together until we reached the point where we started. Auntie Julie hung the skirts up on a hanger to dry. They looked beautiful—and perfectly matched the ones that the other girls and women wore to hālau each week.

For Chloe, who was seven years old at the time, stamping paint along our new pāʻū was like doing a fun art project together for the afternoon. But for me, the process of creating our hula skirts felt like both an honor and a joyous cultural indoctrination. It was not an easy process; it was designed to make me appreciate that the care and dedication to the hālau was also about the care of creating the most important item I'd need for my hula practice. It was also not lost on me how the process required three generations of my family to create—I could not have done it without my mom, who brought her knowledge of sewing and appreciation for our family's culture. And I could not have done it without my daughter, who wanted to wear the pāʻū and make hers just like I'd made mine. It also took the wisdom and guidance of Auntie Julie, who volunteered her time each week to welcome newcomers like me and help us feel part of hālau. Once it was done, I'll never forget the pride we had in walking into the next hālau with our official red pāʻū and Silas in his red-and-black hālau attire. It felt like we had officially joined Team Hawaiʻi.

This weekly class—this hālau of like-minded families and individuals who shared a love for Hawaiʻi—became my escape and my joy. It was an escape from my busy life of working in a high-stress job full-time while also being a full-time mom. At hālau, I enjoyed being a hula student and not having to plan something or manage anything. It felt good to be learning something new, even if at first I wasn't very good at it. The kids and I quickly transformed from being the "new" family in the group to one that was welcomed in and suddenly absorbed in everything the group had to offer. The alakaʻi (ah-la-kah-ee), or leadership of hālau, broke the group up to teach different hula to wāhine (wah-hee-neh), or women, and kāne, men, and keiki (kay-kee), children. There were enough keiki in the group who were around Silas's and Chloe's ages so that it worked out perfectly. And I joined the beginner wāhine group. After a couple of hours into hālau, we'd break for a potluck lunch, and I loved that, in the middle of the DC suburbs, this was our weekly chance to enjoy a little taste of Hawai'i. Each week, it was different, but the kids and I enjoyed eating foods that we only got to eat in Hawai'i or on rare occasions—foods like kalua pork, Spam musubi, and mochi desserts. The food was laid out on a long table, and we piled our plates high, then formed smaller circles to eat sitting on the floor, with food on our laps.

Sitting in the circles and learning hula together, I got to know different members of the group. We each had very different stories and lives. There was an interesting mix of families, couples, and young adults who lived around the region—from an hour's drive away in Northern Virginia, to near Baltimore. Most people had moved to the area from Hawai'i: we had researchers who worked at the Smithsonian, workers at different federal agencies, members of the military, teachers, and retirees. For some, their reason for being at hālau was that they recently moved to DC and were homesick— hālau was a way to feel less so. Others, like our kumu hula and many of the alaka'i, grew up in Hawai'i but now had settled in the DC area. They were now like me, raising kids here and not moving back anytime soon. And a few others—about a half dozen older single women, mostly—didn't have Native Hawaiian ancestry, but they had visited Hawai'i and fallen in love with the culture. Hālau brought them a connection that they were missing in their lives, and they had found friendship, community. For all of us, hālau was healing in some way.

As we settled into the group, I got to know our kumu hula, a man named Kaimana Chee, who grew up on Oʻahu and had started the group in 2014 after a circuitous career led him to the Washington, DC, area. He was working as a government contractor when he was suddenly launched into fame on a celebrity cooking show. He loved preparing the kinds of food that he ate in Hawaiʻi but found it difficult to find good food from the islands on the mainland. When he heard about an open audition for the TV show *Master Chef*, he was determined to give it his best shot. He packed up his cooler and joined an enormous line of people who were eager to prepare a small dish in front of a panel of judges, tell a story about it, and land a rare spot on the show. After a few rounds of impressing the judges with some witty responses on his feet during the interview and telling his story about Hawaiian food and culture, he was in.

It launched him to TV food fame, and he found his way onto other shows, and eventually an entirely new career as a "chef ambassador" for different food brands. Even with all of that success—flying around the world in business class and doing TV interviews—he remained committed to leading the hula community in the community center every weekend.

"We serve a different purpose in our hālau compared to the hālau you will find in Hawaiʻi," he explained. "There, in Hawaiʻi, the purpose is to learn hula. But ours, it is not to envelop themselves in hula but discovery of identity, community, camaraderie, finding people who are at a similar position in life when they are lacking some identity and they want to bring that to the forefront. There's a catalyst in their life that has sparked curiosity, or longing to be connected to their roots. Once a week, they get their aloha filled."

I felt like he knew my story before I had even told him. And as

I got to know him, I knew that this was true for him, too. Kumu, as we called him, started dancing hula at a young age and trained for years in a hālau near his home. As I watched him each week, I admired his unique gift of mastering the movements, and he intuitively understood how to fine-tune a hula into a larger vision of choreography, performance, and a show. He had the gift of musicality that enabled him to direct us to sing in different octaves like a choir teacher, and to pick up an 'ukulele to sing at perfect pitch and strum the music to any hula we were dancing. Often, he would arrive at hālau jet-lagged and exhausted after a twelve-hour flight. Without knowing all the details of his life outside hālau, I could tell he was burning the candle at both ends but dedicated to leading hālau because it brought him so much joy. I had invited him to my house one day so he could share more about his story and why he decided to launch hālau.

"My goal is to share hula," he told me, sitting at my dining room table over coffee and cookies. "I feel it is my kuleana, my responsibility to share what I know and what I have and what I love. When I stop teaching hula, I feel an emptiness." One of the challenging things about running a hālau in the DC area, he said, is that there's a balance between welcoming newcomers with aloha to the group and ensuring that people understand what it is about.

"The struggle is the people who grew up here [on the US mainland] and think of coming to hālau as a dance class. It is not just about learning a dance. Hula is *not* a dance," he explained. "It's storytelling. It's an oral history put to movement, it's how we passed down things from generation to generation . . . It's not like, 'Can I come and just do a drop-in to learn hula?'"

"Do people really inquire about that?" I asked.

"Oh, yes," he said. "That's why we started to have calls with people before inviting them to hālau. They need to know what we're about. It's not a dance class.

"Being Native Hawaiian on the mainland means we should be educating people, we should be debunking misperceptions and misconceptions about Hawai'i. We should be educating people about cultural practices, about what hula is," he said. His role, he said, is "to seize every opportunity to open someone's mind a little bit."

————

The origin of the hula is not universally settled. But there's a story in Hawaiian oral tradition about the Native Hawaiian goddess Pele, who rules over the volcanoes of the islands. The story goes that the goddess begged her sisters to dance and sing, but they demurred, saying they did not know how. But the youngest sister, Hi'iaka (Hee-ee-ah-ka), surprised everyone by dancing on the sands of the beaches as she improvised, having secretly learned from her friend Hopoe (Ho-poh-eh).

As I began to pull together research on hula and Hawaiian history, what stunned me at first was that some of the first sketches, the earliest images of hula dancing, were of men, not women. They were first drawn in the late 1700s by British explorer James Cook's artist, and it was clear that Westerners were witnesses to hula performances and they were captivated by the Hawaiian men, who are depicted as dancing in groups of three or more, with geometric tattoo designs up their legs, along the lengths of their arms, across their bare chests, and sometimes also on their faces. The men are wearing elaborate cloths around their waists and in some cases carrying decorative implements that appear similar to shields, each with one leg raised in unison and arms in chorus with one another. The men look strong and serious, and by the crowd sketched around them, they appear to be performing a dance of great importance.

American historian Nathaniel B. Emerson wrote one of the first comprehensive books about the practice of hula and mele (mehleh), singing or song, in 1909. He observed:

> The [Hawaiian] people were superstitiously religious; one finds their drama saturated with religious feeling, hedged about with tabu, loaded down with prayer and sacrifice. They were poetical; nature was full of voices for their ears; their thoughts came to them as images; nature was to them an allegory; all this found expression in their dramatic art. They were musical; their drama . . . cast in forms to suit their ideas of rhythm, of melody, and of poetic harmony. They were, moreover, the children of passion, sensuous, worshipful of whatever lends itself to pleasure.[1]

Moreover, in ancient times, hula was not practiced by all Hawaiians but only those selected for that purpose and dancers were required to commit to hours of practice at hālau, which had its own strict set of rituals, led by the kumu and his appointed leaders. Within hālau, there were strict rules to uphold the honor of the role to be storytellers of the Hawaiian people, which required memorizing and performing chants, rules about restrictive foods and abstinence before performances, and traditions and rituals surrounding the collection of certain plant leaves and flowers used to create the dancers' costumes.[2] Men and women were chosen to dance hula, and it was an honor to have hula as one's kuleana.

The hula was forever changed with the arrival of foreigners, and in particular, the arrival of Christian missionaries. In 1819, Hawaiʻi's regent Queen Kaʻahumanu accepted the Protestant missionaries who had come from New England, and she persuaded her son,

King Liholiho, to end the kapu system, which in essence got rid of the Hawaiians' religious system and the societal structure built upon it. There was no formal name for the Hawaiians' religion, but they believed in many gods who had power to control the elements of nature that surrounded them and that were critical to their survival. Those gods included Pele, the goddess of fire and volcanoes; Lono, the god responsible for the harvest; and Ku, the god of war, among others. The ancient Hawaiians built heiau to manifest rituals and prayers to these gods. And the hula was a form of expression to tell stories about their gods and honor their creations.

But once their religion was declared over and the kapu system of rules abandoned, the Hawaiians were left with a vacancy by which perhaps only other religions and cultural traditions and norms could fill the void. Enter Christianity. Just as King Liholiho declared the end of the kapu, waves of New England missionaries were sent to Hawai'i ready to convert and "civilize" the Hawaiian people. Boats full of emissaries of the American Board of Commissioners for Foreign Missions (ABCFM) arrived on the Hawaiian Islands in 1820, with their disapproval of the hula. Learning hula was a waste of time, some of their leaders wrote. And even though some appreciated hula as an art form, they were horrified at the practice of women dancers not wearing clothing on top of their pā'ū as they traditionally performed. In 1830, Queen Ka'ahumanu issued an edict banning public hula performances, but she died two years later, and the Hawaiian people never stopped dancing hula even if it became, for a time, less visible on public occasions. As a result, for a time the hula was also banned in Hawai'i on the Sabbath. But accounts make clear that the hula was still being performed by hālau, and the dedication to the practice never wavered.[3] In fact, during the period beginning in the mid-1800s, a new form of hula emerged that was less focused on telling stories of gods and goddesses and led by just the tapping of the gourd to keep the beat to one set to the strum of musical instruments such as the 'ukulele and the slack-key guitar. Instead of lyrics that told stories of the goddess Pele or other deities, the stories focused on the honor of Hawai'i's monarchs and the beauty of places around the islands. Hula and the mele evolved with the times and would continue to do so with each century to reflect a changing culture influenced by foreigners.

In 1883, King Kalākaua—who was a Christian but also believed in keeping alive Hawaiian culture, music, and hula—made a break with Queen Ka'ahumanu's view and launched a public effort to revive Hawaiian traditions in song, dance, and music. With his coronation, birthday, and other public occasions, he famously called for hālau to come and perform hula and bands to perform music and luau, which he loved and earned him the title as Hawai'i's "Merrie Monarch." (He also loved to drink.) Photos from that period show women and men dancing on mats in front of the Iolani Palace, with traditional lei po'o on their heads and around their ankles, big pā'ū made of ti leaves around their hips, and white long-sleeve tops. However, the Hawaiian kingdom was overthrown just a decade after the king's effort to revive the hula and culture, and again, hula became targeted by foreign settlers who were taking over with an illegal provisional government.

After the overthrow, Hawai'i entered a period where its culture would continue to be attacked, diminished, and shamed, which included the hula, as well as the banning of learning or speaking the Hawaiian language, Native Hawaiians' use of land and water resources, and other cultural practices. An article in the anti-monarchy Honolulu newspaper *Hawaiian Gazette* three years after the overthrow stated that the hula "is essentially an immoral dance. How immoral only those who have seen it can understand. It cannot claim for itself a poetry of motion or a poetic idea. It is nothing but pure and unmitigated filth."

In 1899, an article in the *New-York Tribune* headlined "DYING HA-WAIIAN CUSTOMS" detailed how "the only way to see true hula now is to see it in some faraway town in Hawai'i where the whites have not yet come." And it was not just the laws of a new provisional government but the culture that was replacing that of Native Ha-waiians. They were made to feel that their old ways—the chanting, dancing, singing, living—were in the past, irrelevant, and no longer valued or worth keeping. It was more than laws; it was a psychology that seeped into Hawaiian identity. It is captured by many histori-ans but also in this example of the decline of "olioli singers," as put by the *Tribune*. "The Caucasian regards these olioli singers as bird howlers. He laughs when they raise their plaintive voices but does not understand what they say and the hoary antiquity of their tales does not appeal to them. The young Hawaiians, very imitative, very sensitive, do not feel proud of the fact that there is an olioli singer in the family, and refuse to take lessons in the dying art. Instead of learning to sing history they learn to jiggle the typewriter, which may be more useful, but is lacking in picturesqueness."[4]

But it wasn't as though the hula was over. As travel to Hawai'i became more accessible in the early 1900s, with events such as large exhibitions across the United States, hula began to fascinate Amer-icans. And a new kind of hula that blended Hawaiian dance and storytelling mixed with Polynesian dances and more tourist-focused lyrics and songs began to set in. It was called *hapa-haole hula*, which translates as literally "half-white" or "half-foreigner hula," because the lyrics were in English or mostly English, set to a blend of stringed instruments, and incorporated other Western styles of music of the time. Songs like "My Little Grass Shack" and "Honolulu Baby" became popular not only in Hawai'i but across the mainland. All of this set the groundwork for, during the early and mid-twentieth century, a caricature of Hawaiian culture that became the focus of development for the purpose of tourism. Newspapers at this time across the United States described traveling "hula hula" dancers captivating and shocking crowds across the mainland. Large passenger ships made their way across the Pacific from California to Honolulu, and hula became synonymous with Hawai'i and seeing it performed became an iconic cultural experience for tourists. Large hotel resorts began to put on hula shows or luaus for guests, and these shows incorporated more of a Polynesian experience—for example, with fire dancing and fast-moving Tahitian dancing.

In 1964, a group of Hilo businessmen and community leaders started what they called the Merrie Monarch Festival to invite and showcase the top hālau and hula dancers to perform. Every year, during the slow month of April, the festival organizers name the top hula dancers, who perform a number of styles of Hawaiian hula represented by different eras of its evolution. Named in honor of the king who is credited with keeping alive the hula and Hawaiians' beloved musical traditions, today it is one of the most treasured cultural events of Hawai'i. What's more, it's not just hālau from Hawai'i who participate; serious, dedicated, and talented dancers from hālau across the United States are invited to perform on the stage to honor their heritage and keep not only the tradition alive but the art form, the storytelling, the kuleana of hula.

———

Joining the hālau came at a time in my life when I'd also begun to find my groove again and a new confidence in journalism. I had long moved on from my feelings about *The Washington Post*, and, after a few years working at the Pew Research Center, I returned to work in daily news again at a place I'd always admired—NPR.

I found NPR to be a very different kind of newsroom than *The Washington Post*. In the *Post's* old building on Fifteenth Street NW, down the street from the White House, the open newsroom felt like it was upholding the tradition of Woodward and Bernstein from the Watergate days. It felt like walking into an institution where every reporter was trying to hustle for their shot to be like the famous reporters who brought down a president. It had a certain scruff to it, too, that I loved, where reporters sat crunched into cubicles filled with disheveled papers and takeout from lunch that day, and a ring of televisions around the room reminded you that the place was on top of the news around the world.

NPR, on the other hand, was all about the production and the quirky mix of what they created every day—from international news to the review of an obscure ragtime musician. The enormous new white building on North Capitol Street took up nearly the entire block. The center of it was an impressive, beautiful, soundproof studio where the hosts and producers made the flagship shows twice a day. In the center was the team I oversaw, the digital news team, writing up breaking news for the website and posting on social media. By the time I'd arrived at NPR, it had evolved from a radio-only company to a multimedia one that was on top of the news online, even producing *Tiny Desk Concerts* at the fourth-floor music section nearly every week. Once, I even got to take Chloe out of school early so that she and I could see Taylor Swift perform her *Tiny Desk* concert—a cool NPR perk that I knew she'd never forget. Someone at NPR once compared the persona of *The Washington Post* to the serious, know-it-all political science major in college while

NPR was the quirky, tea-drinking, philosophical, tattooed French major. I laughed because it was true; I did notice a lot more tea drinking instead of coffee drinking at NPR. The team at NPR took themselves a little less seriously, and I found them to be funky and creative—they knew the stereotype they represented and leaned into it. They were also serious journalists. It was the public charter and public mission of the place that gave it a special twist.

I arrived at the beginning of a consequential election year in 2016 and a time of internal highs and lows. The news each week was relentless, and I found myself again running on the adrenaline of making sure we were on top of it. That first year I was there, the newsroom was devastated by the loss of two of our own journalists killed in an ambush while on assignment in Afghanistan. It was not only a gut punch to the many colleagues who were also personal friends but also a stark reminder of how dangerous our work could be. Some months later, we were covering the presidential election. In true NPR fashion, since we didn't have and couldn't compete with the likes of CNN and cable news with their fancy zoom-in Election Night graphics, NPR decided it would paint the results of the election on a giant canvas map of the country that we had installed in the newsroom for the evening. As results came in, our team would paint the state red or blue, and we live-streamed it to our website and Facebook page. Fans loved it. So nerdy and creative. So NPR. When the election was called for Donald Trump that night, the newsroom was in shock, and I knew that we'd entered a very different journalism era. We now were working nearly around the clock to keep up with his nonstop tweets—each of which seemed to rock the world into a new state of disbelief. In other words, it sucked me back into the center of the action, and there was no place I'd rather be. I loved it because even though I was no longer reporting—I was now managing a large team of sixty digital news journalists—the mission of journalism never felt more critical.

The relentlessness of the news also made every Sunday afternoon even more precious. Hālau was my only time to turn off my phone—even for a few hours—and live in another world—one with people who wanted to come together to celebrate the Hawaiian culture. I didn't have to answer emails about the latest tweet from the president. Somehow, I'd found the next best thing to being in Hawai'i—to close my eyes and move my bare feet to the beat of the gourd.

11

HŌ'IKE

I'm not a natural performer. I have a hard time faking a smile and making it look authentic and, while I am comfortable being on a stage, I'm not necessarily the gal to ham it up. So I was a little surprised when, one week, Kaimana, our kumu hula, announced at hālau that our hō'ike (ho-ee-kay) would be on Mother's Day weekend, in May. *Hō'ike?* I thought to myself. *What is that?* I had to google it: *hō'ike* translates as "to show, to tell, to demonstrate one's knowledge." *Gulp*. Every year, Kaimana explained, the entire hālau put on a performance with multiple hula for friends, family, and the Washington, DC, community. It serves as the annual fundraiser for our hālau and a way to share our aloha with the community. This year, we were to perform at a public high school auditorium that seated six hundred people.

Dear God.

Suddenly, it felt like the stakes were high. It took me many months, every weekend attending hālau, to feel more confident in hula and in learning to oli (oh-lee), or chant. It was one thing to learn the language, to understand the lyrics of the song, to feel confident in moving my body correctly, and to tell the story and to feel the story. It was quite another to do all this on a stage. Not just for me but for the kids, who'd gone along to hālau with me for weeks even if they complained that it cut into their weekend time with friends. Now, I explained to Silas and Chloe, we were going to be dancing hula in a performance. I smiled and projected confidence for them. *Oh, how fun! We'll be performing in hōʻike*, I told them. For myself and for them, I was giving NBD vibes. Inside, I was panicking a little bit. I had signed up to learn hula, to reconnect with my roots and to expose my kids to a deeper sense of Hawaiian culture. I didn't know I was signing up to perform on a stage. But we didn't really have a choice. There wasn't anyone in hālau who wasn't going to be part of hōʻike in some form or fashion.

The hālau had started meeting in early fall 2018, when the school year began. And the kids and I had committed to making hālau "our thing," just a mom-and-kids weekend event. We were all enjoying learning hula and the weekly Hawaiian food potluck and fellowship among the fifty or so members, even if, at times, the kids seemed bored by the third hour. I had even relented and let them use a Kindle during downtime when we weren't dancing. But once the snow started to melt and the spring of 2019 was upon us, the hālau took on a more serious focus about the big hōʻike. We formed committees to help prepare for the big event. One group focused on sewing or ordering costumes for each person in each hula. Another group focused on marketing the event to various local media and on social media. Yet another was conscripted for designing and building the sets. It was as if our hula group of volunteers turned into a mini production company. In addition to Sunday hālau, the alaka'i set up Saturday workshops dedicated to making costumes, and many of the women brought their sewing machines; I found myself measuring and cutting yards and yards of cloth to make pā'ū. The kids enjoyed making "fun fur" lei that were meant to be draped around one's shoulders like a lei made of flowers, only these were made out of a fuzzy string. We all learned how to tightly wind a special soft yarn around and around a McDonald's ice cream shake straw (which was just the right diameter) that, when you slid it off, made a thick fuzzy lei.

Kumu assigned everyone in hālau their hula and performance roles for their parts of the program. Our focus now became perfecting those hula and practicing our stage entrances and exits as we went through the show's program. Chloe and Silas would be performing a chant while clapping kāla'au (kah-lah-oh), two wooden sticks, together to make the beat, as well as a keiki hula about a frog with the other kids in hālau. Separately, eight-year-old Chloe learned a seated hula that she'd perform wearing a kind of mermaid costume with the other girls. I would dance a couple of different hula with some of the other beginner dancers. Then, just a few weeks before the big day, Kumu called me aside and announced that he wanted to add one more hula to the performance: a special mother-son hula. Would Silas and I be part of it? It was an easy hula, he explained. I felt honored to be asked, as we were both beginners. Yes, of course, I told him. Silas and I would wear matching red-and-black Hawaiian-print outfits, as would four other mother-son couples.

Now I was really excited. I knew I was asking my normally shy son to step up in a big way. I talked with Silas, then age twelve, and he agreed to do it with me. Because he is our only son, I enjoyed the opportunity to do something with him. After all, our house of three kids was always busy, and it was hard to find one-on-one time together. Silas is a quiet and brilliant kid who is curious about the world and plunges himself into passion projects, almost obsessively. Michael and I marveled at how he would set his mind to an obscure pursuit, like learning to solve a Rubik's Cube in under a minute, and he'd devote hours and hours to the task until he mastered it. (He even learned to do it blindfolded!) His earlier passions included learning magic tricks, and later, he became consumed by mastering trick shots, like extreme basketball stunts and water-bottle-flipping games. Later on, in middle school, he became intensely interested in ice hockey. Then he announced that he wanted to become an expert at playing chess and practiced online every day and at matches around the region. But at hālau, I felt he was at the age where it was my last chance as a mother to really connect with him before he became a teen and, I feared, he'd not want to spend as much time with me anymore. At twelve, he'd still hold on to my hand if I grabbed it. At night, I still lay down in bed with him before he closed his eyes and went to sleep, and he still begged me to read to him. A mother-son hula sounded like a special way to capture this precious moment in time that, in the back of my mind, I knew was fleeting but important. Hopefully this hula would be something he'd remember forever.

Around this time, I applied for Silas to attend a unique summer program in Hawai'i run by the Kamehameha Schools, a private school system and campus endowed by the late Princess Bernice Pauahi Bishop, one of the last members of the Hawaiian royal family. Princess Pauahi did not have any children of her own, and she had acquired hundreds of acres of land in Honolulu through the Mahele, and her role as a mo'i, or member of the royal family. After she died, she bequeathed her land to two important institutions that still exist today: the Bishop Museum, which houses the most important Native Hawaiian and Polynesian artifacts in the world, and the Kamehameha Schools, whose mission is to provide excellent education to children of Native Hawaiian descent. Admission to the school is incredibly selective. Students who are admitted receive a truly unique education steeped in Hawaiian language and culture at their beautiful college-like campus in the hills overlooking Honolulu. Graduates go on to the top colleges and universities in the United States. To be admitted, students must be at least one-sixteenth Native Hawaiian, which my children are.

Although it would be hard for Silas to attend the Kamehameha Schools year-round without us living in Hawai'i, he was eligible that year for the summer program called ho'omāka'ika'i (ho-oh-mah-ka-ee-kah-ee), a weeklong immersive cultural program where rising sixth graders spend a week at the dorms on campus. The program, which began more than fifty years ago, invites Native Hawaiian children who don't attend Kamehameha to learn taro farming at a lo'i (loh-ee), an irrigated terrace, learn Hawaiian music, and sing Hawaiian songs, among other cultural traditions. I wished that I'd had the chance to attend something like this when I was a kid, so I wanted to offer the opportunity to Silas. Having been to Hawai'i many times, Silas liked the idea of "Hawai'i summer sleepaway camp," and I noticed that he'd started to grow his hair long, like his Hawaiian cousin. It would be his first time spending a week away from us, and far away from home. But I also knew that it was the opportunity of a lifetime. The program is offered to kids at this important, formative age, and as a parent, I badly wanted this for him. Several of my cousins—including Auntie Maureen's kids—and other cousins who live in Hawai'i had attended the same program when they were Silas's age. Some of my other cousins in Hawaiʻi were accepted and attended the school. Auntie Maureen helped me gather all the family documents required to first prove his Native Hawaiian ancestry and then navigate the application process.

That spring, thick in the planning for hōʻike, we got word that Silas was admitted to hoʻomākaʻikaʻi in an email. Silas and I high-fived, and I began to plan a trip to take him out to camp—just the two of us. After his camp ended, we planned for the entire family to join us for a summer vacation. One week, during announcement time at our hālau in DC, I told the group that Silas would be attending hoʻomākaʻikaʻi, and everyone clapped and whooped for him. I could tell he was proud. "I did that program, too!" several people said. It was as if we'd entered a special society. As a parent, for the first time, I finally felt like I was starting to figure out how to more intentionally pass on my family's culture to my children. There were things I could teach him myself from my parents and my grandparents. And there were things I'd have to learn with him, like hula dancing at hālau. And there were things I'd have to lean on others to teach him, like hoʻomākaʻikaʻi.

Meanwhile, the big day for hōʻike was approaching. Week by week, I was mentally preparing myself to be onstage performing dance routines and singing—something I hadn't done in about twenty-five years since high school, when my friends and I performed in the school air guitar contest. What had I gotten us into? I felt really out of my depth. On one hand, I told myself it was just a high school auditorium. It's not like we were asked to perform at the Kennedy Center. But on another level, I felt an anxiousness that I hadn't felt in a long time. The thought of messing up a hula while in the front row on a stage before a few hundred people was running around in the background of my head for weeks leading up to hōʻike. And yet, in front of the kids, I performed my best "I've got this" mom vibe. This whole thing was gonna be fun, I told Silas and Chloe. It was gonna be fine; it was gonna be a special thing we would do together. I invited my parents, our friends, and our neighbors to hōʻike. "I'm so excited for you to come. It would mean a lot to me if you could be there," I coaxed. I made my pitch. Every time I said it, it felt like I was adding another layer of expectations and pressure on my shoulders. I also knew that we'd spent months learning hula, and it was a special thing to be able to share that with those we loved.

On the day of our hōʻike, Silas, Chloe, and I were all excited and nervous to perform. We pulled into the Northern Virginia high school's parking lot hours before the performance was set to begin and unloaded all our costumes into an empty classroom that served as our hālau's dressing room. The whole room was abuzz, and dozens of members of our hālau hung up their costumes on clothing racks and got their hair and makeup ready. Before we started letting the audience into the auditorium, Kumu gathered the entire hālau onto the stage with the thick curtains drawn. The room was quiet, and he began to chant.[1] The chant was one that we said together at the beginning of every gathering of our hālau as a way to enter the space and to be seen by our ancestors. We all joined hands, forming a circle, and our voices joined into something unexpectedly powerful.

> *E ho mai ka ʻike mai luna mai e (Grant us the knowledge from above)*
> *O na mea huna noʻeau no na mele e (Concerning the hidden wisdom from songs)*
> *E ho mai (Grant)*
> *E ho mai (Grant)*
> *E ho mai (Grant us these things)*

The chant grounded us, reminded us that this performance was more than just about remembering the steps of our hula. This hōʻike was not about me and my individual stress about how I'd perform but about the wisdom of these Hawaiian songs and the stories we were about to tell with our voices and our body movements, from our people to share with new people who had come to receive it. As we chanted, I felt myself grounded in that generational line again, learning the stories of those who'd come before, and holding my children's hands, on either side of me, giving this to them and sharing it with the world. I stood there with my bare feet cold from the stage, but my arms were lit up with electricity. I squeezed Silas's and Chloe's little hands and looked them in the eyes, knowing that my own were a bit watery. My emotions surprised me, but they shouldn't have.

"You're going to do great," I told them. "I'm so proud of you."

Chloe and Silas went first, and my heart filled with pride as they lined up onstage, ready to perform "Ke ao nani" in their costumes and holding the kālaʻau, two wooden sticks used as musical instruments, in their hands. From the side of the stage, the lights blinded me from seeing into the crowd, but I knew that my parents, my husband, my sister, her husband, and her kids were in the audience, ready to record the moment on their phones. The audience clapped when their song was over, and all the kids, in their white shirts and colorful lei, walked off the stage with proud smiles on their faces. The rest of the hōʻike program went by fast, and with each song, our hālau got into a groove. I danced to "Kipona Aloha" with a group of wahine beginner dancers. And once the music started, somehow my body just relaxed. I smiled and tried not to think too much about the crowd that was behind the bright lights glaring in my eyes. I just tried to think about the story I was telling and what the lyrics meant. The lyrics directed my arms and legs what to do and what to say. As I danced, I had a giant smile on my face that was impossible to wipe away.

Next, it was time for me to dance with Silas. We walked onstage together, in mother-son units. In our matching outfits, we danced to "E Huli Makou" (Eh hoo-lee mah-ko) a fun call-and-response modern hula that was just about taking turns this way and that. When the 'ukulele played, the moms danced one part and the sons, on their right side, danced theirs. "Go, Silas!" I heard my dad yell from the crowd. The lyrics were kind of like a kid's song: "E huli, e huli makou" means "Turn, let's all turn." And later, "Kou maka, kou lima, me kou kino e, he aloha mai" means "Your eyes, your hands, and your body, hello there from your heart." It was a hula that was like a starting point. And it was fitting—here we were, mother and son, doing this fun basic thing together, on this hula journey together. At the end of the hula, the boys all gave their moms a big hug. We could hear the crowd go, "Awww!" My smile couldn't have been bigger on my face. I realized in that moment that there was nothing performative about what I was doing on that stage. I was truly loving every minute. It felt like it was where I belonged. I was learning the stories of my ancestors, alongside my children, and sharing those with the world.

What could be more Hawaiian than that?

But the show, as they say, was not over yet. Our kumu, Kaimana, had planned something more contemporary for us to sing as our final number. He loved the message from the movie *The Greatest Showman*, about a group of circus misfits trying to prove their worth to society and the pride they discover about themselves against the odds. Because he is a gay man who has struggled with personal losses in his life, who has had to make it on his own from scrappy roots, I understood why he wanted us to sing the movie's signature song, "This Is Me," as our final number. It was a way for us, as a hālau, as a community of Native Hawaiians far from Hawai'i, to say something about who we were. As a family, the kids and I had watched the movie, and we practiced singing the lyrics in English as well as some in Hawaiian that Kumu had translated for us.

I maintain that I'm not really a singer. I'm not really a dancer. But at that first hō'ike, I felt that I understood the power of hula and hālau. I felt the pride from my grandma, who I knew would be watching from above. I felt the lineage through my bones that made me so happy to sing and dance my heart out. It was as if I were just borrowing that spirit and it was coming through my body onto that stage. After the show was over, Dad stood waiting for me, ready for a hug, with a bouquet of flowers in his hands.

"Wow, you're a natural," he said. I immediately felt the emotion begin to gather in my throat. "Your grandma would be so proud, Sara."

I nodded because I knew he was going to say it before he even said it. I felt like, in my middle age of life, I was in a way finally in my own skin. I felt my feet grounded on this earth and connected to it in a new way. I also felt the charge of power from this song, which spoke to me just as loudly as other Hawaiian chants, when I sang it in front of the crowd on the cold stage of the high school in suburban Virginia. The song's lyrics speak about marching to the beat of one's own drum, a pride in who you are, and not being afraid to be seen. I felt it through my bones as our hālau sang it loudly:

I make no apologies
This is me

———

That summer of 2019, Silas and I boarded a flight to Honolulu together, just the two of us. We arrived a few days before the camp started to get adjusted to the time difference, and I enjoyed taking him to all my favorite places around Oʻahu.

I pulled into the strip mall parking lot in the Waikele shopping center and made a beeline for the hot pink–colored food truck parked next to the Old Navy. We were in luck; the truck window was open. It was time for Leonard's malasadas.

"Ooh, Silas, you're going to love this," I told him as we followed our noses to the smell of hot oil, doughnut batter, and sugar.

Malasadas are a gift from the Portuguese immigrants who came to Hawaiʻi in the late 1800s to work in the sugarcane fields. With them, they brought their light, sweet bread baked into round tins that puff up into a half-globe shape when baked. (Today's King's Hawaiian bread rolls are made from that same dough.) Even better, they brought malasadas—a holeless round doughnut—but adapted them to local flavors, rolling them in sugar and cinnamon or li hing and filling them with haupia (coconut cream), dobash (chocolate), or custard. Just like Grandma treated me to these island favorites, I felt giddy now sharing this with my son.

At the truck, Silas and I scanned the simple menu, and when they called our name, I smiled at the familiar pink box the malasadas came in.

"Now, it's hot, so be careful!" I warned Silas, handing him a chocolate-filled one, rolled in a dusting of sugar and only a sheet of waxed paper to hold off the anticipation of the messiness that was about to follow.

Silas closed his eyes as he bit into the hot doughnut, a warm gush of chocolate pudding–like filling squeezing out the side. I did the same, but mine was filled with my favorite, haupia. Hot, sweet, messy. 'Ono.

'Ono is the Hawaiian word for tasty, but the sound of the word "oh-no" conveys more than that—"mouth pleasure" is more accurate.

We ate our doughnuts in silence, sitting in the car in the parking lot, our fingers covered in fine sugar dust, our mouths trying to mop up the filling before it fell on our laps. I looked up and noticed an elderly couple in a car across from us doing the same thing.

A rim of chocolate and sugar encircled Silas's mouth, and his eyes smiled at me. "Thanks, Mom!"

I took Silas to the North Shore, where we sprawled out on some beach mats and towels on the same Haleiwa sand where my grandparents had taken me about eighteen years before. I told him the story of where my grandparents and his great-grandparents met at that very beach for the first time. He nodded at me while I tried to picture Grandpa in his army uniform, walking down the beach with his buddies, and Grandma sitting in the same spot as me, with her girlfriends, playing the 'ukulele.

We hiked up Diamond Head, getting there early to beat the tourist crowds and take in the powerful view of Waikiki beaches all the way down to Pearl Harbor. Another day, we hiked far out to the westernmost tip of the island past Makaha for a breathtaking view of the Pacific Ocean on three sides of the island's peninsula.

I had never been to the Kamehameha Schools campus at Kapālama. But when we pulled into the campus, past the security gate, and up the winding hill, it was truly breathtaking. There were students in blue-and-white uniforms walking the campus's expansive set of walkways and buildings, with the lower part of the hill for elementary students and the upper part for high school students. The athletic facilities included an enormous football stadium with a hilltop view of the ocean as far as one could see. And at a giant outdoor swimming pool, the swim team was busy at practice. I removed Silas's giant duffel bag from the car and started to follow the other kids to the enormous gym, where we checked in. But it wasn't just the campus that impressed me. I realized that I'd never been surrounded by so many Native Hawaiian kids before, and it was exciting to see that this program had drawn kids, all Silas's age, from not only every island but across the US mainland. The kids looked like him. The families looked like us. It was an entire gym full of us, brought together for the same reason—to make sure our kids could have a week immersed in culture with one another. This could only happen here, because of this program. It was, of course, no ordinary summer camp.

I sensed Silas's nervousness, because he grew quiet and was embarrassed every time I asked someone a question about where we were supposed to go or which group he was in. We eventually found our way to the line of boys who would be spending the week together and the camp counselors who would be looking after them. When I checked him in, the young man whom I presumed to be the counselor gave us a warm aloha and greeted Silas with a shaka and a "Hey, man!" and then pointed to the line of kids sitting next to their duffels behind him on the gym floor. I was still asking the counselor questions when Silas snuck by me, made his way to the line, and promptly sat down. I wasn't fully ready to say goodbye yet, and I tried to pull Silas aside to remind him to comb his hair every day and give him a few extra rubber bands to pull his long hair into a ponytail. I wanted to tell the counselor that my son was kind of shy and could he make sure he actually ate something every day? But I did not.

"Mom, you can go," Silas said to me.

"You sure?" I wondered if he'd make friends and like the food and keep his dorm room clean. Now it was my turn to feel the butterflies. I knew that as soon as I left the gym, I wouldn't see him for a week; I'd decided to work from NPR's Culver City, California, office. I'd be half an ocean away.

"Yeah, it's good."

I gave him a big hug. I reminded him that he was going to have an awesome, special time. I wanted him to have fun. I couldn't wait to see him at the end of the week. The sound of my flip-flops hitting the pavement was all I could hear as I walked back to that parking lot. There are a few moments in time when, as a parent, you feel like you just have to let go a little bit to let your kid grow, even if it's totally uncomfortable. As much as I wanted to assure him and ease his anxiety, I also knew that all of this was part of the process for him to learn independence. And I think he knew it, too.

A week later, I drove back to the Kamehameha campus. Now it was time for another hōʻike—this time, it was the students' turn to show us parents what they had learned at the end of their week away from us. I returned to the same large gymnasium, which must easily seat several hundred people, as the hoʻomākaʻikaʻi campers sat in groups on the floor. I noticed that each group held a different musical instrument in their hands. *Wow*, I thought, *this is going to be a bigger production than I imagined.*

I scanned the kids and found Silas sitting at the end of the gym, so I sat on the bleachers just a few rows back from him. He saw me right away, and when our eyes caught, he smiled behind his long hair. "Hi, Mom!" he yelled and waved, with a look of relief in his eyes. Over the next hour, I was totally unprepared for a performance that took my breath away. As soon as the music started, the gym was quiet. And then suddenly, it was filled with children's voices singing in Hawaiian. They raised their instruments above their heads and swayed from right to left. The children picked up small ipus or gourds, slapped them as they chanted in Hawaiian with their sweet young voices, creating a beautiful sound across the room. I noticed that some parents knew the chant and chanted along with them. The chant was so clear, so powerful, that it seemed to cut through the roof, calling to be seen from the heavens. I realized that my child had never had the chance to be together with other Native Hawaiian children before in his life like this. I realized I had never been with other Native Hawaiian families in a setting like this. They sang the mele of Kamehameha Schools:

> *We are the youth of Hawai'i nei*
> *We are the chosen sons and daughters*
> *Who are brought together by rich tradition*
> *[Clap, clap]*
> *That's us!*
> *E nei*
> *Look at us!*

I saw Silas in the crowd, and he was beaming. I could tell that my child had been transformed from this week, without even speaking to him. Later in the program, the announcer thanked all the families who had traveled from far corners to let their children be part of hoʻomākaʻikaʻi, and as they sang a final number, the ʻukulele strummed as they called on the students to stand when they called out where they lived. Dozens of kids stood up when they called out Oʻahu, Maui, and the Big Island; a handful more stood when they called out the smaller islands of Kauai, Molokaʻi, and Lānaʻi. They then called out California, and dozens more kids stood up; followed by Washington State and Oregon, Nevada, Arizona. Just a handful stood up for Colorado and Texas. It was amazing to see the scattered diaspora of Hawaiians across the US who were eager to keep their culture alive. By the time they called the East Coast states, Silas was just one of about ten kids who stood to be recognized as the crowd cheered. Indeed, we had all come a long way to be here. It had been a long journey, in more ways than one.

After the program was over, I brought Silas a special orchid lei and draped it around his neck as we embraced on the gym floor. I couldn't have been prouder of him, and I knew he was proud of himself, too. I snapped some photos of him, and he showed me the ipu he had made himself, as he explained how he and the other kids had climbed a tree to find gourds, scrubbed them clean in the stream, and then cut off the tops to make his musical instrument that he had just played in hōʻike. They then took the top of the gourd and attached strings to it, so it formed a kind of hanging pouch. My normally quiet kid couldn't stop talking all the way home in the car about the experiences he had learning about taro at the loʻi and the long days traveling around the island on the bus. (I also learned he only showered twice the entire week and slept in his clothes because he was too tired at night to change into his pajamas! Oh well.) I felt my mission was accomplished—our son had a memorable experience learning about what it meant to be a Hawaiian that he'd remember for the rest of his life. It was more than

I could teach him myself, and I was so grateful to Kamehameha Schools and the late Princess Pauahi, that she had the wisdom and vision to give the gift of this experience to generations of Hawaiian children like my son.

Thank you, Princess, I thought, *for this gift to generations of Hawai'i's children*. Her kuleana was to the Native Hawaiian children, and it was alive and well.

After Silas's ho'omāka'ika'i camp at Kamehameha, Michael flew out to meet us in Hawai'i with our girls, Chloe and Isa, for a family vacation. We drove to Hāna to visit Uncle Take. Uncle Take was now well into his nineties, and he still remembered us and met us with his easygoing chuckle. He greeted us at the door of his modest home on the main street in town that leads down to Hāna Bay.

"Welcome to heavenly Hāna." He smiled, standing at the front door in his bare feet, shorts, and an old collared shirt. He gave us each a hug and a kiss on the cheek. "Come, come," he said, gesturing us inside. The TV was on, with the volume up too high, probably because Uncle's hearing wasn't so good. So we sat on the couch and talked loudly over it.

"So you play sports? You play football?" he asked Silas, bending his arm like a quarterback.

"No, Uncle, not football but other sports like baseball," I answered. Silas looked at Uncle Take, smiled, and nodded.

We made small talk in the family room, and I shared with Uncle about Silas's time at Kamehameha Schools. I was pretty certain that Uncle Take recognized our family, but at times in our conversation, it seemed as if he was going along. I think he knew we were relatives but perhaps couldn't place us.

"You go down to the heiau?" he asked.

We nodded, and I explained we would drive over later in the day.

"You play sports, like football?" he asked again, gesturing like a quarterback.

"Papa, you already asked that," Auntie Lei chimed in from the kitchen. Both Auntie and Uncle were moving slower than I remembered, but I loved that they still had the same banter. Uncle Take smiled and nodded. I noticed a walker with tennis balls on the bottom in the corner.

We sat in this awkward conversation loop for a bit before deciding it was time to leave. As we said our goodbyes, I looked at my kids' faces and could tell they were concerned by what had just happened. Before we arrived, my auntie Gizelle, Uncle Take's daughter, had told us that he was having problems with his memory, and caring for both of them had become more difficult. I wondered how long Uncle Take and Auntie Lei could live out in Hāna in this house all alone without some kind of help. Uncle Take had stopped driving, so they relied on my cousin Gabe, who worked at the resort in town, to get them to church. Auntie Gizelle drove out from her home on the other side of the island, two hours each way, nearly every weekend, to visit with them and take them to doctors' appointments. Living in Hāna had its benefits, but being so far away from a hospital in this remote town was now a major concern for Uncle Take's family on Maui. Not to mention, it was hard to find a caregiver who could help Auntie and Uncle as they were able to do less on their own.

On that visit, I smiled and looked Uncle Take in the eyes and took a picture in my mind. I remember thinking, *This may be the last time that I see Uncle Take*. It's strange, but I had the same feeling the last time I saw Grandma before she passed away suddenly from a stroke. She was healthy and able-bodied, and we had spent some time together after a holiday. I could hear her nervous giggle in my ear as I hugged her small body that smelled like cocoa butter lotion. I remember taking a step back and looking at her and thinking, *Soak this moment in, Sara. This is the last time you will see her.*

Why did I get that feeling at that particular moment and that intrusive, disturbing thought entered my head? As soon as I felt it, I was annoyed at myself for the negative idea. But both times, it was as if God were intervening in my life and holding up a flag to say, "It's time. This chapter of your life is about to end. This time, it's your kūpuna, Sara, who is turning the page."

———

Eight months after that 2019 trip, the COVID-19 pandemic took hold of our lives, and it effectively shut off Hawai'i from the rest of the world. The islands—with their large elderly population and limited health care system—did not want to take any chances with millions of visitors who came each year and risk that they could bring the deadly disease with them. The state imposed one of the strictest quarantine rules in the country, requiring visitors to test and remain isolated for weeks before being able to mix into the regular population. Hawai'i is especially vulnerable to infectious diseases, and waves of them—cholera, smallpox, measles, leprosy, tuberculosis—wiped out large swaths of the Native Hawaiian population who, like other native people, had no immunity to them. So I understood why it enacted strict measures. For a time, local officials set curfews to discourage people from gathering together, even outdoors at the beach.

As a result, of course, my connection to Hawai'i became more distant. It was impractical to travel back to my beloved Hāna. I worried about Uncle Take and Auntie Lei, especially in the early days when there was no vaccine and because elderly people were especially at risk. And even if I deemed it safe for myself, it wouldn't be logistically possible for the family and me to return for nearly two years.

It was challenging to maintain my Hawai'i connection in other ways. Our hālau canceled its annual spring hō'ike that first year in 2020. Kumu tried to keep classes going on video meetings, but I quickly learned that trying to dance hula on Zoom just didn't work for me. On video, everything was backward. A movement to the right was actually a movement to the left and vice versa. It felt strange to chant at home with the Mute button on. I saw all the squares of names I recognized from hālau, but half of them were blacked out with no camera on. And we couldn't really talk to one another. We were trying to show up, at least I was. But Zoom hula was challenging, to say the least. It was hard to feel the same connection, the same unity while chanting Hawaiian words alone in my empty attic. It felt strange, distant, removed. Everything in COVID felt like that. I gave up and told Kumu that I'd have to take some time off.

I stopped dancing hula. I stopped chanting. I told myself that I'd get back to it later.

12

END OF AN ERA

In 2020, the first year of the global pandemic, I felt the gravitational pull of the news drag me quickly into my Washington journalism world. It was like a tidal wave had swept in, picked me up, and taken me away. I knew it was happening, as it has so many times before, and I let it drop me into the deep world of nonstop news. I had just started a new role at Axios, a digital news start-up that I had joined as executive editor just months before the pandemic set in. My job was overseeing our national news coverage, and we pivoted hard to cover several major news stories at once. First, we journalists were trying to understand what a global pandemic was and get accurate data on how many people were dying, who was dying, and how to help people understand the new lockdown rules that varied from state to state. Then we watched in horror as a Minneapolis teenager's cell phone video captured a Black man, George Floyd, being slowly deprived of air and dying on the street as a police officer knelt on his neck. Crowds across America took to the streets in protest, and it lit a fire under the nation's fragile discussion about race relations and police, and also the history of racism. And then, of course, the presidential election between Donald Trump and Joe Biden was its own hot mess. Between 2020 and 2022, I didn't really sleep, and I didn't really stop working, because the nation's news cycle was a constant inferno. All I remember is that Michael and I bought a Nespresso coffee machine, and we used it so much, day and night, that it broke down after a year. I noticed that my right eye would start to twitch, almost like a freak pulse of its own. When I googled "Why is my eye twitching?" the answer was: too much stress, too much caffeine, not enough sleep. The remedy was: reduce stress, less caffeine, more sleep. *Yeah, right,* I thought. *That won't happen anytime soon.* Physically, emotionally, and mentally, my body was in overdrive with the news fueled by adrenaline and caffeine. It remained in that state for all of 2020.

Our "newsroom" continued to work remotely, although our White House reporters continued to report from the White House and our congressional reporters did the same from the US Capitol, with constant COVID testing and while wearing masks. I set up a makeshift office in our home attic, and sometimes it felt like I lived up there and never came down. My news colleagues and I worked from our homes all day, every day. I started at 6:00 a.m. and didn't stop until 11:00 p.m. Weekdays and weekends blurred together. During this time, Michael's work was no less busy. He was leading a regional public health institute, and suddenly, his organization was tasked with overseeing large-scale COVID response programs in Virginia. His organization went from a few dozen employees to more than five hundred in the span of six months. Our small brick home in Washington, DC, became ground zero for COVID coverage, in more ways than one. Meanwhile, our children were restless, anxious, stuck in video classes that didn't seem to include much learning—although I was grateful that they were at least doing something.

I have to say, I wasn't the best parent during COVID. Chloe, who was nine when the pandemic began, would climb the attic stairs to my office and sit at my feet, bored to tears, while I told her I had "just one more Zoom call" after another. She memorized all the names and faces of my coworkers because she listened in on so many work video calls that I had. I set up an old easel in the attic so that she could draw pictures while I talked on the phone, directing our team on a new investigation or a new podcast we were launching or a new person we were hiring as we doubled the size of our newsroom. "I'm so bored," she would complain often. I didn't have a lot of solutions. She and her brother, Silas, had no one to hang out with but each other. I decided to give them more freedom—for example, by allowing them to ride their bikes a half mile away to the corner store. I'd give them cash and ask them to buy flour or some small item that we needed, and they loved the newfound independence that came with the task. I admit I'd also, when totally engulfed by work calls, give them cash and tell them to go buy lunch or an ice cream at the store, too. They had to learn, in more ways than one, to fend for themselves to a certain extent. The pandemic forced us all to learn to adapt, like it or not.

I learned how to multitask in a new way to juggle work and home responsibilities. I learned how to make lunch or dinner while on a work call, by finding the Camera Off button and the Mute button. I'd work until my Apple earbuds' batteries died, playing a sad "fade to black" tune in my ears. When I wasn't thinking about the news, I was stressed about how I felt I was neglecting my children. In my mind, if I kept working, it meant that I was surviving the pandemic and helping other people survive the pandemic, too. In my strange news brain, this made perfect sense to me at the time and kept my adrenaline running and my entire being focused on making it through to the end of the insane new upside-down world we had just entered.

Isabella was in her second year of college and decided that it made more sense to move in full-time with her mother when the campus shut down. That way, she'd have her own quiet space, free of interruption from little siblings, to attend her own Zoom classes. Her mother lived close by, and we still saw her, but we were also mindful at the beginning that we didn't want her to risk infecting her other household.

I did have time—because we all had too much time at home during those years—to observe and reflect on how Silas and Chloe bonded in a way that I also knew probably wouldn't have happened without the forced isolation together. They became partners in crime and in creativity to pass the time. They started to take long bike rides together through our neighborhood alleys and found secret ways to get through the maze of our city. They built enormous forts all over the house. I let them sleep inside the cardboard apartments in the basement even though it looked like they were sleeping inside coffins. They had slumber parties in each other's rooms. They created a family band, with Chloe on the piano and Silas on the drums, writing songs together, even though Michael and I did not like that Silas moved his drum set into the family room. One rainy weekend, they created small wooden boats with sails made of plastic grocery bags and raced them down the rushing gutters of our street. When the rain stopped, they hiked through

Rock Creek Park and caught minnows in the creek—things they otherwise never would have thought to do. In a way, I saw them thriving while I felt I was just paddling through one big news story at a time, one day at a time. I found myself at the deepest I'd ever been in my Washington news world, and I wasn't sure when I could ever surface.

Hawai'i, for the time being, was very, very far away.

———

The first diseases arrived with the first boats. British captain James Cook is credited by the Western world for "discovering" the Hawaiian Islands, which he named the Sandwich Islands, while on a yearslong quest around the globe to discover a northwest passage that could cut across the North American continent. Cook knew that several men aboard his ships *Discovery* and *Resolution* were infected with venereal disease. In his journals, he worried about his men infecting the local population. And for good reason. A year after his first visit, he and his men returned from Alaska and recorded physical evidence of disease and complaints from Hawaiians. Cook's men had initially visited Kauai and Ni'ihau, and now they saw evidence of the diseases having spread to the island of Maui. One sailor wrote that it was clear they had given "an eternal and everlasting curse" to the Hawaiians, "a set of poor harmless and innocent people."[1]

In addition to the venereal diseases introduced by the men on Captain Cook's ships at the very first encounter with Hawaiians, there were at least three major epidemics that killed thousands of Hawaiians during the early to mid-1800s.[2]

The first was in 1804, which the Hawaiians called *ma'i 'ōku'u*

(mah-ee oh-koo-oo), likely cholera or dysentery. It killed an estimated five thousand to fifteen thousand Hawaiians, and it's unclear
how it arrived and how it spread.

The second was in 1848, likely a combination of diseases—
measles, whooping cough, dysentery, and influenza—hitting the
islands at once to a population with no immunity. It is estimated to
have killed more than one-tenth of the population.

The third was the smallpox epidemic in 1853, what the Hawaiians called *ka wā hepela* (kah vah heh-peh-lah), believed to be
caused by an infected passenger or passengers who arrived on a
ship in Honolulu.

And finally, in addition to the three epidemics, Hawai'i's most
well-known tragedy of leprosy, or Hansen's disease, became a crisis by 1865, although Hawaiians had been infected and disfigured
by the disease for several decades prior. The Hawaiians called it
ma'i ho'oka'awale (mah-ee ho-oh-kah-ah-vah-leh), or the separating
sickness. The outbreak of leprosy led to dramatic isolation measures during which infected people were sent to a penal colony on
a small peninsula called Kalaupapa on Moloka'i. More than eight
thousand people died there, living in permanent exile from the rest
of the world.[3]

In 1867, Hawaiian historian Samuel Kamakau wrote about the
waves of disease and death that afflicted the Hawaiian people and
his theory as to why. He observed that the foreigners had brought
a bloodless but devastating coup with them to the islands: "The
reason that this misfortune and demise has befallen the Hawaiian
people is clear: the foreigners are nation killers. The love of glory
and wealth are the companions of deadly illness. Submission to
other races makes hospitable offices for contagions and cancers,
and these have spread desolation upon this people, bringing on fear

and terror and making the whole race shudder and tremble from the impact of fatal illnesses, epidemics, contagions, and cancers that cannot be cured by native healers."[4]

After experiencing one deadly disease after another—to which foreigners were immune but from which only Native Hawaiians died, I'm sure the Hawaiians could only ask: *Why us?*

Imagine, thousands of people like you, who look like you and were born of native blood, dying in epidemic after epidemic. The Hawaiians quickly went from being the majority in their own lands to a minority. All the while, foreign missionaries—who were not dying—preached that their wicked, backward ways needed saving. At the same time, the diseases decimated the population as many Hawaiians lost their connections to land under the Mahele. And this pattern of disease and mass dying continued for more than a *century*.

I thought a lot about this during the early months of the global pandemic. As the death toll in the United States reached one hundred thousand after a few short months,[5] I was finally able to wrap my head around what that amount of death really does not only to those affected but to the nation and world of survivors.

The death toll from the coronavirus reminded us of our physical bodies' limited ability to fight a new disease. But there's another casualty that we often don't talk about and maybe are only now beginning to understand: How does so much dying and fear of an uncontrolled, unseen epidemic damage our collective psyche?

I remember very clearly the time before vaccines were available when I would put on a mask before leaving the house. Neighbors, with smiles under their masks, would swerve out of their way to maintain a respectful distance. The few stores that were open had "distance drop-off," where nervous employees dropped plastic bags full of items after opening the door slightly, skimming every second possible from our interaction.

For a time, we were a nation, a world that felt unprotected and afraid.

This is something native people know more than most.

With modern technology, data, and scientific modeling, the pandemic taught us how infectious diseases spread so that we could try to reduce our chances of getting sick and getting others sick. Although not always perfect or easy to follow, there were many sources of government and public health data to help people understand the disease and what it did to our bodies, as well as the risks. Not all of that turned out to be 100 percent accurate. But with data, we could measure the spread of diseases on curves in charts. We understood risk based on demographics of age, health, and behavior. We took steps to shield higher-risk elderly people. And we understood that children were largely spared.

But now imagine life in the 1800s or early 1900s, without any of that information. Without data, vaccines, or immunity, you could only look around and make your own conclusions about what was killing your family members, your neighbors. You would be left to draw only your own conclusions about why some were dying and some remained healthy.

There were many Hawaiian newspaper accounts from the 1800s that remarked on the dramatic rate that the kanaka maoli were dying and infant mortality was rising while white foreigners remained healthy and strong.

In the 1800s, Westerners were constantly predicting when the entire Hawaiian race would be gone from the planet. Indeed, just 20,000 Native Hawaiians were left by 1920. By most recent data analysis estimates, the Hawaiian population was around 680,000

when Captain Cook first arrived to document the Hawaiian people's existence to the outside world. Only 7 percent of the Hawaiian
population remained within one hundred years of foreigners arriv-
ing to the islands.[6]

My great-grandmother was part of that 7 percent. All the Native
Hawaiians today are part of that tiny surviving group. I began to
understand the miracle not only of the land that survived to this day
in our family, passed down from generation to generation, but that
the feat of survival of the Hawaiian people—my father's side—was
part of the same story of indigenous people around the world just
struggling to exist.

As I learned about the decimation of the Native Hawaiian
people, I also understood the COVID pandemic differently. I
understood that one branch of my family tree had survived the
equivalent of many pandemics, against many odds, generation after
generation. The people of Hawaiian bloodline I'd come from had
somehow survived to this day. The land we had been granted had
somehow survived to this day, too. Now that I understood, I wanted
to pay tribute to that history of survival.

———

My family had successfully built a farm on our Hāna land in an
effort to save it. Now we needed to start some real discussion about
what we'd do with it if we could hold on to it.

Even if the county granted us agricultural status, it would only apply to the ten acres of Grandma's land that Dad and the farm brigade
had cleared. To bring the taxes down to the original $200-per-year
amount, we'd also need a much larger investment in time and money
to clear more land and plant more crops. The idea of doing that
seemed daunting, maybe impossible. But we also knew that the farm

plan was just a Band-Aid, anyway. As a family and multigenerational branch of the Kahanu family, we needed a long-term plan: What was the vision for the Hāna land? Did we want to build a house there? Should we leave it undeveloped as long as possible? Should we build something more temporary, like an Airstream trailer or a yurt as a first step before building a permanent home? Should we invest in bringing utilities such as water and electricity to the property?

It was time for Gen 2 to weigh in. My cousins and I aren't very close—mostly because I'm the oldest of them by many years. But most of us remember the days when we all lived in Southern California and would get together for every holiday with Grandma and Grandpa, eating our traditional Hawaiian food in a house that smelled of sweet teriyaki. Grandpa would make the teriyaki beef and spareribs, starting the night before with a shoyu marinade. Grandma would make the mac salad and potato salad and her famous Chinese chicken salad. And there was always dessert—lots of pie—custard pie, cheesecake, blueberry cheesecake that Grandma made. Plus one of my aunties would stop at King's Bakery—the company that makes those famous Hawaiian sweet rolls has a restaurant and bakery in Los Angeles—and pick up a cake with lilikoi (passion fruit) icing. Because Dad has seven siblings, our gatherings were large, often loud, and each holiday celebration lasted for days, not hours.

Our Spanish-style house in San Juan Capistrano, California, was often the gathering spot for our extended family because Dad loved hosting his siblings and having family over for days and days. And that's when we had lots of cousin time: Samantha and Jonathan from Auntie Maureen and Uncle Tim; Stevie and Jordan from Uncle Darrell and Auntie Linda; Shannon, Marie, Vincent, and Anna from Uncle Duane and Auntie Jackie. Because Dad grew up as the third-born child among eight siblings, they formed a tight unit who hung out a lot and were one another's closest friends. Most of my cousins are about seven or eight years younger than me, and as everyone grew up and went off to college, we fanned out from our Southern California roots across the country—to Massachusetts, Georgia, DC, and elsewhere.

During the pandemic, Dad and Auntie Maureen organized the Gen 2 group calls to, for the first time, talk about the land that we all had a stake in. On our first few calls, Dad focused on explaining the tax situation to the cousins and his ideas for solutions. Quickly, it became clear that among my cousins, there were varying degrees of understanding about the family land and its history. Everyone knew about Grandma's land, but how the Kahanu family got the land from King Kamehameha was not universally understood. Because I had been doing a lot of research, I ended up "talking story" about what I had learned from Uncle Take and from researching the larger context of how Native Hawaiians received or lost their land in the Mahele. I was both delighted and surprised at how my cousins reacted to what I had to share. They thanked me. They asked for more. They wanted to know if they could have copies of what documents I had. They wanted me to organize more calls to share what I knew.

My younger cousins, whom I remember as toddlers and elementary-age kids, were now adults inquiring about the history of the land. One cousin, who lived in California, enthusiastically proposed we could build a tiny house on the property. My brother, who lived in Virginia, proposed building a larger farm of koa and sandalwood trees, to bring back native trees known for prized hardwood. Another cousin in Massachusetts shared photos of how you could convert a shipping container into a small studio apartment with a tiny kitchen. Auntie Maureen researched the cost of bringing electricity to the property: the electric company said we'd need to pay for them to install utility poles to reach our land. It would cost $5,000 per electric pole and we'd need at least five. Yikes. That would be $25,000 before we even put a shovel in the ground. We'd need a plan for water, too.

We had no shortage of ideas. But we did have a shortage of money.

We agreed to start a joint fund for whatever came of our ideas. Auntie Maureen set up a bank account, and we agreed to contribute a small amount of money each month or each year toward a Hāna land fund. Hopefully, this fund would over time replenish our family trust that our grandparents had created before they died to take care of taxes and maintenance, which was quickly dwindling because of the tax hike. What was $20,000 in the fund was now about $15,000 because we had paid the first year's higher taxes and then paid for renting the equipment that Uncle Keith brought over at his own expense and time to help us clear the land. If the county didn't approve our lower tax status, we'd be losing more than $2,000 a year from the account. So at the very least, we needed to raise more funds just to pay the tax bill. Dreaming of bigger ideas, such as the "luxury" amenities of electricity and water, would require not only a lot more capital but a plan for how we, collectively as a family, would assign financial responsibility for it. Ironically, we learned that building a home on the property would lower our tax rate, but of course it would be a lot more expensive and complicated to build the house itself. What we didn't address were the even trickier questions, such as: How would we divide financial ownership and

interest, and perhaps just as importantly, responsibility for maintenance when none of us lived on Maui or would anytime soon?

We began to talk through different scenarios beyond just building a structure. The additional costs of building a house on Maui
would incentivize us to generate some revenue from the property
by renting it out, for example, to pay for maintenance. But Hawai'i
was cracking down on short-term rentals, such as Airbnb, and a new
law backed by the hotel lobbyists and hotel union workers made it
harder to get approval for homeowners to rent out their properties.
Even if we were to pursue that path to build a home and rent it
out occasionally, with it would come additional responsibility and
headache. Anyone who owns a home knows that houses require
constant maintenance both on the inside and outside. We'd have
to find someone in Hāna to manage the property and take care of
the land, which wants to return to its natural state as a rainforest
every time you cut down a branch. In my dream world, I would
want to build a small home that each of us cousins could use to take
our families to stay and visit Hāna. A small house would provide
an incentive to go maybe even more frequently to the place of our
grandma's birth and nearby proximity to the heiau.

Without a physical place to stay and visit, it's harder to maintain
the appreciation of the land and our family's history in Hāna as the
generations pass. But as we tried to come up with a plan, it seemed
we were boxed in by bureaucratic rules on both ends: we either
had to run through hoops to keep the taxes lower on undeveloped
land, or spend hundreds of thousands of dollars to build a house
and deal with the challenges of trying to make any income from
our own property. The logistics of how it would work is where we
eventually got stuck.

My Maui cousin Mark has an expression for stupid rules that only seem to benefit the powerful, no matter how large or petty, whether it's some government fee or a rich person's fence. "Dem damn Pilgrim rules," he says. In this case, he was damn right.

I was encouraged that my cousins were motivated to find a solution. My younger cousins, many of whom were just starting to work in their first postcollege jobs, wanted to fork over a small part of their hard-earned paycheck to help the cause. I learned that several of my cousins who grew up in Massachusetts hadn't even been to Hawai'i before, and now, when the pandemic was over, they had plans to finally book that trip and visit our ancestral lands. My cousin Vincent, who was studying at the University of Massachusetts, signed up for a program to study for a semester at the University of Hawai'i to spend more time there. My brother and my cousins Stevie and Samantha started organizing a family reunion.

I found myself answering their many questions about the land and even about Grandma. What was she like? What did she say about what she wanted to do with the land? I had forgotten that, as the oldest grandchild, I had spent more time with our grandmother than any of the other grandchildren and probably knew her best. Some of my cousins were very young when she died, so their memories were smaller, faded, or only existed in the stories that other members of our family told. It felt like a privilege to answer their questions and share my experience. I felt them hanging on my words, forming pictures in their minds. We shared these grandparents, which was special. But we now also shared this story and this land. Could we band together and find a solution we could all get behind?

After we hung up from these extended-family meeting calls, I felt an optimistic warmth inside, knowing that my aunties, uncles, and cousins wanted to understand our family story, to embrace the kuleana that was part of their heritage, and wanted to take the torch. With each generation, our family had become more spread out. And distance requires more effort, more intentional learning and connection. One by one, my siblings, my cousins, my parents, my uncles and aunties nodded. *Yes.* It was like we were all putting a hand in the circle, one on top of the next for team Kahanu.

We were all in.

13

ALOHA ʻOE

I never thought that my next trip back to Maui would be to attend Uncle Take's funeral. He and Auntie Lei, now in their nineties, survived the pandemic. But in 2022, my mom called with the news that Uncle Take's mind and body had deteriorated. By then, Uncle Take's children had moved him and Auntie Lei out of Hāna to Wailuku, a town on Maui near the airport, where they could get regular, professional health care and help from their grown children and grandchildren. In the end, Uncle Take suffered from dementia, and he died on January 19, 2022, at ninety-six years old. On the island of Maui, the limited funeral services were overwhelmed, even as the pandemic eased. There was only one hearse on the entire island that would make the trek from the funeral home near the airport all the way down the Hāna Highway to Uncle Take's final resting place. So we had to wait more than a month to schedule Uncle's funeral.

Bad news continued to spiral down from there. About two weeks after Uncle Take died, we heard back from Maui County about our application for the tax relief. We all had been hopeful that the newly created ʻāina kūpuna law that was designed to help people hold on to ancestral or family lands would provide us a Hail Mary just when we needed it. But perhaps in reading about the law and all the enthusiasm to get our family members to apply, it was too good to be true.

Auntie Maureen, who was working with Dad to get our application together and submit it, sent us an email with the rejection letter on February 1. The form letter typed on government letterhead delivered a gut punch. Addressed to the Goo Family Trust, it read: "Your application was denied for the following reason(s)." The fourth line down had an X next to the statement: "The aggregate real property taxes assessed on the property for the 10 years prior to the initial application does not exceed $50,000." Auntie Maureen had sent an email sharing the rejection letter to me, my dad, and my uncle Duane. We learned that Auntie Bobbie, whose property is next to ours, also received the same letter. Essentially, the county determined that we hadn't paid enough in taxes to qualify to pay lower taxes. Why did the government always seem to apply this kind of cruel logic? It was a big strikeout.

Dad relayed the bad news in an email to all of us. "Sorry to say our ʻĀina Kūpuna Exemption application was rejected. So on to further Home and Ag development of Hāna property strategy." In other words, our Hail Mary plan B failed. So it was back to plan A: we'd continue to hope that our agriculture exemption would be approved after Dad sent in all those photos of our new farm.

Maui County Council member Keani Rawlins-Fernandez had told me how she wasn't sure exactly how many families would get relief nor how much it'd cost. This was the first year that the bill would be implemented, so they'd have to wait and see how many property owners applied. So perhaps a lot of people applied and we just didn't make the cut? I reasoned that many other families had higher tax bills than we did, so perhaps this was a fair verdict. But who knew? It was a new program, and dealing with the government was unpredictable but usually lousy for the little guy. Was I a fool for thinking—and hoping and praying—that this new bill that passed would give Hawaiians like us with generational property a break from the taxman? It kind of seemed like it.

But I put that aside for now.

Mom and Dad said they were unable to make Uncle Take's funeral. But Auntie Maureen told me that she and my cousin Samantha, who lived in Atlanta, would be attending. I decided that I needed to be there, even if I had to go alone; it would be too difficult to pull all the kids out of school at the beginning of the year and make the twelve-hour flight. And besides, it would be too expensive. Together, the three of us would represent our branch of the family to pay tribute to Uncle Take. I arranged to get to Maui a few days before the funeral.

The day I arrived, I settled into the apartment I had rented, and it felt so strange to travel to Maui alone, without my kids, without any purpose but to say goodbye. As soon as I'd heard the news about Uncle Take, I knew that I wanted to honor a man who had served as my surrogate grandfather, my teacher of all the things about our Hawaiian land and the heiau. And I was trying to also process what might be in store for our family's land now that our latest hope for tax relief had been rejected. Jet-lagged and foggy-headed, I walked to a nearby beach cove in Pa'ia and sat down on the cool sand, not yet heated by the bright morning sun.

It felt like the end of an era, because it was. Uncle Take had always been a fixture for me in Hāna. To me, he *was* Hāna. It seemed like just yesterday he was driving me around town in his pickup truck, his arm out the window and people on the street yelling out to him, "Heyyy, Uncle!" He'd smile and give the shaka sign or sometimes just stop in the middle of the road to chat and introduce me. I felt like I was driving around with the mayor. Everyone knew him. Everyone knew his advocacy for Hawaiian lands and the restoration of the heiau that had once been part of our family lands. I could still hear his baritone voice, his words, his admonition, his worries in my head about what would happen to the land after he passed away.

"It is our kuleana," he had said.

Sitting on my towel, I marveled at the incredible scene on display in front of me. A few surfers were trying their luck to catch a wave just past the reef. The sky was perfectly blue, with a gentle breeze. The ocean waves rolled in with a beautiful blue-green color that I could see through when the waves crested. And suddenly, as if the scene weren't perfect enough, a rainbow appeared just above the ocean down from the sky; a straight, brightly colored beam shot into the sea just in front of me. I looked out at the sand where the waves lapped onto the shore, and I noticed that a large black lump, just a stone's throw away, was moving. A Hawaiian sea turtle, called a *honu*, wiggled its flippers as it awoke from a beach nap. The scene was too perfect, like a movie, designed just for me and for this moment. It was as if Uncle Take were waving to me from heaven— *Aloha! I'm here, I see you. Mahalo for coming all this way.* In Hawaiian culture, the honu, which lives to be eighty years old, is a symbol of resilience, wisdom, and peace. They are also a sign of luck. Even though I feel lucky enough to spy a honu every time I'm in Hawai'i, it still thrills me each time to see these beautiful creatures. I'm normally too skeptical of everything to believe in divine signs from God, but this was an exception. I felt like I was crawling out of my COVID cave back on the East Coast and finally had a chance to breathe and feel alive again—to connect with Hawai'i again. It felt fitting, like I'd come full circle, to find myself here on Maui to have a moment alone with Uncle Take. As much as it felt surreal to sit here on the beach in the middle of winter, on this quiet morning with this sea turtle, it also felt right to be here. To spend some time reflecting on a man who had done so much for our family, our history, and our people.

The next morning was the funeral. One more trip down the road to Hāna. This time, Auntie Maureen, cousin Samantha, and I began the two-hour drive under a torrent of rain. Before dawn, we filled our coffee mugs, brought along banana bread and snacks for the road, and set out on the curviest road in America. Uncle Take died in Wailuku, but he would be buried in his beloved Hāna. This time, the road was wet, and the darkness hid the normally beautiful vistas of the ocean. I insisted on driving, knowing my own proneness for car sickness, and couldn't help but revisit in my mind how different my journey today was from all the other times I'd been down this road. Instead of breathtaking vistas of waterfalls and green mountain cliffs, this time, all I could see was the curve in the road ahead of me. The steady drizzle of rain kept my windshield wipers busy, and the tall, rustling bamboo that lined the cliffs in the darkness blocked any view. This trip wasn't about appreciating the views, anyway. This was about our determination to show up for Uncle Take.

I drove cautiously and purposefully and tried not to worry too much about possible cliff landslides or the steep drops that separated our car from the inky ocean below. I focused on my hands gripping the wheel, navigating the narrow strip of road as far out as my headlights could show me. Curve after curve after curve, we would get there. This trip was not for stopping or lingering; there were no tourists in rental cars to navigate around this time, either. My auntie and cousin distracted me and caught me up on their lives in California and Atlanta. Auntie Maureen was now an empty nester back home in Santa Barbara, and was trying to relax into retirement. Cousin Samantha was working her first job out of college, a grisly assignment as a forensic expert in a police department. And I was trying to find my way out of seclusion from my Washington news world, clearing the cobwebs of COVID and the panic of the January 6 insurrection, and eager to awaken my soul by being back in Hawai'i for the first time in years. I'd found myself in the deep end of news coverage again. This time, it was a traumatically stressful period of a pandemic, civil unrest, and political violence. We rounded one curve after another in the rain, navigating dozens of single-lane bridges with ease. I could make out the rushing water streams falling down the cliff on my right side as we drove past. I felt like a worm moving from one world to another through this dark maze of a road, only I knew the way and pointed my rental car with a purpose to get us there. Somehow, I always found my way back to Hāna just when I needed it.

By the time the road started to stretch out into straighter lines and fewer curves, the sun had begun to come up. Almost like clockwork, the rain stopped when we pulled into Hāna town and into the driveway of Saint Mary's Church. The sky grew bright and cloudless, as if to announce the glory of this day with great fanfare. Of course it would be a beautiful Hāna morning for Uncle Take. We pulled up to the simple white Catholic church on the hill that

I knew all too well. Saint Mary's was where Uncle Take attended services dutifully nearly every day his entire life; where a young Uncle Take married Auntie Lei; and now where Uncle Take would be remembered in a final Mass.

Saint Mary's sits facing the ocean, with a beautiful view of Hāna Bay, the Pacific spread out to the horizon like a panoramic photo. I walked to the front of the church and took in the view of the shining water in the distance. The morning sun painted the sky a bright orange and white, and the air smelled like it was freshly washed from the rain, a blessing on a new day after the long, dark drive. A giant banner out in front of the church had a picture of Uncle Take wearing a white flower lei, giving the shaka sign—a perfect image of him. It read "Edwin Take Umesaboro Matsuda, July 29, 1925–January 19, 2022." We met up with our aunties and uncles and cousins who had driven in from across Maui and flown in from Oʻahu and Las Vegas. The crowd greeted one another with kisses, hugs, and alohas, and it looked like the entire town of Hāna was there. Then I saw my cousins and uncles, the pallbearers, wearing white gloves, carry Uncle's casket from the white hearse into the church. We followed them in and took our seats in the wooden pews. True to form, each person in the church was handed a square slice of Auntie Lei's shortbread wrapped in cellophane with Uncle Take's picture on it. I'm sure he wouldn't have it any other way. The church quickly filled up to standing room only, a sign not only of Uncle Take's family in attendance but really the entire town who had come to pay their respects to a man who had served in many capacities as a kind of unofficial mayor.

As I sat in the pew, I thought of the last time I was in this church, when Uncle Take took me to light a candle for Grandma.

We prayed for her, and as I remembered that moment, I closed my eyes and drowned out the funeral service to say my own quiet prayer. I prayed that Uncle Take knew how much he had helped to guide me to understand who I was and where I came from. I prayed to thank him and thank God for the example he laid for me and his entire 'ohana. I prayed that I could live up to his and Grandma's expectations to do the same over the course of my life. I opened my eyes and hoped my prayers would land somewhere and mean something.

After the service, we got back in our rental car and followed the hearse down the Hāna Highway. I had heard Auntie Gizelle mention something about a small detour we might have time to make on the way to the burial site. Sure enough, the hearse turned right off the road toward the Kahanu Garden and the Pi'ilanihale heiau. The long string of cars followed the hearse across a shallow stream and onto the grass to the base of the majestic heiau—the ancient site that Uncle Take and his brothers and sisters had fought so hard to get restored to its original grandeur. It was a fitting moment as we rolled down our windows to let Uncle Take pay his respects one final time. Or was it the other way around—so the ancient heiau could pay respects to its caretaker, Uncle Take? My uncles, cousins, and aunties and local townspeople—in their pickup trucks and SUVs and I in my rental car—rolled down the windows, and we honked our horns. We formed a circle of cars at the base of the ancient place of our people. "Love you, Uncle!" We raised our arms out the car windows with the shaka sign and smiled. I got the "chicken skin" as I took in the scene—a final goodbye beneath the shadow of the ancient place of our ancestors. Now, Uncle Take had joined them. The scene was unforgettable: a white hearse trailed by a circle of cars beneath the towering rock structure built centuries ago. A final goodbye. The circle he left behind, I hoped, were all of us following him who would pick up the torch in his absence.

"He took me in after my grandma died," I told Auntie Gizelle and my cousins Brande and Gabe at the grave site later. "He helped me understand the heiau and the land in ways Grandma could not do. He was like a grandfather to me and taught me about kuleana."

They each nodded to me with wet eyes. I hugged each of them and felt the grief of their bodies sigh with me in the moment. We took a deep breath as we embraced a moment of simultaneous sadness and aloha. The word *aloha* means "hello," "love," and "goodbye," but it also literally means "an exchange of breath."

The rest of that day was a fitting tribute to Uncle Take. His final resting place is at Wai'ānapanapa State Park, today known as a beautiful black-sand beach tourist stop that is also sacred ground for Native Hawaiians. We celebrated his life with an incredible feast of Hawaiian food—kalua pork, lau lau, lomi salmon, the works—at Hāna Bay, which was a short walk down the street from his house. In my memory now, the day was a tour of all of Uncle Take's favorite places—his church, the heiau, the park, Hāna Bay, with family and great food. He would have loved it.

But most of all, I remember getting on the plane back from Hawai'i thinking that our family would never be the same, much as it was never the same after my grandma died. In 2022, it was not just Uncle Take who died but also his only surviving sibling—Auntie Dolly died several months later. There was now no one left from that generation who had received the ancestral land from their mother, my great-grandmother, Martha Kekauililani Kahanu Matsuda. All that was left was the next generation of their children—Dad, Auntie Gizelle—who are now retired or reaching retirement age themselves. It was hard to imagine not only Hāna but Hawai'i without Uncle Take. Uncle Take was our fixture, our rock, who lived in Hāna his entire life. We still had a few other relatives who live in Hāna, but Hāna was not the same without Uncle Take and Auntie Lei. It felt like a chapter was ending in our family—the torch was being passed. As we processed our grief, we all knew this was our new reality. It was now clear how much responsibility Uncle had taken on for all these years. It was, like Grandma had said, now up to us.

———

Working the room inside the church at Uncle Take's funeral was an unmistakable visitor: Chipper. As I sat in the pews, I saw him walk in with his wife, Hau'oli, as they hugged our family members one by one. Despite the family's ups and downs with the Garden and Chipper over the years, it felt pono and appropriate for him to be there. After all, he and Uncle Take had worked for years together to get the heiau restored. And now Chipper had shown up for a rare chance to see as many family members as possible—and to remind them of our unfinished business.

A couple of months after Uncle Take's funeral, Chipper and Dad arranged for a video call with our entire extended family to meet the new director of the Kahanu Garden, a young haole man named Mike Opgenorth. With the funeral fresh in our minds, our family's unfinished business was now clear to everyone. I was impressed with how many relatives—many of whom hadn't met one another—showed up. By this time, Dad and Auntie Maureen had already accomplished a big task—they had gotten in touch with every branch of the original mo'opuna, the grandchildren, who originally received land from their grandfather back in the 1960s. My great-grandma Mileka was just one of these grandchildren, so we had to find contact information for children or grandchildren of my great-grandma's brothers and sisters. Using old family records, my mom's sleuthing on Ancestry.com, old paperwork from Dad and Chipper, and the coconut wireless, we finally assembled a list of relatives. The good news was that we managed to track down someone from each of the family branches who was interested in joining the heiau conversation. Our first Zoom call included about thirty faces—like a mini family reunion—for the first time, many of us were learning who was who. Each person introduced themselves and shared, often with tears, why they were interested to "talk story" about the heiau again.

Mike explained that the state of Hawai'i had reached out to the Garden because they had identified some iwi (ee-vee)—or bones—that belonged to the ahupua'a of Honomā'ele and would like to return them to this place. The state agency wanted to know: Could the Garden recommend what to do with the iwi?

"This is the kind of thing," Mike explained, "that the Garden would like to work with the family on. We'd like to have a family representative—a kahu—to provide input to the Garden" in a formal way. But it would be easier if we had some kind of formal relationship established. All the more reason, Chipper and Mike said, for us all to finish what our kūpuna did not finish.

"I always knew it would be the next generation to resolve this, and I'm hopeful that we can get it done," Chipper said.

The representatives were from each of the heirs and their families. On the call, I saw Uncle Terry, the one who had sold his land and was living in Papakōlea; and Brande, my cousin and Uncle Take's granddaughter living in Honolulu; and Auntie Sann, Auntie Dolly's eldest daughter, living in Las Vegas; Auntie Bobbie and my cousin Joni on Oʻahu. And I met new relatives—Auntie Echo and Auntie Maude—granddaughters of Uncle Henry, my great-grandmother's brother, and cousin Kealiʻi—Uncle Sonny's son. Just seeing Kahanu names and faces on the call was exciting because I knew it wouldn't be possible without the video technology and a shared desire to support the heiau that brought us together.

Everyone understood that it was in our interest to regroup as a family to finish the document that would codify the relationship between the Kahanu family and the Garden that bore our family name. Our kūpuna were buried there. Our kūpuna worked for generations to take care of the heiau and ensure that it would be restored. We were currently operating without an agreement that spelled out our relationship to a garden with our ancestor's name on it. We were operating on a handshake, but could we do what Chipper said—what our kūpuna couldn't do themselves?

At that first meeting, as each family member introduced themselves, there were a lot of tears as, one by one, each relative shared how they wanted to represent their kūpuna by connecting again with the Garden and the heiau. Each brought their own memories, and I realized each of their parents and grandparents had told them the same stories about protecting the heiau and the land that I had heard, too, from Grandma. They had shown up because of a sense of duty. More than one person on the call broke down in tears over the memories of loved ones now passed away but also the memory of their kuleana to our shared place.

But sadly, the story here is not a happy one, nor is it resolved. Some of our subsequent meetings devolved into arguments and tears, as years of distrust within the family resurfaced from our kūpuna who did not get along. At one point, Dad organized a group of family representatives from each branch to finally sign an old agreement that their parents or grandparents had drafted with the Garden. But the Garden didn't accept it, because not all members of each branch of the family had signed off. It's possible the Kahanu family will eventually reach an agreement with the Garden, but the complicated web of feelings and relationships across our family and distrust has made that difficult for now.

———

Around the time of Uncle Take's funeral in 2022, the world began to emerge from our pandemic hibernation. Back in DC, I was relieved—for their sake and mine—that our kids would be back in their classrooms with teachers and friends. Isabella returned to her college campus in Atlanta, moving in to share an apartment with a friend. In the spring, Chloe would finish her final year of elementary school, and Silas would finish his final year of middle school. Both of them were looking forward to their promotion ceremonies, which would be held outdoors this year.

As a surprise gift to make their ceremonies a little more special, I decided to make fresh-flower lei for Chloe and Silas to wear at their commencements. I found a floral warehouse and ordered dozens of purple orchids and bought a special lei-making needle and thread, getting out a towel and trying to remember the way Grandma taught me to make the lei. Once the kids were asleep, I got all my supplies out and began the delicate process of removing each flower from the stem, then threading the long needle through the middle of the stem. Once the flowers stacked up in a row long enough to make the lei, I tied the string together, wrapped them in a moist paper towel, then a plastic bag, like Grandma taught me, and put them in the fridge to stay fresh. I remembered how years ago we sat at her kitchen table in Nānākuli and I strung a carnation lei for Michael, who was coming to visit and meet my grandparents for the first time. I looked at the kitchen stove clock when I was done: 1:00 a.m.

The next morning was Chloe's promotion ceremony day. But when I presented the lei to her over breakfast, her reaction shocked me.

"Mom, really, do I have to?" Chloe asked. Her face looked pained, like I was trying to make her eat something she really didn't want to. "No one else will be wearing one."

It felt like a stab in the heart.

"Chloe, a lei is a sign of love. It's a sign of your Hawaiian-ness," I explained, trying to keep my voice unemotional, covering the deep wound in my chest. "It's an honor. It's a tradition. You should be proud, not embarrassed."

As I said those words, I tried to think quickly about how to react. I debated the best parenting tactic: I could try to convince her of the meaningfulness of wearing a lei on an occasion like graduation, although I didn't feel this was going to work; or I could decide to *make* her wear it and tell her she didn't have a choice, which felt kind of against the spirit of aloha. Or a third tactic could be to give her the guilt trip and tell her how much it would hurt my feelings if she didn't wear it. Out of desperation, I ended up doing some combination of pleading and guilt-tripping.

Her brother's attitude was no different. I explained to him how I was making one for him, too, to wear in his promotion ceremony the following week.

"Mom, you shouldn't go to all that trouble," he said. He exchanged a knowing look with his sister.

"No one else will be wearing one," Chloe repeated. She did not want to stand out. "Do I have to?"

Ugh. I tried to suppress my feelings of utter failure inside.

Where had I gone so wrong? It never occurred to me that anyone would not want to wear a lei—let alone my children. What had
happened to the little girl who was dancing hula on the stage right
before COVID hit? What happened to "E huli"—that mother-son
hula I danced with Silas? Perhaps two years of not going to hālau
had messed up that cultural connection for them both. I blamed
COVID for lots of things, including the end of the Easter bunny.
But now, had COVID killed this part of their identity?

"Yes, and that's what is so special about it," I told her. "Please, for
me, it's important that you wear it. I made it just for you. You don't
have to wear it the whole day, just during the ceremony."

"Okay," she said with a deep sigh. She looked resigned, like
she was making a big sacrifice because she didn't want to hurt my
feelings. "Fine."

This reluctant agreement made me feel only slightly better. And
yet I somewhat empathized. As much as I wanted her to be excited,
appreciative of the lei I had made for her, I also understood that she
was at an age where it's normal to feel hypersensitive and anxious,
even, about what your peers think of you. Conformity with the group
often means acceptance. I understand not wanting to stand out. I remember how, when I was in sixth grade in Southern California, our
class similarly had a celebration for us when we finished elementary
school. The parents had put together a luau-style party for us at
the harbor, and everyone was encouraged to wear Hawaiian-style
clothes. Around that time, my mom was excited because Grandma
had recently found a bunch of hula costumes that my aunties used
to wear when they traveled around performing in the area. I loved
looking through these costumes, which included brightly colored
sarongs, flower-print muumuus, and even grass skirts with bikini
tops lined with fake flowers. I remember how excited I was to try

on the costumes, and I decided to wear an "authentic" grass skirt to the luau party. Because I had three aunties, we had three costumes each. I let one of my friends borrow another one of the grass skirt costumes, and we attended the luau together and even put flowers in our hair. Although I was a little self-conscious to wear a bikini top and grass skirt to the party (and, I remember, a little cold), I felt proud that we were the only ones who wore "the real thing." Plus, my girlfriend declared it was cool.

When I dug up that old memory, I was probably the exact age that Chloe was now. Maybe it was an East Coast thing where Chloe had no frame of reference for wearing a lei in a graduation ceremony. In Southern California, where I grew up, everything related to Hawai'i *was* cool, and it was and still is very common to see kids wearing flower lei at ceremonies—even around the shoulders of people who had no connection to Hawai'i. But on the East Coast, I suppose this was not something Chloe imagined for herself on her big day.

On the morning of her promotion ceremony, she took the plastic bag with the lei inside it to school, and I warned her to be careful with it so as not to squash the delicate petals. In the afternoon, Michael and I arrived at the grassy field outside the elementary school, where rows of chairs had been set up and a small stage where the "graduates" would get to shake the principal's hand when their name was called.

It felt just like yesterday when I pushed the kids around in strollers around this same field, lugging bottles, diapers, and a giant bag of snacks. It didn't seem long ago when I'd dreamed of the day when they would get to attend elementary school here. It seemed like months, not years, since I'd taught Silas, and then Chloe, how to ride a bike without training wheels on the cement that encircled the field. Now, Michael and I were saying goodbye to this chapter. Chloe was our youngest, and after this day, we'd no longer have any kids at the elementary school. It was all "big kid" parenting from here on out, and soon, the dreaded "teen parenting" would follow. The pandemic had blurred the previous two years, so it was surreal how time had seemed to both slow down and speed up to get us to this moment, standing in the bright sun on the grass with all the other smiling parents. At least COVID didn't ruin this moment for our kids. At least they got to finish the school year in the classroom, with one another, experiencing a ceremony like this.

I saw the kids from Chloe's grade begin to walk out from the school building, single file toward the field. *Here goes nothing*, I thought. *Please, please, be wearing the lei.*

I saw some kids in her class whom I recognized, so I scanned the line to find her. That day, she was excited to wear a new jade-colored jumpsuit that I bought her, as well as some new sandals. The trip to Nordstrom had felt like a big treat when we went together to pick out an outfit for the special occasion. That morning, she had asked me to do her hair into two french braids. I spotted her in line, with her new outfit and her braids. But she was not wearing the lei. My heart sank. The purple orchid flowers were dangling from her hand.

"She's not wearing it," I said. Michael looked at me in sympathy and shook his head. He knew it was tearing me up inside.

Then I locked eyes with her. I smiled and waved at her and gestured for her to put the lei over her head onto her shoulders. She looked away.

The fifth graders filed into their seats facing the audience near the stage. When Chloe took her seat, she had put the lei over her shoulders. She looked like she wanted to shrink away.

She listened to me. But she did not get it.

A few weeks after what I've come to refer to as "the parenting fail with the lei," I was on a plane back to Hawai'i for the first time in three years with eleven-year-old Chloe. She was accepted into the same Kamehameha Schools ho'omāka'ika'i program that her brother attended three years earlier, and we decided to stay at my late grandparents' house for the week while she attended. Because of lingering caution about COVID-19, the school modified the program to a day camp and arranged for buses to come pick up the kids across the island every day instead of spending the night in on-campus dorms. Without housing provided for kids in the program, this time, it was mostly local kids who attended.

Like Silas three years before, Chloe was excited to go on a special trip to Hawai'i with just me. Silas had given her plenty of notes about the special summer camp for Native Hawaiian kids (fun activities, long days, good Spam musubi). Chloe and I arrived to my late grandparents' Nānākuli home a few days before camp started to get ourselves settled in and adjusted to the time zone. My parents had cleaned up the place a little bit by removing the faded carpet, adding new flooring, a new kitchen table, and even air-conditioning upstairs to cool off the humid summer days. Some parts of the house still looked frozen in time, with family photos hung on the walls of my aunties' senior high school graduation portraits and the old family photo albums sitting on the coffee table. I was most pleased to see Grandma's mango tree in the backyard full of fruit. Every few minutes, we'd hear a *thunk!* outside—the sound of another large mango that had ripened and fallen to the ground. I'd rush outside, pulling back the screen door to go pick it up before it was eaten by a bird or rotted into the soil.

Grandma had a pole that was uniquely built to pull mangoes

off the tall branches of her tree; it had a metal trap at the top that would allow you to pull on the mango, and if ripe, the fruit separates easily from the branch and is caught by the trap at the end of the pole. I taught Chloe how to use it as we tried to spy the golden-colored mangoes hidden in the top branches, ready to be eaten. Every morning, I got up before Chloe and before the sun rose and peeked over the mountains behind the house and sliced open a new mango. Grandma had planted this tree and picked this particular variety of mango that I'd never seen at a grocery store: thick skin, large as a grapefruit, more yellow in color than orange, and so sweet and juicy, you had to slurp it up before the juice would spill over onto your plate.

We'd bought some papaya from the farmers market and a local, ripe pineapple. Every morning, I'd cut up the most incredible tropical fruit salad for Chloe and me for breakfast. I sliced the mango's sides off and then cut crisscross into the flesh so that it fanned out into a beautiful set of square pieces ready to bite off the skin. As I did so, I realized that, in a way, I was reliving the same moment, fifteen years before, when Grandma sliced the fruit for me at this very same spot. She never got a chance to meet her great-granddaughter Chloe or great-grandson Silas. But in a way, Grandma was here, feeding her granddaughter and great-granddaughter fruit from the tree that she planted in the backyard.

Aloha, Grandma. We're here.

Chloe seemed to have a great time at camp. Every morning, I dropped her off at the bus stop for the long drive to the Kamehameha campus. One day, she came home with a baby taro plant from the lo'i. She loved stomping around in the mud that day and wanted to find a place to plant the taro in Grandma's backyard. I was pretty sure that the baby taro wouldn't survive, but she was excited to care for it and watch it grow. While she was at camp, I had the day to myself to just chill out and pretend for a week that I was a local. I knew that, at the end of the week, Chloe's group would put on a hō'ike, and I knew I'd have to confront the potential for more lei drama again. In Hawai'i, it is a tradition to bring a fresh flower lei to celebrate someone for any occasion—a birthday, a graduation, any big milestone—and a hō'ike fit the bill.

I knew I was taking a gamble buying a lei for her—it would be more humiliating in Hawai'i and at this camp for Native Hawaiian kids if she refused to wear it or put it on reluctantly. But I had to have faith that the camp would, by the end of the week, make an impression on her. If I was unable to convince her about the meaning and importance of the lei, perhaps the camp would succeed where I had failed. This time, I visited my favorite lei shop in Honolulu to buy a special flower lei for Chloe. It was made of special pink-and-white orchids and, at thirty-five dollars, far more delicate and sophisticated than anything I could ever make myself. Making lei is an art form, and the lei at this particular shop by the airport were beautifully crafted. I took a deep breath when I paid the bill. I didn't tell Chloe that I bought it, of course. After a week at camp, would she appreciate receiving a lei after learning in a weeklong camp about Native Hawaiian culture? I hoped that having had this experience, she would understand the importance of the lei and wear it. But I braced myself to expect the worst.

The Kamehameha campus felt like a college campus, with dorms for students and gorgeous views of the ocean at every turn. The only difference was the kids looked Hawaiian and all the families looked like mine—a mix of haole and Asian and Hawaiian.

Everyone was dressed up—parents and aunties in aloha-print shirts and dresses . . . and flip-flops. I noticed that nearly every family brought a plastic bag with a lei inside for their child.

It was time for the performance. The night before, I heard Chloe singing in Hawaiian in her room with the door closed. I settled into a seat inside the cold, dark auditorium. As the kids came out onstage, I spied Chloe, and she gave me a little wave. The kids' young voices began with a chant—loud and strong—a traditional greeting in Hawaiian to open the performance. Then they picked up the gourds they had made and tapped them against their hands and the floor. In the second row, I saw Chloe's eyes smiling at me from behind her pandemic mask. She was proud, and she sang her heart out in Hawaiian. Afterward, I presented her with the lei. Many kids had a few family members surrounding them, doing the same. This time, of course, she would have been the only one without a lei if I hadn't brought it for her. She put it over her head and removed her mask, and I snapped a picture of her big smile.

I looked around me, and every other family was doing the same thing—placing a lei on their child's shoulders and snapping a photo.

One generation to the next. This is how we survive as a people, as a culture. I'll never forget this day. And I hope to God she doesn't either. It's up to her to decide how much this moment means, to sear it into her memory. Hopefully it's one of many memories I've given her to help show her who she is and those who came before. If there's one thing I've learned, it's that keeping a culture alive means learning it, living it, and passing it on.

14

'ĀINA KŪPUNA

In early January 2023, about a year after Uncle Take's death, my auntie Maureen got a phone call from an unknown person with an 808 area code. Curious, she answered.

"Hello?"

It was an official from Maui County. "Aloha, you are the representative of the Kahanu family, the Goo Trust, correct?" the man said.

"Yes, correct," she answered.

"And you applied for the 'āina kūpuna tax relief and were rejected, correct?"

"Yes," she said, thinking, *Don't remind me.*

"Well, I'm calling to tell you that we have resubmitted your application on your behalf, and your application has been approved," the man said to my stunned and speechless auntie.

Under Maui County's rising property taxes, our annual bill,

which started at $200 per year and rose to more than $2,000 a year, was set to grow to more than $3,000 per year in 2023. But with this surprise phone call, now it'd drop down to about $100 per year, by Auntie's estimation.

Just like that. Without warning or much explanation, the county had decided to grant us tax relief, just as suddenly and inexplicably as they had raised our taxes several years before. We had just won the tax lottery!

As soon as Auntie Maureen hung up with the Maui County man, she called my dad. "Are you sitting down? You need to sit down."

"What, what?" Dad said.

"'Āina kūpuna. We got it! It's good for ten years." Auntie explained the tax relief to Dad, who was too shocked to even reply. "Hello? Are you still there?" she said.

"Okay, now I'm on the floor," Dad said. "I passed out."

Dad and Auntie Maureen sat there, stunned, in disbelief. "We got it? Wow. We did it? I can't believe it!" At last, he said, "Ten years? Well, in ten years, I'm passing this all down to the next generation in 2033!"

They both laughed.

When Auntie recalled the whole conversation to me, she was still in shock, and I was, too. Her voice was giddy, incredulous.

I was dying to know why the county had rejected us and then approved us. But we also felt like we didn't want to ask any questions in case the county changed its mind again and had made some kind of mistake.

Auntie Maureen said when she got the call, she immediately thought of Grandma. "I was like, *Well, Mom, thanks for watching out for us. And happy birthday to you*," she said to the heavens. "You know, this county guy called me on January 3. Mom's birthday is January 6. She's looking out for us."

Auntie Maureen and Dad relayed this all to me while I was at Dulles Airport about to fly out for an international work trip. It was a bizarre, although welcome, ending to our yearslong angst over the Hāna land. It felt like a wave of relief washed over my body—after years of worrying, waiting, feeling in limbo and out of control of our future, we had an answer, a solution, an answer to our prayers. I thought about that generational line and how each branch of our family tree had done something to keep that land in our family. My ancestor Kikaha, who had given the land to his mo'opuna and in his will asked them to hold on to the land, requesting that if they had to sell it, they do so to one another and keep it in the family. I thought of my great-grandmother, who divided her land among her children and tried to protect the heiau. I thought of Uncle Take and his siblings, who pushed the Garden to fulfill their promise to restore the heiau. And now, Dad and his siblings had done their part—fought the tax increase that threatened our ability to hold on to Grandma's land. Each generation, the fight took a different turn and required us to honor the family kuleana in a different way. Each generation had met the moment with a raised fist.

Grandma, up there, you see this, right?

I thought it was fitting, too, that the way we received the good news was just the same as the bad news. In 2019, we got the big tax bill delivered by a faceless and nameless bureaucratic stroke of a pen—a bill that arrived unannounced, without a heads-up or explanation, that threw our family into a panic. Now, four years later, a reprieve arrived in just the same way—without real explanation, just a verdict, a decision. Here you go.

Of course I felt grateful—victorious, even, that we had prevailed and the Kahanu family would hang on to our land without a threat hanging over our heads for ten more years. But it also reminded me of how vulnerable we were. I thought back to all that paperwork Uncle Take had collected—the wills, the land records, the land division, the land donation, the back-and-forth about the heiau and restoring it, the haole CEOs who wanted to turn the heiau into a high-end ecotourism resort and then died, the ancient artifacts discovered but then hidden away in a shed wrapped in newspaper. This latest relief—the ʻāina kūpuna law—was just the latest iteration of fighting for and holding on to our culture. It was our genera-tion's turn at being a vigilant steward of our land and all that is precious to Native Hawaiians, and we had scored a win. From my great-great-great-grandfather Kikaha's will granting his land, to my great-grandmother Mileka's donation of the heiau, to my Grand-ma's dreams to return to her land, to Dad, to me—the stewardship we inherited meant constantly being on guard to the ever-shifting rules, laws, powers that be that we did not control but were just trying to steer around and defend against. It impressed upon me that the survival of the lands, the heiau, all of it, was dependent on not just vigilance but a collective determination that required our family to stay together and work together as a team. Moreover, we had to hand off that stewardship with each generation, and that next generation had to be willing to take it on.

Before, I understood the duty. But now I understood more deeply the bigger picture of the operation that we were up against in the past and going forward. It was a version of the same thing for each generation—we were trying to cling to what we had with the values of our people, while navigating the rules and culture of a com-pletely different Western world that didn't really care. How long could these two things coexist? How miraculous that we have managed thus far?

I thanked God for the stars that aligned to remove the urgent threat facing our ability to hold on to Grandma's land. But I also thought, *Ten more years is just ten more years. It isn't forever.*

———

In the fall of 2023, I returned to hālau after it reopened to in-person hula classes. My pā'ū skirt fit a little tighter than before, thanks to COVID-era weight gain. I missed dancing hula, and even though the hālau tried to keep things going on Zoom, I could not find it in me to learn hula on a computer screen. But now it felt good to be back.

This time, I came alone.

"Aloha, Sara," one auntie at hālau said to me, kissing my cheek. "Where's Chloe and Silas?" she asked.

"How come they no come?" another auntie asked me.

"Oh, they're really busy now with their sports, unfortunately," I said. "So it's just me."

The truth was that my kids lost interest. At age twelve, Chloe was now playing club volleyball and had practice and tournaments on most weekends. At age fifteen, Silas's latest fixation was playing ice hockey on club and school teams. Three to four hours on the weekend at hālau with me was not how they wanted to spend their time. I tried to beg and plead and guilt-trip them. But I got tired of fighting with them about it. Every Sunday, our conversations about hālau would end up with me feeling upset and them expressing how they were bored at hālau and it "wasn't their thing."

So I decided that if I couldn't change their minds, I would have to change my own attitude about it. I was over the drama about hālau with them.

I wasn't going to force my kids to come to hālau ever again. They may decide to join me one Sunday in a few weeks or months—or years. Hula is the physical practice of Hawaiian culture, the stories of its people, and the expression of aloha. To learn the moves of my aunties and grandmother and great-grandmother to tell the story of the hula, I had to learn the Hawaiian words and what they meant so that my body could tell the story with just the right emotion. I was still learning each of these things and delighting in it for a new reason—but now it was for myself. It was my joy and my connection. And if they weren't feeling that, then my forcing them wasn't going to make them appreciate it. And frankly, I needed my own joy that was just mine—my time to turn off my phone for a few hours, to not have to make dinner or answer an email or drive a carpool or anything else. Some women call that "me time" or "self-care." And this was my new frame of mind.

One day, while in the car running errands, Chloe said to me, "Mom, I know you're sad that we don't go to hālau with you anymore."

"Yes, you're right. I am sad about that."

"Well, I want you to know that it's not that we don't appreciate Hawaiian culture. We do. It's just that hula dancing is not our thing," she said.

"Okay. I get it," I told her. "Thanks for telling me. I'm going to do it for me because it brings me joy and it's important to me. I really hope that someday you find a way to practice your culture and stay connected to it."

But they will decide when the time is right for them. That's what I learned from this experience—to let each person come to their own relationship with their ancestry. For now, a few hours each Sunday was my time to put my bare feet on the cold linoleum floor and learn a new story through hula.

At hālau, I noticed how all the other kids that my children learned hula with had grown so much taller and bigger. They were no longer tiny kids running around.

I have come to realize that my Native Hawaiian identity is not something from my blood quantum or from the Mahele or something dictated by where I was born. It's not for others to tell me who I am, relatives or not, Hawai'i or mainland. It's not something a government agency decides, nor frankly is it something for locals or mainland residents to judge. It's something I was given by my kūpuna and also had to seek, accept, and understand on my own. It's something I must choose to practice and pass on—or not. Each of us makes that choice—particularly parents—consciously or not.

For many years, I had just the breadcrumbs of my Hawaiian culture left for me, and I am grateful for what Grandma kept alive as best she could while raising her family in California. She gave us the land, but we are not really the owners. That truly is the challenge ahead. The land is just the physical part left from our culture—our honor and family lineage manifested in a place we can visit, walk on, touch, and care for. But it won't remain, and our culture won't remain unless each generation—grandparent to parent to child to grandchild—keeps it burning. I was desperate to not let that flame go out, and I will remain committed to that mission as long as I'm alive. In our modern world, there are so many distractions and practical reasons that have caused many members of my own family—those who live in Hawai'i and those who do not—to lose that connection. The challenge for the land and our culture remain the same: we must keep it going.

EPILOGUE

On August 8, 2023, wildfires whipped up by hurricane-level winds raced across the island of Maui, destroying everything in their path with breathtaking speed. Images from that day—of families desperately trying to escape the flames in their cars and people plunging themselves into the ocean, clinging to rocks, are seared into our memories forever. It was the deadliest wildfire in US history in a century. It killed more than one hundred people and wiped out the entire historic town of Lahaina. My family and their homes were spared, although barely. For hours, it seemed as though the fires upland near Kula would take Uncle Keith and Auntie Gizelle's home. They lost power for weeks. Hāna, on the other side of the island, was also spared. Later, we learned my cousin Mark's wife's cousin died in the fire. He was working at a restaurant in Lahaina. He was in his twenties. The fires devastated and traumatized the entire island, which will take years to rebuild.

As government workers cleaned up the ashes and assessed the causes, it made local people angry. Why? There is a lot of anger at inept leadership, government preparedness, safety responses, and failed infrastructure. In the bigger picture, it forced locals to confront bigger questions: Why was all of Lahaina's landscape so dry in the first place? It once had natural water that created a lush, green landscape from the mountain to the sea. The answer: sugarcane plantation owners long ago wrangled rights to divert water upland to serve commercial farms. Another question: When so many families' homes burned down, why couldn't they access all the available housing on the island? Answer: There is enough housing for the thousands who lost their homes; the problem is that a quarter of the housing is for tourists who pay hundreds of dollars per night.[1] Another question: Why were locals paying some of the highest electricity bills in the nation to the state's one electricity company that had cut corners and failed to heed weather warnings about high winds that fateful day? That's now being litigated in court. The fires served as a stark reminder of how, for decades, bigger economic forces on Maui had resulted in neglect of its own local people.

A year after the fires, more than 1,500 families living on Maui who lost their homes or livelihoods have left the island because they had no place to live that they could afford. Since the fires, the median single-family home price on Maui in 2024 has risen to $1.3 million.[2]

Today, across Hawai'i, providing an affordable place to live for local people—especially Native Hawaiians—is a crisis. Housing is the top reason that local people say they can't afford to stay in Hawai'i, and the state struggles to hold on to its professional class to care for and educate those who remain. It has a shortage of doctors, nurses, and teachers. In 2024, O'ahu brought in more than one hundred schoolteachers from the Philippines on short-term visas because it did not have enough teachers to educate public school children.[3] Today, more Native Hawaiians live outside Hawai'i than in their homeland. And of those who remain, a large share live in homes with multiple family members because rents and mortgages are too hard to afford on one family's salary. Meanwhile, Native Hawaiians are overrepresented among the homeless population, living on the beaches in Waianae, Nānākuli, on the streets of Honolulu, and on other islands. There are tents along the beach with older-model SUVs parked out front, baby cribs under trees, kids' bicycles parked along the public beach parking lot. When I see this get worse and worse with each year, it makes me angry at a society that has failed its community. Too many Native Hawaiians are displaced from their homelands. And this crisis is invisible to the millions who visit each year—they embrace the aloha culture—and then leave, blissfully unaware of the desperation among those who drive the airport shuttles, clean the hotel rooms, and serve the hotel food every day. It makes you wonder how long this can go on.

After all, what is Hawai'i without Hawaiians?

There are small glimmers of hope. Not far from my grandparents' homestead in Nānākuli, in 2023 the Department of Hawaiian Homelands broke ground on a new housing development in Kapolei for the first time in thirty years. In 2024, fifty-two homes on Maui were made available to applicants on the waiting list. The state approved $600 million for new housing that will also be built across the islands, but with inflation, and plans that have already shifted course, how many homes will that money support? Today, more than thirty thousand Native Hawaiians are waiting for an opportunity to have land of their own through the

Hawaiian Homelands program started by Prince Kuhio more than a century ago.

The Pi'ilanihale heiau has expanded its program to support visitors interested in learning about Native Hawaiians' early way of life, the canoe farm, the ahupua'a structure that sustained its people, and the temple—a relic of the power, of its chiefs, and of its religion. There's a beautiful visitors' center at the Kahanu Garden that proudly displays some of the poi pounders, 'ulu maika, and other artifacts found at the heiau grounds that I held in my hands more than a decade ago. And at the office headquarters, all other artifacts are now carefully labeled and displayed in proper glass cabinets, not wrapped in newspaper inside Costco cardboard boxes. My family—the Kahanu family—still has not come to an agreement with the National Tropical Botanical Garden, which operates the Kahanu Garden, to ensure access, burial rights, and a formal role with the organization going forward. Chipper has since retired from the Garden. Dad's working with the new CEO of the NTBG, and head of the Kahanu Garden, in hopes that our extended family can come to an agreement with them.

Not too far down the road from the Garden is Uncle Larry's property and the small, dilapidated house he left behind. Once listed for sale by his heirs for $1 million, real estate records show that it was sold in August 2024 for $300,000, after being on the market for nearly a year. No one ever heard from Uncle Larry's heirs about who they sold to or why the price dropped so much. The heirs never reached out about selling to other members of the Kahanu family. But according to the coconut wireless, word is that the property was sold to a local family.

Today, I'm proud to see a new generation of Native Hawaiian leaders running for public office, taking on leadership roles, and shaping many aspects of Hawai'i's future—including its laws. More children and adults speak the Hawaiian language than have in a century. There are twenty-eight Hawaiian language immersion public schools, in addition to other privately run and nonprofit programs. Hawai'i's tourism agency is now focused on educating visitors about Native Hawaiian culture. The Native Hawaiian Legal Corporation has made inroads in protecting water rights and land rights for Native Hawaiians, through state supreme court cases and helping Hawaiian families. It says it has represented more than 2,300 individuals in more than four hundred quiet title cases.

Local and environmental groups have imposed more visitor limits on ecologically sensitive areas, such as Hanauma Bay and Lē'ahi, or Diamond Head on O'ahu and Hā'ena State Park and the Nāpali Coast on Kauai. Protests by Native Hawaiians successfully stopped construction of a massive telescope at the top of Mauna Kea, one of the most sacred mountains on the Big Island. The *Hokule'a*, the voyaging canoe built in the style of Hawai'i's first original inhabitants, has traveled the world, part of an effort to teach a new generation of wayfinders how to navigate the ocean by only using the stars, tides, and birds—just like their ancestors did. A group of Native Hawaiian cultural practitioners have revived kākau, or Native Hawaiian tattoo, using a hand-tap method to imprint markings that reflect one's Hawaiian genealogy—keeping alive an ancient art form and tradition.

The kuleana of perpetuating Hawaiian culture is alive and well but remains—as it always has—a struggle. After attending Uncle Take's funeral, I came across a book called *Nānā i ke Kumu* (translation: pay attention to the teacher) in a Native Hawaiian bookstore on Maui, a book written to document Hawaiian cultural values, practices, and traditions. "The ancestors in our family select us to fulfill certain kuleana, though it's up to us whether we choose to accept those responsibilities or aspirations. This is one way we understand spirituality in the Hawaiian cultural context: as the fulfillment of obligations to our family lineage, which we cannot always know in a conscious sense, but which the ancestors can reveal to us if and when we are self-reflective, prepared, and centered."[4] This passage stopped me in my tracks because it put into words what I had felt and experienced over the course of my life but had no words to describe. It's what led me to want to share my family's story in this book—not to write about myself but to share the real story about Hawai'i that the world needs to understand.

My story is a story of land lost but also kept and honored, a culture nearly stamped out but fighting to endure. My story, and my Hawaiian family's story, is also one of survival, struggle, and fulfillment. It's about what you owe to those who come before you and those who come after you and coming to understand the privilege of that responsibility. Even if it's hard to grasp in the modern world we live in, I believe kuleana is a part of Hawaiian culture that also has universal understanding that speaks to one's larger, grounding purpose. At least, it is to me.

As for the Hāna land, Grandma's land remains the same as it has been since King Kamehameha III granted it to my ancestor in the 1840s—wild jungle, but now with an overgrown farm of various plants. Dad and I, along with all my aunties, uncles, and cousins, are still researching options for our land and whether to invest in building a modest home on it. If I had to bet, we will end up building something someday. Now that Uncle Take is gone, we need a new anchor to keep us coming back to Hāna. A home would get some use, and it would be our best chance to honor Grandma and her wishes that her children and grandchildren would come to know Hāna as she did. To cherish something, you've got to be close to it, to build a connection to it and appreciate all the kuleana that comes with it.

But more than that, my journey has led me to believe that the land and all that it represents has been the anchor for our Native Hawaiian family from which everything else is related. The heiau, the artifacts, the genealogy, the extended family connections—they have all been anchored in our shared history with the land. That has been the case for generations and generations, and it is true for me. The land called me back. My grandmother, Uncle Take, and so many family members and the extended lāhui of the Hawaiian people helped me along the way back to Hāna. The land taught me where I came from and informed who I am.

On a recent visit to the land with my sister Haley, we met up with Uncle Keith and his son, my cousin Luka. It had been years since Haley had been to Hāna and seen Grandma's property. Uncle Keith had offered to take us, since we needed a truck with four-wheel drive.

Luka's truck, blasting local island music of Maoli, rolled down the steep pitch of grass along his family's property on its way to ours. A few roaming cows stared at us as we drove by.

On our property, we found Uncle Keith riding a lawn mower, trying to tame the thigh-high grass that had already taken over the "road" that he, Dad, our brother, Ben, and the farm brigade had bulldozed just a couple of years earlier. After a few rows of mowing, Uncle Keith turned off the motor and beckoned me to get into the driver's seat. He showed me how to let go of the clutch as the machine lurched forward, munching up the tangles of the jungle in front of me as I tried to steer a somewhat straight line.

"Nice job!" Haley laughed as she snapped photos and videos of me.

We stopped at an area where the wild bushes had grown taller than me, but I could still make out several red ginger plants growing in clusters. I could feel the sweat dripping down my neck and onto my arms.

"Is this the farm that you built with Dad?" I asked.

"Yeah, pretty sure," Uncle Keith said, reaching back into his truck.

Uncle Keith and Cousin Luka cracked open cans of beer, handing one to me and the other to Haley.

"Cheers to the 'āina," Uncle Keith said. It was 11:00 a.m.

"To the 'āina," we said, clanking aluminum cans.

I have no illusions that the tax abatement we received through the 'āina kūpuna law will remain. In fact, I'm quite certain that Haley and I and my cousins Gabe, Luka, Brande, Keali'i, Toni, Tia, Joanie, Julie, and Auntie Gizelle, Uncle Keith, Auntie Bobbie, Auntie Echo—all of us—someday will have to face the next government, bureaucratic, or financial hurdle in our generation to hold on to the land. And I'm sure there will be yet another challenge for my kids and Haley's kids and all our cousins' kids, too.

But back in Hāna, when I stood on that land, I inhaled a deep breath of the luscious air. I looked around at the wild papayas, Mohawk tops of red ginger popping out from the tree branches, the bluest ocean that reached into the horizon just beyond, and I thought of all my kūpuna who stood on this very land before me. Behind me, the hala forest rose up the mountain until it hid behind the clouds. From mauka to makai, mountain to the sea, the glorious beauty of Hawai'i, preserved just as it was for centuries, still endures today, and I imagined the ghosts of our ancestors looking out on this very same spot.

When I stand on that land, it's just as majestic, special, and honorable as it was the day I climbed the arch along the rocky shore with Grandma all those years ago. We haven't built her house. But we still have the land in our hands.

Mālama i ka ʻāina, Grandma. Take care of the land, and the land takes care of you. *Mālama i ka ʻāina*.

MAHALO AND ACKNOWLEDGMENTS

This book took more than a decade to research, report, write, structure, and edit. I owe a debt of gratitude to all the people who helped to educate me, lead me, guide me, and support me along the way.

First, mahalo to my agent, Howard Yoon of WME, who believed in my story years ago and was patient with me as we shaped the story into this book. He was the first to identify the important theme of what we owe those who came before us and those who come after us—and he understood kuleana before I told him about the Hawaiian word that became the title. Thank you to Bryn Clark for loving my story and helping me structure the two narratives together. I am so grateful to Flatiron Books publisher Megan Lynch and Flatiron editor Kukuwa Fraser for taking me on, supporting my story, and seeing it to the end. Thanks to Jeremy Pink for the eagle-eyed edits, and to the Flatiron and Macmillan editors, designers, and marketing and publicity teams, for all your support of Team *Kuleana*!

I'm indebted to the incredible anthropologists who informed this book with their work studying the Pi'ilanihale heiau, starting with the late Dr. Yoshi Sinoto, Eric Komori, Ross Cordy, and Michael Kolb. I relied heavily on Patrick Vinton Kirch for his incredible research on the ancient chiefs, the study of heiau across Hawai'i, and love for Kahikinui. Kirch's books were essential in helping me understand the Pi'ilanihale heiau in the context of ancient Native Hawaiian societal structure. Mahalo to all the anthropologists who sought to understand, document, and share with the Hawaiian people what they are able to learn about the ancient wisdom of those who have come before us.

I relied on the work of other researchers, such as David Arthur Swanson, University of California, Riverside professor of sociology, for his fascinating research on the Native Hawaiian population over time and a new way of estimating the precontact population of Native Hawaiians. I'm grateful to my former colleagues at the Pew Research Center who were supportive of my nerdy interest in population shifts of Native Hawaiians and overall supportive of me taking time to work on this book. Like you, I heart data.

On the subject of the Hawaiian language, I'm lucky to have met Larry Kimura, who spent many hours talking story with me about the radio show he started in the 1960s so that others could hear the Hawaiian language being spoken and his efforts, along with so many others of his time, to revive it. Mahalo, Larry, for your support and for checking me on my Hawaiian language use in this book. Also much love to NPR's *Code Switch* team for their incredible, thoughtful, and delightful coverage of the revival of the Hawaiian language. It was pure joy to work with you on that and hear it come into the world.

On the Mahele, special mahalo to Lilikalā Kame'eleihiwa for her incredibly thorough research on the topic and leadership. Mahalo also to Meyer Cummins for helping me understand the history of land and quiet titles in Hawai'i. Our family's fight to hold on to lands and fulfill our kuleana with regards to the Pi'ilanihale heiau would not be possible without the Native Hawaiian Legal Corporation and its staff, including executive director Makalika Noholowa'a, former executive director Moses Haia, and Camille Kalama and Li'ūla Christensen, who have personally helped the Kahanu-Uaiwa-Matsuda family. I also relied heavily on the incredible databases that have digitized history and culture of kanaka maoli, including the Ulukau English-Hawaiian online dictionary database; the Papakilo database and Hawaiian newspaper archive; Hawai'i State Archives; staff of the Bishop Museum; Ancestry.com; and the University of Hawai'i at Mānoa library.

Mahalo to the incredible journalists in Hawai'i who continue to address the issues that need attention, especially affordable housing, the Hawaiian Homelands, and homelessness, in addition to the recovery of Lahaina and Maui from the 2023 wildfires. I appreciate the work of reporters such as Ku'uwehi Hiraishi, Russell Subiono, Jason Ubay, and the staff of Hawai'i Public Radio under the leadership of the incredible Meredith Artley; Anita Hofschneider of *Grist*; and Kirstin Downey and so many others at *Civil Beat*. Special thanks to former *Mana* magazine editor Ke'opulaulani Reelitz, journalist Naka Nathaniel, and former *Honolulu Star-Advertiser* photography chief Greg Yamamoto for your support, encouragement, and friendship.

I'm grateful to *Axios* cofounders Jim VandeHei and Mike Allen and so many others who encouraged me to pursue this book, even if it meant fewer hours of sleep to recover from the nonstop news in Washington. My *Axios* fam, I love you all, and thanks for being my teammates in building the next great media company. It's been an honor.

Even though our family's relationship has been rocky at times, I am grateful for Chipper Wichman and his years of leadership at the National Tropical Botanical Garden. Chipper has built an important legacy at Kahanu Garden to restore the heiau as promised and make the grounds as beautiful as ever, along with a wonderful visitors' center. Thank you to Mike Opgenorth for the use of his incredible photos and for taking on the next chapter at the garden. Mahalo to Lipoa Kahaleuahi, director of Ma Ka Hana Ka 'Ike, for touring us around to see conservation lands and the incredible work by you and others to perpetuate the culture in the Hāna community. And mahalo to former director Kamaui Aiona. Mahalo to researcher Maria Kaimi Orr for her incredible work to write up the history of the Pi'ilanihale heiau.

I've been grateful to have the support and sage advice of many fellow writers and journalists over the years. Big hugs to my dear friend Brooke Warner, founder of She Writes Press, and Linda Joy Myers, who read earlier drafts of this book when it was a baby of a book finding its way. Dear friend David Greene introduced me to my literary agent, Yuki Noguchi encouraged me at every step, and so many journalism friends have given me great advice. Thanks to Matt Allinson for his helpful legal review in all my contracts. Thank you to my DC mom friends—too many to name—who have endured hearing about this "book project" for years, and for that I thank you for keeping me accountable. Thanks to Jon Yaged and Catherine Daly, who enlightened me with book industry wisdom and encouraged me for many years on this project.

I'm grateful to the entire Kahanu family for trusting me to tell our family story as honestly and thoroughly as possible in these pages. I must start with the late Uncle Take, for spending nine years in probate court, reviewing land records, working with lawyers and the Hāna Ranch to sort out our family's land title history and coming to an agreement with the NTBG to protect the heiau. I am grateful for my late Auntie Dolly, who pushed for the NTBG to honor its promises. I also thank my larger extended kūpuna, many of whom I never met but whose guidance and blessing I felt with each door that opened. Great-grandma Mileka Kekauililani Kahanu Matsuda, we only met once, but I hope I have made you proud. I have felt your guidance along the way.

Sadly we lost the last members of the Matsuda Goo kūpuna over the last two years before this book was published: Uncle Take, Auntie Dolly, Uncle Richard, and Uncle Sonny. Mahalo for showing us the way with your leadership and aloha. Your 'ohana will take it from here.

I truly wouldn't know Maui without the aloha and support of the Kuailani 'ohana—special mahalo to Auntie Gizelle and Uncle Keith Kuailani and cousins Mark and Luka. Auntie Marsha Tomoshiro helped me get started in understanding the Kahanu and Matsuda genealogy with her research. Aunty Bobbie Harada talked story with me about old days in Hāna and O'ahu—and her fight, with my cousins Joni and Julie, to hold on to their lands, too. Uncle Richard and Uncle Sonny cracked me up with their stories as "pineapples" in the military. Mahalo to Uncle Terry, who welcomed me to his home and trusted me with his story of the tough decision to sell the land.

Special love and gratitude to my cousins Brande and Gabe Ribilia, for all their love and support. Mahalo, Gabe, for hooking me up with the kama'aina rate at the hotels where he has worked, and Brande, who talked story with me and got the Kahanu family organized so many times out of the goodness of her heart. Aloha to my cousins Tia and Toni Matsuda on Maui for feeding me at their incredible food trucks! I'm grateful to have connected with extended members of the Kahanu family through the writing of this book, namely Auntie Echo DelaPena and Auntie Maude Kaholi; and Kealiʻi and Kawika Kahanu Uaiwa.

My journey would of course not be the same without finding my ʻohana in DC at Hālau Nohona Hawaiʻi: Kumu Kaimana Chee, Napua Kamakele, the Barker family, Uncle Isaac and the entire Hoʻopiʻi family, the Viernes family, the Sripipatana family, Robin Veracruz, Josh Gabonia, Terry Walker, Cecilia Kramer, and Shani Puanani. Aloha to my hula family: Cayrn Haukea Walker, Jamie Chen, Kanani Rannels, Alan Hew, Judith Wang, Gem Daus, Amber Maikui, Ashley Macaysa, Lenn Cruz, Mallorie Fiero, Nona Lee, Danielle Heiny, and many more. Mahalo to all my hula sisters and brothers, for forgiving me for not remembering my hula. I promise to do better next week. Auntie Julie Coleson died in 2023, and I am forever grateful to her and Uncle Peter Coleson for welcoming us to hālau.

Mahalo to the entire Goo ʻohana across the mainland for your love and support along this journey: Rick and Joanie Goo; Darrell and Linda Goo; Maureen and Tim Gaasch; Duane and Jackie Goo; Doreen Goo; and Ross Goo. And to my cousins Samantha Gaasch, Jonathan Gaasch, Stevie Goo, Jordan Goo, Vincent and Stef Goo, Marie and Johnnie Zhu, Shannon Goo, and Anna Goo.

I want to thank my parents, Dennis Kokoʻolani Goo and Susan Goo. Thank you, both of you, for babysitting the kids so I could write for so many weekends and for supporting this project when it seemed like it might never happen. I'm lucky to have parents like you who support me and believe in me. I knew as a child that I would someday write a book; your love and support made it possible. My mother-in-law, Janie Rhein, a librarian and book lover to her core, has been an ongoing source of support, and I'm grateful to her and my late father-in-law, Joel Rhein, for everything. And finally, my incredible kids Isabella, Silas, and Chloe. Thank you for letting me write about our lives. I love you with everything that I am. And finally but most importantly, this book would not be possible without my husband, Michael, who allowed me to take many solo research trips to Hawai'i in order for this book to happen, who picked me up and encouraged me for years. You are an incredible 'ohana man, fisherman, father, public servant, and partner for life. It wouldn't have been possible without you.

GLOSSARY OF HAWAIIAN WORDS

The Hawaiian language has thirteen letters, including the ʻokina, or glottal stop, usually represented by a reversed apostrophe. The ʻokina signals to the reader to pause, often to pronounce each vowel, before and after the ʻokina. The plural "s" in English is not used for spelling Hawaiian words. This glossary represents only the meanings for the purposes of this book. It is not meant to be the complete or final representation of how each word is understood.

—SKG

Ahu (ah-hoo)—Pile.

Ahupuaʻa (ah-hoo-poo-ah-ah)—A division of land, usually triangular in shape, the tip starting from the mountain then running to the sea, designed to be self-sustaining by the natural resources within it.

ʻĀina (aye-nah)—Land, country.

Hālau (huh-louw)—A long house for a canoe or a hula school.

Haole (how-lee)—Foreigner; white person.

Hapa (hah-pah)—Portion, fraction, mixed, such as a person of mixed race.

Heiau (hey-ouw)—A Native Hawaiian temple constructed of stacked lava rocks without mortar. A pre-Christian place of worship used by Hawaiians for ceremonies, rituals.

Hewa (heh-vah)—Wrong.

Hōʻike (ho-ee-keh)—To show (v.) or a show (n.), such as a hula or musical performance.

Honomāʻele (ho-no-mah-el-leh)—The name of the ahupuaʻa, or land area, granted by King Kamehameha III to Kahanu.

Hoʻomākaʻikaʻi (hoh-oh-mah-kah-ee-kah-ee)—To visit, tour. Name of Kamehameha Schools "Explorations" program.

Hoʻoponopono (ho-oh-poh-no-poh-no)—To make right; a Native Hawaiian practice of forgiveness and healing.

Hui (hoo-ee)—(as a verb) To convene, join, unite.

Kālaʻau (kah-lah-oh)—Pair of wooden sticks used as musical instruments.

Kanaka (kah-nah-kah)—Human, person.

Kanaka maoli (kah-nah-kah mah-oh-lee)—Native Hawaiian, or native human.

Kane (kah-neh)—Man, male. Plural form is kāne.

Kahu (kah-hoo)—Protector, guardian.

Kāhuna (kah-hoo-nah)—High priest with special knowledge or gifts from the gods.

Kamaʻāina (kah-mah-aye-nah)—Person, people of the land. In modern terms, refers to local people. Stores in Hawaiʻi will offer lower "kamaʻāina" prices for residents with a Hawaiʻi driver's license.

Kapu (kah-poo)—Forbidden, not allowed.

Keiki (kay-kee)—Child.

Konohiki (koh-no-hee-kee)—Chief, or headman of a land division to oversee specific ahupua'a.

Kuleana (koo-lee-ah-nah)—Responsibility, privilege.

Kumu (koo-moo)—Teacher.

Kupuna (koo-poo-nah)—Grandparent, ancestor. Plural form is kūpuna.

Lāhui (lah-hoo-ee)—People of a common identity, race.

Lo'i (loh-ee)—An irrigated terrace, used for growing taro.

Luakini (loo-ah-kee-nee)—Traditional temple where sacrificial rituals took place.

Maka'ainana (mah-kah-aye-nah-nah)—Commoners, citizens of a place.

Makahiki (mah-ka-hee-kee)—Year, annual. Native Hawaiians' annual mid-fall to early spring celebration in honor of the harvest and return of the Pleiades constellation to the night sky.

Mākaukau (mah-kow-kow)—To prepare, be ready.

Mālama (mah-lah-mah)—To take care of, maintain, protect.

Mālama i ka 'āina (mah-lah-ma ee-kah aye-na)—A phrase to take care of the land, inferring that the land takes care of you.

Malihini (mah-lee-hee-nee)—Visitor, stranger, foreigner.

Manapua (mah-nah-poo-ah)—Hawaiian word for sweet pork bun, or bao.

Mauka to makai (mow-ka to mah-kai [rhymes with eye])—Hawai'i local English meaning from the mountain to the sea; a Hawai'i English phrase incorporating the locative preposition *ma* precedes the word *uka*, indicating toward the mountain, and precedes *kai*, indicating toward the sea.

Mo'olelo (moh-oh-lel-loh)—Story or tale, often referring to Hawaiian history or legend.

Mele (meh-leh)—Song.

Mo'opuna (moh-oo-poo-nah)—Grandchild.

'Ohana (oh-hah-nah)—Family.

Oli (oh-lee)—Chant.

'Ono (oh-no)—Delicious; tasty.

Pau (paoh)—Done.

Pā'ū (pah-ooh)—Skirt.

Pi'ilani (Pee-ee-lah-nee)—Sixteenth-century chief of Maui who united east and west factions of the island. His sons Kiha and Lono fought for control of the island after his death.

Piko (pee-koh)—Navel.

Pono (poh-no)—Balance, state of harmony.

Pua'a (poo-ah-ah)—Pig, pork.

Tūtū (too-too)—Common pronunciation of kūkū; grandparent, male or female.

Wahine (wah-hee-neh)—Woman, female. Plural form is wāhine.

NOTES

Introduction

1. Patrick V. Kirch, *How Chiefs Became Kings: Divine Kingship and the Rise of the Archaic States in Ancient Hawai'i* (Berkeley: University of California Press, 2010).

2. "Largest Landowners by Type and by Island: 2017," Hawai'i State Department of Business and Economic Development, accessed September 19, 2024, https://files.hawaii.gov/dbedt/economic/databook /db2023/section06.pdf.

3. "The Hawai'i Housing Factbook," UHERO, June 2023, https://uhero .hawaii.edu/wp-content/uploads/2023/06/TheHawaiiHousingFactbook .pdf.

4. Brittany Rico, Joyce Key. Hahn, and Paul Jacobs, "Detailed Look at Native Hawaiian and Other Pacific Islander Groups," US Census Bureau; September 21, 2023, https://www.census.gov/library/stories /2023/09/2020-census-dhc-a-nhpi-population.html.

5. "The Hawai'i Housing Factbook."

6. "How Hawai'i's Cost of Living Impacts Homelessness," HomeAid Hawaii, July 11, 2024, https://homeaidhawaii.org/articles/hawaiis -cost-of-living-impacts-homelessness.

7. "The Hawai'i Housing Factbook."

8. "How Hawai'i's Cost of Living Impacts Homelessness."

9. "Increased Food Security and Self-Sufficiency Strategy," Hawai'i State Department of Business and Economic Development and Tourism, accessed September 19, 2024, https://files.hawaii.gov

/dbedt/op/spb/INCREASED_FOOD_SECURITY_AND_FOOD
_SELF_SUFFICIENCY_STRATEGY.pdf.

10. Kadin Mills, "#NativeVote24: Indigenous Candidates Fight for Seats in
Hawai'i," ICT, August 12, 2024, https://ictnews.org/news/nativevote24
-indigenous-candidates-fight-for-seats-in-hawaii.

11. Mahealani Richardson, "'We Are Still in a Crisis': 1,500+ Families
Believed to Have Left Maui Since August Wildfires," Hawaii News
Now, February 19, 2024, https://www.hawaiinewsnow.com/2024/02
/20/we-are-still-crisis-1500-families-believe-have-left-maui-since
-august-wildfires/.

1: The Heiau

1. Nicole Campoy, "10 Tips for Driving the Hana Highway," Fodor's
Travel, February 11, 2013, https://www.fodors.com/news/10-tips-for
-driving-the-hana-highway-6423.

2: Mauka to Makai

1. "Wage Standards Division | Minimum Wage and Overtime," De-
partment of Labor and Industrial Relations, accessed September 19,
2024, https://labor.hawaii.gov/wsd/minimum-wage/.

2. Brittany Rico, Joyce Key Hahn, and Paul Jacobs, "Detailed Look at
Native Hawaiian and Other Pacific Islander Groups," US Census
Bureau, September 21, 2023, https://www.census.gov/library/stories
/2023/09/2020-census-dhc-a-nhpi-population.html.

3. Sara K. Goo and David Swanson, "After 200 Years, Native Hawaiians
Make a Comeback," Pew Research Center, April 6, 2015, https://
www.pewresearch.org/short-reads/2015/04/06/native-hawaiian
-population/.

4. Patrick V. Kirch, *A Shark Going Inland Is My Chief* (Berkeley: University
of California Press, 2012).

5. U.S. House of Representatives Committee on Foreign Affairs, Blount
Report: "Affairs in Hawaii" (Washington, DC: Government Printing

Office, 1895), accessed via the University of Hawai'i at Manoa Library, https://libweb.hawaii.edu/digicoll/annexation/blount/br0402.php.

6. "Pearl Harbor," National Park Service, https://www.nps.gov/perl /learn/historyculture/pearl-harbor.htm.

7. Maya Yang, "Mark Zuckerberg Adds 110 Acres to Controversial 1500-Acre Hawaii Estate," *Guardian*, December 28, 2021, https:// www.theguardian.com/technology/2021/dec/28/mark-zuckerberg -110-acres-hawaii.

8. Russell Subiono and Catherine C. Pactol, "A Look Inside Life on an Island Owned by Larry Ellison, the 4th Richest Person in the World," Hawaii Public Radio, July 28, 2023, https://www.hawaiipublicradio .org/local-news/2023-07-28/a-look-inside-life-on-an-island-owned -by-larry-ellison-the-fourth-richest-person-in-the-world.

4: Ua Mau Ke Ea O Ka ʻĀina I Ka Pono

1. "American Community Survey 5-Year Estimates," Census Reporter Profile, http://censusreporter.org/profiles/16000US1511350-hana-hi/.

5: Getting Pono

1. Elizabeth Grieco, "Newsroom Jobs and Employment in the U.S.: 10 Charts About the Industry," Pew Research Center, April 28, 2020, https://www.pewresearch.org/short-reads/2020/04/28/10-charts -about-americas-newsrooms/.

6: The Road to Hāna

1. Thomas K. Maunupau, *Huakai Makaikai a Kaupo, Maui*, ed. Naomi N. Clarke Losch, trans. Mary Kawena Pukui and Malcolm Naea Chun (Honolulu: Bishop Museum Press, 1998).

2. Maria Kaʻimipono Orr, *Piʻilanihale Heiau: An Ethnographic Survey and Cultural & Historical Background Review* (Hāna, HI: National Tropical Botanical Garden, 1999).

7: The Mahele

1. Curtis J. Lyons, "Land Matters in Hawaii—No. 1," *The Islander*, July 2, 1875, https://hilo.hawaii.edu/maunakea/library/reference.php?view =1223.

2. Lilikalā Kameʻeleihiwa, *Native Land, Foreign Desires, Pehea Lā E Pono Ai?* (Honolulu: Bishop Museum Press, 2013).

3. Gavan Daws, *Shoal of Time: A History of the Hawaiian Islands* (Honolulu: University of Hawaii Press, 1974).

4. James L. Haley, *Captive Paradise: A History of Hawaii* (New York: St. Martin's Press, 2012).

5. Daws, *Shoal of Time*.

6. Michael Dougherty, *To Steal a Kingdom: Probing Hawaiian History* (Waimanalo, HI: Island Style Press, 1994), 186.

7. Dougherty, *To Steal a Kingdom*, 115.

8. Kameʻeleihiwa, *Native Land*.

9. *Chronological Sugar Mill Data Sheet, Hana-Kaeleku* (Hāna, HI: Hāna Cultural Center, 1985).

10. Julia C. Wong, "'A Blemish in His Sanctuary': The Battle Behind Mark Zuckerberg's Hawaii Estate," *Guardian*, January 17, 2019, https://www.theguardian.com/us-news/2019/jan/17/mark-zuckerberg -hawaii-estate-kauai-land-rights-dispute.

8: Clues in the Rocks

1. Patrick V. Kirch, *A Shark Going Inland Is My Chief* (Berkeley: University of California Press, 2012).

2. Piilani Heiau National Historic Landmark, National Register of Historic Places Inventory—Nomination Form, US National Park Service, 1987.

3. "Finds Hawaiian Sworn to Silence on Heiau Sites," *Honolulu Star*, August 19, 1919.

9: Hawaiian Renaissance

1. Sara K. Goo, "How the Hawaiian Language Nearly Died and Activists Brought It Back," NPR, June 22, 2019, https://www.npr.org/sections/codeswitch/2019/06/22/452551172/the-hawaiian-language-nearly-died-a-radio-show-sparked-its-revival.

2. "History of Hawaiian Education," Hawaii State Department of Education, accessed September 19, 2024, https://www.hawaiipublicschools.org/TeachingAndLearning/StudentLearning/HawaiianEducation/Pages/History-of-the-Hawaiian-Education-program.aspx.

3. Ānela Iwane, "Hawaiian Language Immersion Program," Hawaii State Department of Education, accessed September 19, 2024, https://www.hawaiipublicschools.org/TeachingAndLearning/StudentLearning/HawaiianEducation/Pages/translation.aspx.

4. "About 1—'Aha Pūnana Leo,"'Aha Punana Leo, accessed September 19, 2024, https://www.ahapunanaleo.org/kula-kamalii-1.

5. "Some Little Known Facts About the Hawaiian Language," United Language Group, accessed September 19, 2024, https://www.unitedlanguagegroup.com/learn/little-known-facts-about-the-hawaiian-language.

6. "The World Atlas of Languages," UNESCO WAL, accessed September 19, 2024, https://en.wal.unesco.org/world-atlas-languages.

7. "Some Little Known Facts."

8. Keani Rawlins-Fernandez, "'Āina Kāpuna Bill Aims to Keep Ancestral Lands in Kānaka 'Ōiwi Hands," Council of the County of Maui, October 25, 2021, https://www.mauicounty.us/councils-3-minutes/aina-kupuna-bill-aims-to-keep-ancestral-lands-in-kanaka-oiwi-hands/.

10: Learning to Hula

1. Nathaniel B. Emerson, *Unwritten Literature of Hawaii: The Sacred Songs of the Hula* (Honolulu, 1909).

2. Emerson, *Unwritten Literature*, 16–22.

3. Rachel Ng and Michael Maslan, "The Surprising History of Hawai'i's Hula Tradition," *National Geographic*, March 22, 2022, https://www.nationalgeographic.com/history/article/the-surprising-history-of-hawaiis-hula-tradition.

4. "Dying Hawaiian Customs," *New-York Tribune*, April 16, 1899.

11: Hō'ike

1. Edith Kekuhikuhipu'uoneo'naalikiokohala, "E Hō Mai," Aloha 'Āina Project, accessed September 19, 2024, https://blogs.ksbe.edu/alohaainaproject/e-ho-mai/.

12: End of an Era

1. Hampton Sides, *The Wide, Wide Sea: Imperial Ambition, First Contact and the Fateful Final Voyage of Captain James Cook* (New York: Doubleday, 2024).

2. Kerri A. Inglis, "Kōkua, Mana, and Mālama 'Āina: Exploring Concepts of Health, Disease, and Medicine in 19th-Century Hawai'i," *Hūlili: Multidisciplinary Research on Hawaiian Well-Being* 2, no. 1 (2005): 215–37.

3. "The History of Hansen's Disease in Hawaii-Kalaupapa National Historical Park," National Park Service, https://www.nps.gov/kala/learn/historyculture/hansensdisease.htm.

4. "Renowned Hawaiian Historian Kamakau Explains in 1867 How Diseases Ravaged the Population of Aboriginal Hawaiians in the Kingdom," Hawaiian Kingdom, August 30, 2021, https://hawaiiankingdom.org/blog/renowned-hawaiian-historian-kamakau-explains-in-1867-how-diseases-ravaged-the-population-of-aboriginal-hawaiians-in-the-kingdom/.

5. "Provisional Death Counts for Coronavirus Disease 2019 (COVID-19)," CDC, accessed September 19, 2024, https://www.cdc.gov/nchs/nvss/vsrr/covid19/index.htm.

6. David A. Swanson and Kamehameha Schools, "A New Estimate of the Hawaiian Population for 1778, the Year of First European Contact," *Hūlili: Multidisciplinary Research on Hawaiian Well-Being* 11, no. 2

(2019): 203–22, https://kamehamehapublishing.org/wp-content/uploads/sites/38/2020/09/Hulili_Vol11.2_Swanson.pdf.

Epilogue

1. Justin Tyndall and Emi Kim, "Maui Short-Term Rentals, the Minatoya List, and Housing Supply," UHERO, https://uhero.hawaii.edu/maui-short-term-rentals-the-minatoya-list-and-housing-supply/.

2. "Monthly Indicators," REALTORS Association of Maui, August 2024, https://media.salecore.com/GetFile.ashx?p=QmMwhQMKyFaa.

3. Jonathan Y. Okamura and Danny de Gracia, "Hawaii's Teacher Shortage Persists Despite Recruitment from the Philippines," *Civil Beat*, May 26, 2024, https://www.civilbeat.org/2024/05/jonathan-okamura-hawaiis-teacher-shortage-persists-despite-recruitment-from-the-philippines/.

4. Lynette K. Paglinawan, Richard Likeke Paglinawan, Dennis Kauahi, and Valli Kalei Kanuha, *Nānā I Ke Kumu*, vol. 3 (Honolulu: Liliʻuokalani Trust, 2020).

ABOUT THE AUTHOR

Sara Kehaulani Goo is a journalist and senior news executive who has led several news organizations, including *Axios*, NPR, and *The Washington Post*. She is the former editor in chief at *Axios*, where she launched the company's editorial expansion into national and local newsletters, podcasts, and live journalism. Before *Axios*, Goo led online audience growth as a managing editor at NPR, overseeing the newsroom's digital news operation. At *The Washington Post*, she served as the news director and also a business editor and reporter. Originally from Dana Point, California, she graduated from the University of Minnesota's journalism school. She lives in Washington, DC.